POLICY ISSUES
in
WORK
and
RETIREMENT

Herbert S. Parnes
Editor

The W. E. Upjohn Institute for Employment Research

Library of Congress Cataloging in Publication Data
Main entry under title:

Policy issues in work and retirement.

Conference held Oct. 1982 in New Brunswick, N.J.
1. Age and employment—United States—Congresses.
I. Parnes, Herbert S., 1919-   . II. Rutgers
University. Institute of Management and Labor
Relations. III. Rutgers University. Institute on
Aging. IV. National Council on the Aging.
V. W. E. Upjohn Institute for Employment Research.
HD6280.P64   1983   331.3'94'0973   83-4950
ISBN 0-88099-011-2
ISBN 0-88099-010-4 (pbk.)

THE INSTITUTE, a nonprofit research organization, was established
on July 1, 1945. It is an activity of the W. E. Upjohn Unemployment
Trustee Corporation, which was formed in 1932 to administer a fund set
aside by the late Dr. W. E. Upjohn for the purpose of carrying on
"research into the causes and effects of unemployment and measures for
the alleviation of unemployment."

iii

Acknowledgments

Many persons and organizations contributed to the success of the Conference on Policy Issues in Work and Retirement, for which the papers in this volume were prepared. Co-sponsors were the Institute of Management and Labor Relations and the Institute on Aging at Rutgers University and the National Council on the Aging in Washington, DC. I should like to thank Professor James Begin, Director of the Institute of Management and Labor Relations and Professor Audrey Faulkner, Director of the Institute on Aging, for their encouragement and support; Harold Sheppard was a valued ally in serving as our liaison with the NCOA.

Professors Marsel Heisel and Polly Williams of the Institute on Aging provided valuable advice. Within the Institute of Management and Labor Relations, Professor Barbara McIntosh was my partner from the outset in planning and directing the Conference; Marjorie Saari was responsible for all of the local arrangements and for our contacts with the more than 200 persons who attended the Conference; Daniel Sohmer provided valuable advice for publicizing the Conference and collaborated in editing the manuscripts; Joan Riese served as secretary to the project from the beginning and cheerfully accepted the difficult chore of preparing the edited manuscripts for publication. To all of these colleagues I express my deep appreciation.

Finally, I should like to acknowledge with gratitude the financial support provided by the Retirement Research Foundation, which made possible lower registration fees for the Conference than would otherwise have been necessary.

Herbert S. Parnes
April 1983

Foreword

As Professor Parnes states in his introduction to this volume, "the aging of populations creates problems and requires adjustments on the part of society as a whole, just as the aging of each individual creates personal problems and requires personal adjustments." The human resource implications of individual and population aging point up a number of public policy issues—issues relating to health and retirement, to age discrimination in employment, and to methods of financing retirement, among others.

Each of the papers presented at the 1982 Conference explores, from a somewhat different perspective, aspects of individual and population aging. They are subjects which need to be considered in sound policy planning for fuller utilization of older workers as well as broadened options in retirement decisions.

Facts and observations presented in this book are the sole responsibility of the authors. Their viewpoints do not necessarily represent the position of the W. E. Upjohn Institute for Employment Research.

Jack R. Woods
Acting Director

Contributors

Theodore Bernstein, *Director*
International Ladies' Garment Workers'
Union Benefit Funds Department

Anna Marie Buchmann, *Vice President*
Human Resources, Bankers Life
and Casualty Company

Donna Cohen
Director, Division of Aging and
Geriatric Psychiatry and
Associate Professor of Psychiatry
and Neuroscience, Albert Einstein
College of Medicine and
Montefiore Medical Center

Carl Eisdorfer, M.D.
President, Montefiore Medical Center
and Professor, Departments of
Psychiatry and Neuroscience,
Albert Einstein College of Medicine

Anne Foner
Professor of Sociology, Rutgers

Eli Ginzberg
A. Barton Hepburn Professor
Emeritus of Economics and Director,
Conservation of Human Resources,
Columbia University

Daniel E. Knowles, *Vice President*
Personnel and Administration,
Grumman Aerospace Corporation

Leon F. Koyl, M.D.
Medical Consultant to The
de Havilland Aircraft of
Canada, Limited, Toronto, Canada

E. Douglas Kuhns
Assistant Research Director,
International Association of
Machinists and Aerospace Workers

Elliot Liebow, *Chief*
Center for Work and Mental Health
National Institute of Mental Health

Stephen R. McConnell
Professional Staff,
Select Committee on Aging,
U.S. House of Representatives

Barbara McIntosh
Assistant Professor,
Institute of Management and Labor
Relations, Rutgers

Alicia H. Munnell
Vice President and Economist,
Federal Reserve Bank of Boston

Herbert S. Parnes
Professor, Institute of Management
and Labor Relations, Rutgers

Karl Price
Consultant, Towers, Perrin, Forster,
and Crosby

James H. Schulz
Professor of Welfare Economics,
Florence Heller Graduate School,
Brandeis University; President,
The Gerontological Society of America

Bert Seidman, *Director*
Department of Social Security,
AFL-CIO

Harold L. Sheppard
Director, International Exchange
Center on Gerontology
University of South Florida

James R. Swenson
Vice President and Associate Actuary,
Prudential Life Insurance Company
of America

Michael K. Taussig
Professor of Economics, Rutgers

Contents

Chapter 1
Introduction and Overview

Herbert S. Parnes*

Individuals inevitably age, and populations may do so also. The aging of a population refers to a change in its age composition such that the proportion of older individuals becomes larger or the median age of the population rises. The aging of a population may be brought about by an increase in the life expectancy of its members, although this is not the most usual way in which the phenomenon occurs; reductions in fertility are a far more important cause under contemporary conditions. The crucial importance of fertility in affecting age composition has been demonstrated by the calculation that even if humans lived forever, only one-tenth of a population with a gross reproduction rate[1] of 3.0 would be over 60 years of age, as compared with about 41 percent if the reproduction rate were 1.5 and something approaching 100 percent if the rate were 1.0.[2]

Whatever the causes, the aging of populations creates problems and requires adjustments on the part of society as a whole, just as the aging of each individual creates personal problems and requires personal adjustments. As a matter of fact, the personal and social implications of aging are not completely separable; population aging, by definition, means that larger absolute and relative numbers of individuals are experiencing the personal problems associated with aging, and this in itself may be part of the problem with which society is compelled to deal.

*I am indebted to Frank Mott and Michael Taussig for the improvements that resulted from their review of an earlier draft of this chapter.

The papers in this volume are all concerned with what might be called the human resource implications of individual and population aging. They view aging, in other words, from the perspective of the productive roles of human beings, and explore some of the policy issues that confront society in this regard—issues relating to health and retirement, to age discrimination in employment, to methods of increasing work opportunities for the elderly, and to methods of financing retirement, including the very thorny contemporary issue of how to resolve the financial problems that currently confront the Social Security system.

The purpose of this introductory chapter is to provide a backdrop for the remaining papers. It begins with an examination of the demographic trends that establish the framework for much of the subsequent discussion, and assesses the degree of confidence we can have in the projections that have been made. After a brief discussion of the roles of analysis and value judgment in policy prescription, it then offers a series of generalizations about the labor market and retirement experience of older male workers derived from a longitudinal study of a national sample of middle-aged men (45-59) over a 15-year period during which many of them moved into retirement. The concluding section contains a summary of the remaining papers in this volume.

Demographic and Retirement Trends

The population of the United States and of most other industrialized societies has been aging, and the prospect is for a substantial intensification of this trend over the next half century. The proportion of the U.S. population 65 and over rose from about 4 percent in 1900 to 8 percent in 1950 and 11 percent in 1980. Depending upon what assumptions are made about fertility and immigration, this proportion is projected to range between 17.2 percent and 20.2 percent by 2025[3] as a result of the maturing of the "baby boom" generation born between the end of World War II and the mid-1960s.

Projected Age Structure Ratios
Assuming Replacement-Level Fertility

Age ratio	1976 (actual)	2025	2050
0-17/18-64	.51	.42	.42
65 and over/18-64	.18	.30	.30
18-24/18-64	.22	.16	.16
18-24/55-64	1.40	.78	.81
55-64/18-64	.16	.20	.20
20-39/40-64	1.16	.88	.88
75 and over/65 and over	.38	.39	.44

SOURCE: Based on Robert L. Clark and Joseph Spengler, "Economic Responses to Population Aging," in Robert L. Clark (ed.), *Retirement Policy in an Aging Society.* Durham, NC: Duke University Press, 1980, Table 2, p. 13.

Assuming replacement level fertility (which yields the lower of the two estimates for 2025 mentioned above), Clark and Spengler have calculated a number of ratios that capture the most significant demographic changes from the standpoint of the labor market, some of which are reproduced in the table above. The increase in the ratio of persons 65 and over to those 18 to 64 between 1976 and 2025 signifies the prospective rise in the *old-age* dependency ratio, but this is to a considerable extent offset by a drop in the *child* dependency ratio (0-17/18-64), so that the *total* dependency ratio is only 3 percentage points higher in 2025 than it is now. Among the bright elements in the picture are the decline in the number of young people (18-24) relative to the total working-age population and the even greater decrease in the ratio between the young and those approaching retirement age (55-64). These trends promise an easing of the youth unemployment problem as well as the possibility of an improvement in the tradeoff between inflation and unemployment. Finally, the reduction in the ratio of "prime age" workers (20-39) to older workers (40-64), along with the drop in the proportion of young workers, should operate to increase job opportunities for older workers.

To these prospective demographic changes one additional factor must be added in order to provide the necessary backdrop for the issues to be addressed in this volume, and that is the trend in retirement. The institution of retirement as we know it today is a relatively recent one in the history of human societies.[4] Even as late as 1947, the labor force participation rate of men 65 and over was almost 50 percent. From this level it dropped to slightly below 20 percent in 1981. Among men 55 to 64 there was also a notable decline, from 90 to 71 percent. Thus, to put both elements of the picture together, at the same time that the proportion of older persons in the population has increased, the fraction of that group that has continued to work has shrunk. This means that the actual old-age dependency ratio has increased by a greater degree than the demographic trends alone would suggest. And by the same token, if the trends that have prevailed in the past continue, the potential labor shortages of the future are also greater than the changes in age structure alone portend. It must be kept in mind, however, that these predictions assume the continuation of existing trends.

Will the Trends Continue?

Fertility trends. Forecasts of the age structure of the population *of working age* can be made for a period of, say, fifteen years into the future with a great deal of confidence, simply because all of the potential members of that group have already been born, and because dramatic changes in mortality rates over a 15-year period are unlikely. When the forecast period goes beyond 15 years, however, or when the mission is to forecast the age structure of the *total* population even for shorter periods, the task becomes much more difficult because of uncertainty about what will happen to the fertility rate—and, as has been seen, this is the crucial element in inducing changes in age structure.

As Alicia Munnell's paper in this volume makes clear, the projected costs of the Social Security program depend very substantially on the assumption that is made about the fertility rate—ranging from 11.4 percent to 26.9 percent of covered payrolls in the year 2050. The upper bound assumes a fertility rate that remains in the neighborhood of the lowest level to which it sank in the 1970s (1.7); the lower bound assumes an increase in the fertility rate to 2.4, somewhat above the replacement level (2.1) at which the total population would ultimately remain constant, but well below the rates achieved during the baby boom (3.5-3.7).

However, there is by no means any assurance that the fertility rate will actually fall between these two limits. It is well known that demographers failed to predict either the "baby boom" of the post-World War II period or the "baby bust" of the late 1960s and the 1970s. Perhaps the most dramatic illustration of the potential for error is the following quotation from the 1975 Report of the Panel on Social Security Financing, a group of experts appointed by the Senate Committee on Finance to make an independent actuarial assessment of the Social Security program:

> In 1946 it was authoritatively estimated that the 1975 United States population would perhaps be as low as 147 million, or perhaps be as high as 191 million; in 1958 the corresponding low and high forecasts of the 1975 population were 216 million and 244 million; the event—a population of 213 million has confounded both those prophecies.[5]

It is not only that the actual fertility rate *may* fall outside the range of the official estimates; what is more intriguing is the fact that at least one theoretical explanation of the determinants of fertility predicts that it *will*. Richard Easterlin has argued that the size of a birth cohort—i.e., the individuals born in a particular period of years—has an important effect on a number of aspects of the lives of the members of the group, including their marriage and fertility rates. The argument can be summarized very briefly in the following propositions expressed in Easterlin's own words:

1. Marriage, childbearing, and many other aspects of family formation and growth depend crucially on how the "typical" young couple assesses its "relative income," that is, the prospects for achieving the economic life-style to which they aspire. The more favorable this assessment, the freer a couple feels to marry and raise a family. . .

2. A young couple's relative income depends in large part on the supply of younger workers relative to older when the partners are in the early working ages. . .

3. The supply of younger workers relative to older depends chiefly on their generation size, the national birth rate about 20 years earlier. . .[6]

It follows that a "baby boom" generation will as adults have a relatively low fertility rate and produce a "baby bust" generation which, in turn, will have a relatively high fertility rate and produce another baby boom. Easterlin points out that his theory explains both the baby boom of the post-war years and the baby bust of the 1970s, and he foresees the possibility of a succession of "self generating fertility swings," and a population that will "continue to grow in roughly stepwise fashion."[7]

Easterlin is cautious, however. He acknowledges that the amplitude of future swings may well be lower than those of the cycle that has just been experienced. Moreover, Easterlin's theory of fertility by no means represents a consensus among demographers. Nonetheless, in reviewing

Easterlin's book, another leading demographer has advised that

> It is unwise to take Easterlin lightly. His 1962 explanation of the baby boom is the only one supported even weakly by the data. When there was a sign of fertility decline in the early 1960s most observers thought it was a temporary, short-term adjustment, and that baby-boom-level fertility would persist. Easterlin was virtually alone in predicting the baby bust. . . . Easterlin should be taken seriously, but perhaps not too seriously.[8]

In any case, the purpose here is not to decide upon the merits of the Easterlin thesis, but rather to stress the need for a healthy skepticism about some of the major premises underlying the debate on important policy issues. One can understand Michael Taussig's amusement at "intelligent and well-informed people who take . . . official Social Security projections so seriously. . . ."

Retirement trends. Whether the trend toward earlier retirement will continue is also uncertain. There is clear evidence of a pronounced downward trend in retirement age during the past decade not only in the official BLS data on labor force participation, but also on the basis of the intentions expressed by a representative national sample of men approaching retirement age. Of men 55 to 59 in 1976, 60 percent either were already retired or expressed the intention of retiring prior to age 65; the corresponding proportion of the *identical group of men* had been 27 percent in 1966 (when they were 45 to 49 years old) and 38 percent in 1971 (when they were 50-54).[9] This trend, moveover, continued between 1976 and 1978.[10] Many observers have speculated that the persistence of high rates of inflation would lead to a reversal of the trend toward early retirement. While a development of this kind would not be surprising, there is no evidence that it had occurred by the end of 1982, although there has been some evidence of a retardation in the trend.[11]

In any case, unlike the trend in fertility, the trend in retirement is subject to change by the manipulation of policy variables. While there is still some disagreement about the relative importance of the several factors that affect retirement decisions, no one can doubt that the high rates of early retirement that have characterized the recent past would drop if the ages of normal and early retirement under the Social Security Act were to be increased by three years as some have proposed. Indeed, as the paper by Schulz in this volume makes clear, there are a variety of less drastic policy options that would likely have similar effects. One of the important issues that society has to resolve, therefore, is what kind of policy it wishes to implement with respect to retirement age. This observation provides an appropriate link to an examination of the character of policy formation.

The Roles of Analysis and Value Judgment in Policy Formulation

As one considers policy issues relating to work and retirement—or indeed in any domain, public or private—it is well to keep in mind that all policy prescription involves both analytical processes and value judgments. The latter are crucial in selecting among competing goals, while the former relate to the means of achieving them. Because both of these intellectual processes are necessary ingredients of policy formulation, research findings alone, no matter how clear, can never point unambiguously to appropriate policy measures. Not until they are blended with values do they tell us what course of action to follow. What makes matters worse, the analytical aspects of policy formulation frequently do not point to unambiguous answers even to nonvalue-laden questions. It is for both these reasons that intelligent women and men of good will can disagree so substantially on policy issues.

These are hardly profound observations; yet they are sufficiently important to warrant an illustration or two from the field with which this volume is concerned. Analytically, it is clear that postponing the normal retirement age under Social Security will reduce the long run costs of retirement. Whether it is a good idea to move in that direction depends on how *effective* that approach is relative to alternatives (an analytical question) as well as how *equitable* it is relative to other cost-reducing measures and to measures designed to increase income into the trust funds (value questions). Moreover, whatever one's value hierarchy, whether postponement of the retirement age is equitable depends upon the reasons for early retirement (an analytical question). For instance, to the extent that the individuals who retire prior to age 65 withdraw from work in good health simply because they wish to enjoy leisure, one might be willing to make the value judgment that, compared with alternatives, the long term financial problem of Social Security is best met by removing the financial support for early retirement. On the other hand, if large numbers of early retirees are really forced into retirement by poor health—or inability to find work—the same set of values might well lead to the opposite conclusion. While this is an analytical issue on which one might suppose the evidence would be crystal clear, unfortunately it is not—or at least not clear enough to preclude difference of interpretation between two competent scholars. For instance, Robert J. Myers, former Chief Actuary of the Social Security Administration, in challenging the research of Eric R. Kingson, argues that the "widespread belief . . . that a considerable number of people who leave gainful employment before age 65 do so because of poor health . . . (is) based on erroneous or inadequate analysis and (is) not necessarily valid."[12] My purpose here is not to take sides in this debate, but merely to illustrate the important role that analytical differences can play in debates on policy.

To illustrate the importance of value judgments where there is agreement on analytical questions, let us consider briefly the policy issue of mandatory retirement. One of the *a priori* arguments in favor or eliminating mandatory retirement or raising the age at which it may legally be imposed is that this would have the effect of significantly increasing the labor force participation of older workers (an analytical proposition). The evidence is fairly conclusive, however, that such an effect is quite small; although almost half of the labor force is covered by mandatory plans, the vast majority of covered workers retire either prior to the mandatory age or at the mandatory age with no desire to work longer.[13] But this (analytical) conclusion obviously does not require one to abandon opposition to mandatory retirement. For one thing, propensities to retire may change in the future. Moreover, even if it were possible to be certain that only a handful of individuals would be involuntarily retired by mandatory rules, a concern for freedom of individual choice (a value) might constitute adequate justification for opposing mandatory retirement.

As if it were not enough that policy disagreements can be engendered either by differences in the interpretation of evidence or by differences in values (or both), they can result also from the way in which individuals choose (or have been taught) to view certain institutions. It is instructive to compare the way in which most Americans view (a) public education and (b) the Old-Age, Survivors, and Disability Insurance program (OASDI), both of which are part of the Social Security system in the United States viewed in its broadest perspective.[14] Public education is widely perceived as an institution that serves a crucially important social purpose and thus justifies social support irrespective of the degree to which a specific individual or family uses it. Property owners without children pay the same school taxes as those with children. When the baby boom generation flooded the elementary schools in the 1950s and 1960s, adults, while perhaps lamenting the required increase in taxes, did not bemoan the fact that they were having to "put in" more than they had (previously) "gotten out" of the educational system.[15]

In contrast, what is now the OASDI program was originally sold to the American public in the 1930s as an insurance system in which one pays in premiums while working in order to withdraw payments in retirement. However, there is nothing inherent in the program that *requires* it to be viewed in this way. Even if eligibility for and size of retirement (or disability) benefits are related to lifetime work experience, there is no reason why the collection of revenues for the support of the program—whatever their source—could not be viewed as an independent process. The support of retired workers, in other words, would be seen as a worthy social objective (like public education), requiring broad social support. And while "baby bust" generations might lament the increase in taxes required to support "baby boom" generations, the issue would not necessarily be perceived and discussed in terms of intergenerational inequities. Moreover, as Alicia Munnell points out in her contribution to this volume, whether one views OASDI as an individual-saving-for-retirement scheme or as a tax-and-transfer scheme has a substantial influence on what one regards to be an appropriate means of financing the program. With all due respect to William Shakespeare, names *do* make a difference!

The Labor Market and Retirement
Experience of Older Males

Although policy cannot be formulated on the basis of fact alone, sound policy obviously must be grounded in knowledge of relevant facts and in understanding relevant relationships. Many of the following chapters explore such matters relating to various aspects of work and retirement, but none of them focuses specifically on the work and retirement experience of older persons. In this section, I should like to distill from the research on this subject that my colleagues and I have done over the past fifteen years a series of findings that seem to me to be most important.

The research has involved a unique data base derived from repeated interviews between 1966 and 1981 with a representative national sample of about 5,000 men who were 45 to 59 years of age when the study began.[16] The longitudinal design of the study has allowed us to follow this sample over a 15-year period during which a large majority moved from full-time, full-year work into complete retirement. By 1981, death had claimed 26 percent of the original sample; the 2,832 respondents who were interviewed in that year were reasonably representative of the men who were then between 60 and 74 years of age.

The fact that repeated interviews were conducted with the same men over a number of years allows much more definitive conclusions on certain types of issues than can be derived from cross-sectional studies. For instance, in a cross-sectional study that obtains information on health and labor force status at the same point in time, an observed relationship between these two variables among men in their fifties may simply reflect the fact that poor health is the only legitimate "excuse" that a man of this age can give for not working. One cannot be certain, in other words, that self-reported poor health really *explains* withdrawal from the labor force, or simply *reflects* a prior decision to withdraw for other reasons. If, on the other hand, a report of poor health in one year is seen to *predict* a labor force withdrawal in a subsequent year, much of this ambiguity is removed. As another example, if a man covered by mandatory retirement tells us *prior to achieving the mandatory retirement age* that he would not choose to work longer even if he could, his subsequent retirement at that age can hardly be construed to be involuntary.

Since five volumes of reports and well over 100 articles have been written on the basis of these data,[17] it is clearly impossible to attempt even an incomplete summary. The following propositions merely cull out some of the more interesting findings that appear to have important policy implications.[18]

(1) A substantial majority of men in their forties and fifties encounter no special labor market problems. They serve in better jobs than the average of all men; a majority have moved up the occupational ladder since having started their careers; unemployment rates are low, although men who do become unemployed tend to remain jobless longer than younger men.

(2) Nonetheless, a sizeable minority of middle-aged men suffer severe labor market disadvantages, holding degrading jobs with low earnings and suffering substantial unemployment. During the 1966-1976 decade, 4 percent of the cohort suffered at least 66 weeks of unemployment, accounting for over 47 percent of all of the unemployment experienced by the total cohort.[19] Even at the beginning of the decade about 8 percent were at the bottom of the occupational hierarchy either because they had started and remained there or because they had slipped down during their working lives.

(3) There are dramatic differences between white and black middle-aged men in all dimensions of labor market

success; and these differences in rewards are greater than what can be accounted for by racial differentials in education and other forms of human capital. Nevertheless, on a more optimistic note, racial differentials in labor market opportunities narrowed over the decade.

(4) Health has an important effect on the labor market position of middle-aged men, being related not only to labor force participation, but to earnings and unemployment experience as well.

(5) There is clear evidence of a relation between education and training and the labor market fortunes of men in this age category, which suggests that whatever labor market disadvantage older workers currently experience will be reduced in the future as the educational attainment of this age group rises.

(6) Despite the inverse relation between age and all forms of labor mobility, the amount of job changing among middle-aged men is far from negligible. Over one-eighth of the 45-to-59-year-old cohort made at least one voluntary change of employer between 1966 and 1971, and an additional one-twelfth had moved involuntarily. About one-third changed occupations during the period. Most of the voluntary job changes appear to be advantageous, leading both to economic gains and to increased levels of job satisfaction.

(7) General economic conditions exert a profound effect on the labor market experience of middle-aged and older men; promoting high levels of economic activity is therefore an effective means of helping the members of this group who suffer labor market disadvantage.

(8) Job loss is particularly serious for those middle-aged and older workers who have accumulated substantial equities in their jobs (i.e., at least five years of service). While unemployment is the most immediate and obvious

penalty, there are also long run consequences in the form of a deterioration in earnings and occupational status.

(9) The secular decline in the labor force participation of middle-aged and older men has been due primarily to increasingly attractive income alternatives to work; the greater decline for blacks than for whites stems from their less favorable labor market opportunities as compared with whites. The evidence suggests that if wage rates for equally qualified whites and blacks were to be equalized, the difference in their labor force participation rates would disappear.

(10) Of the more than six million men 59 to 73 years of age in 1980 who had retired between 1967 and 1978, fewer than 5 percent had been unwillingly removed from jobs by virtue of mandatory retirement, in contrast to more than one-third whose retirement appears to have been induced by poor health.

(11) Irrespective of reason for retirement, only a minority of the retirees in this age group manifest an interest in labor market activity. Sixteen percent were either working or looking for work in 1980; of the remainder only 1 percent explained their absence from the labor market by a perception that no jobs were available, and only 15 percent said that they would (3 percent) or might (12 percent) take a job if one were offered them. Thus, at best about one-third of recent retirees appear to be available for work in any meaningful sense.

(12) A large majority of retirees profess to be able to "get by" on their income, although there is a pronounced difference between nonmarried and married men in favor of the latter—and an even larger one between blacks and whites. Nonetheless, for married men of both races 59 percent report that they do better than just "get by," while 9 percent assert that they "cannot make ends meet." By way of comparison,

the corresponding proportions for nonretired men in the same age range are 72 percent and 4 percent. (In interpreting these data, it must be remembered that no members of the sample are older than 73 years of age.)

(13) While a very large majority of retirees report that their experience in retirement has equalled or surpassed their expectations, about one in five of the whites and one in four of the blacks admit that they have been disappointed. The proportions vary considerably according to reason for retirement; about one-third of the men who retired for health reasons found retirement worse than their expectations.

(14) The proportion of retirees who retrospectively endorse the age at which they originally retired is also very large, but in this case there is clear evidence of a decreasing trend in responses between 1976 and 1980—from three-fourths to two-thirds.

(15) Life satisfaction among retirees varies systematically according to a variety of characteristics—especially in the case of white men. In particular, satisfaction varies directly with health, financial status (income and assets), preretirement occupational level, extent of leisure time activities, and being married. The circumstances under which retirement took place and the respondent's general attitudes toward work and retirement are also significantly correlated with degree of life satisfaction. Other things being equal (including current state of health), men who retired for health reasons are considerably less satisfied than voluntary retirees. The more favorable the retiree's attitude toward retirement in the abstract (as measured two years earlier) the more highly satisfied with life he was likely to be in 1980.

(16) These attitudinal differences are also important in assessing the impact of retirement on life satisfaction. Retirees who had displayed favorable attitudes toward retire-

ment (about one-third of the total) had significantly higher levels of life satisfaction than comparable nonretired men.

Remainder of the Volume: A Summary

The remaining papers in this volume were prepared for and presented at a Conference held in New Brunswick, New Jersey in mid-October 1982. Both the program participants and the approximately 200 persons who attended were broadly representative of management and labor in the private sector, government and social agencies concerned with problems of aging, and academic researchers. In developing the several sessions for the program, an attempt was made to assure representation of each of these constituencies.

In the first paper, Eli Ginzberg raises a fundamental question of values: "Life Without Work: Does It Make Sense?" On the basis of his own remarkably productive career one might expect an unqualified negative response. Actually, Ginzberg's answer is more tempered: it depends. He illustrates the possibility of individuals hanging on to positions longer than what can be justified by the welfare of the organization or, indeed, the individual's own self interest. But the importance of work as a determinant of income, status, personal achievement, interpersonal relations, and the allocation of time argues against denying work opportunities to those who want them, irrespective of age. To Ginzberg the crucial objective of social policy in this respect is the broadening of options, although in the light of demographic trends he sees merit in a gradual rise in the retirement age to 68, provided there is adequate protection to those who are unable to continue work to that age.

Aging, Health, and Work Performance

In his paper on this general topic, Leon Koyl comments on human life span and life expectancy, and then discusses some of the physiological and psychological aspects of aging. He emphasizes the fact that from both these perspectives the vast majority of individuals are capable of work beyond the conventional retirement age. In this context he calls attention to the potential contribution of ergonomics in altering the work environment to make it more congenial to the older workers.

The paper by Carl Eisdorfer and Donna Cohen examines the interrelationship between health and retirement. Whether one asks about the effect of health on the retirement decision or the effect of retirement on the health of the retiree, the evidence does not permit simplistic answers. The influence of health on retirement depends upon the demands of the present job and the nature and severity of the health problem, as well as on the individual's previous work experience and prospective retirement income. As to the effect of retirement on health, an unambiguous answer is even more difficult. For some individuals retirement may constitute a crisis; for others it may lead to improved well-being.

In her discussion of the issues raised by these two papers, Anne Foner suggests several principles that relate to interpretations of data on aging, health, and work performance: (1) to understand the elderly, they must be viewed in the context of the entire age structure, not only for purposes of comparison but because the elderly necessarily interact with other age groups; (2) the way in which people age depends on the way in which they grew up and matured, including the broad cultural context in which the process occurred; and (3) since no two cohorts age in exactly the same way, the very definition of aging as well as the problems that are associated with it are largely social. She concludes with the warning that if current social problems result in a "new orthodoxy" that older workers should remain in the labor force well past age 65, this may have unforeseen and unfortunate consequences for both younger and older persons.

Elliot Liebow expresses the view that traditional assessments of the work potential of the elderly—including Leon Koyl's—give too much attention to the characteristics of workers and too little to the characteristics of jobs and the work environment. To a considerable extent, he argues, the former are a function of the latter, for "our factories and offices produce not only particular goods and services but particular kinds of people as well." In reacting to the Eisdorfer-Cohen paper, Liebow emphasizes the importance of both financial considerations and workplace safety and health to the effects of retirement on individual well-being. Because he is pessimistic about the effects of recent and prospective policy decisions on the wholesomeness of the work environment and on post-retirement incomes, he fears that future cohorts of "older and retired workers are headed for poorer health, not better."

Theodore Bernstein draws upon his rich experience with the International Ladies' Garment Workers Union to illustrate his conviction that the "employability and adaptability of the healthy older worker has been clearly and firmly established." For him, the most crucial public policy issue lies in assuring full employment. In this context he argues against raising the Social Security retirement age on the ground that it would penalize those older workers in poor health. A full employment economy, on the other hand, would induce more older workers who enjoy good health to remain in or return to the labor force and thus improve the financial position of the OASDI program.

Improving the Utilization of Older Workers

Daniel Knowles' paper on "Keeping Older Workers on the Job: Methods and Inducements" is of especial interest because one does not expect the Vice President of Personnel and Administration of a major U.S. corporation to acknowledge that both industry and government have treated the middle-aged and older worker with "benign neglect"; that age discrimination is pervasive and "the most insidious type of labor market discrimination taking place today"; and that industry "will have no one to blame but itself if Congress enacts further legislation requiring an annual formal affirmative action plan similar to that required for the other protected groups." Except to remedy past discrimination, Knowles finds no need for programs to induce older workers to remain on the job. Indeed, his objective is to create complete freedom of individual choice, rather than to "manipulate older workers in order to achieve other objectives."

Anna Marie Buchmann's paper relates to "Maximizing Post-Retirement Labor Market Opportunities." In it she stresses the potential contribution of pre-retirement counseling programs and discusses the components of a good one. She then turns to (1) a description of a wide variety of "alternative work programs" to accommodate retirees who desire less than full-time employment, (2) a discussion of the possibilities of developing full-time "second careers," and (3) a treatment of volunteerism as an activity that may be attractive to retirees. Although Buchmann is rather optimistic about the employment opportunities for older workers and retirees in the long run, she acknowledges that the current state of the economy makes short term prospects rather bleak.

Harold Sheppard, in reacting to the Knowles and Buchmann papers, cites three basic reasons for the increasing interest of employers in the subject of older workers: (1) the Age Discrimination in Employment Act, (2) demographic change that threatens labor shortages, and (3) the dissemination of research findings that tend to dispel the negative stereotype of the older worker. He predicts a continuation and intensification of this trend, and reports on the basis of his recent research that older workers are receptive to opportunities for continued employment and the acquisition of new skills.

Karl Price's discussion emphasizes the importance of alternative forms of post-retirement activity, since there is no single pattern that is appropriate for all retirees. Barbara McIntosh makes the important point that all aspects of personnel policy need to be scrutinized for the ways in which they might be modified to promote increased utilization of older workers. Douglas Kuhns notes what he describes as paradoxical behavior on the part of many companies—resisting early retirement provisions in pensions on the ground that they result in the loss of highly productive workers, but being eager to be rid of the same workers when they reach age 65. In any case, Kuhns is not optimistic about job opportunities for older workers, given the national economic policies that are currently being implemented.

Stephen McConnell, in his paper on the Age Discrimination in Employment Act, asserts that age discrimination is pervasive despite the provisions of the law. After analyzing official data on the changes that are brought under the Act, he goes on to describe and illustrate the forms that age discrimination takes and examines recent efforts to strengthen the law. Noting that each of these efforts has been thwarted by special interest groups, he pleads for improving the legal protection afforded older workers not only in the interest of individual freedom "but as a means of contributing to the nation's economic welfare."

Social Security and Pension Policy

Alicia Munnell's paper on OASDHI financing presents a penetrating analysis of the sources of the short run and long term financial problems that confront the Social Security program and catalogues the possible remedies—all of which involve hard choices between increasing taxes of one kind or another and curtailing benefit rights. Munnell mentions three categories of short run options: modifying the cost of living adjustment; increasing revenues by advancing the dates of scheduled increases in payroll taxes, extending coverage, or taxing some portion of Social Security benefits; or using general revenues to finance part of the program. The longer run problem associated with the changing age structure of the population may be met by (1) decreasing the ratio of benefits to earnings as the latter increase over time, rather than maintaining constant replacement rates as the current scheme of calculating benefits has the effect of doing; (2) adjusting the benefit formula to provide a lower replacement rate (but one that would remain constant over time); (3) extending the retirement age; and/or (4) increasing tax rates. While Munnell does not make explicit policy recommendations, it is not hard to infer that she would prefer either of the latter two alternatives to the first two. With respect to extending the retirement age, she emphasizes the importance of protecting those who, by virtue of disability or unemployment, will not have the option of working. In regard to increasing tax rates, she notes (1) that the projected increase in the old-age dependency rate is offset by a reduction in the child dependency ratio and (2) that the long run projected costs in terms of percent of payroll are below the level that already prevails in a number of European countries.

James Schulz opens his paper on "Private Pensions, Inflation, and Employment" by expressing some doubts as to the likelihood of substantial increases in the employment of the elderly. Acknowledging that demographic changes may tend to produce this result, he points to two factors operating in the opposite direction: workers' preferences for earlier retirement and the possibility of more significant health barriers to employment as longevity increases. In attempting to keep older workers in the labor force, Schulz has a strong preference for the "carrot" rather than the "stick." Specifically, he urges (1) demonstration projects designed to help workers understand the feasibility and desirability of flexible work arrangements, (2) abolition of mandatory retirement (largely for symbolic reasons), and (3) liberalization of the Social Security retirement test.

Michael Taussig's discussion of these papers presents an unconventional view about the long term financial problem of Social Security: he argues against any present action in part because he doesn't trust the projections of the distant future. "Babies may come back into fashion," he suggests, or retirements may be fewer as the character of work opportunities for the elderly becomes more attractive. More fundamentally, Taussig sees OASDI largely as a tax and transfer mechanism, which means that every generation of workers must make its own decision about what level of support to provide its nonworking dependents. He observes that even if current pessimistic assumptions are realized, future tax rates will not be out of line with those that currently prevail in other industrialized democratic countries. Taussig calls attention to a difference between the Munnell and Schulz papers on an important issue that requires further attention: whether, with increasing longevity, the health of future cohorts of older workers will be better or worse than that of the current cohort.

The other two discussants of the social security and pension papers are in fundamental disagreement with each other. Bert Seidman's position on the long term Social Security problem is similar to that of Taussig: there are too many imponderables to warrant any kind of action at this point. In this context Seidman makes the interesting point that Social Security actuaries assume a continuation of the increasing trend in the ratio of fringe benefits to total compensation, which Seidman believes is highly unlikely, and which therefore has the effect of understating payments into the trust funds. James Swenson, on the other hand, is inclined to put considerable stock in the demographic projections, and is not reassured by the fact that the total dependency ratio will be no higher than in the past, since the elderly cost much more to support than dependent children. Accordingly, he would raise the age of normal retirement to 68, but would continue to allow retirement as early as age 62 at actuarially reduced benefits. With respect to the short run problems, Seidman's preferred solution would be to advance the scheduled tax increases, while Swenson would replace the CPI cost of living adjustment with a wage index reduced by 2 or 2.5 percent. Swenson also takes issue with the idea expressed by both Munnell and Schulz that middle income workers will not save to any significant degree for their retirement. He urges stronger incentives to save in order to stimulate this basis for financing retirement.

Conclusion

I am neither sufficiently imaginative nor sufficiently daring to attempt a grand synthesis of all of the above. The topics are disparate, and there are conflicting points of view. Nevertheless, certain themes reappear either explicitly or implicitly in a number of the papers, and there is some merit in simply listing these, for their general tenor is encouraging:

1. From the perspective simply of capability, there is currently a very substantial waste of human resources among the elderly.

2. If the economy regains a healthy pattern of growth, and if fertility remains low, prospective demographic trends threaten labor shortages unless there is fuller labor market utilization of older persons.

3. A primary objective of social policy in a democratic society should be to preserve and to broaden individual options. In the context of the present subject, this implies as a minimum (a) the achievement of full employment and (b) the elimination of age discrimination. In addition, con-

tinued experimentation with flexible work patterns for the elderly is desirable.

4. If greater labor force participation of the elderly is perceived to be socially necessary, incentives are to be preferred to penalties. In any case it will be important to remember that older persons are not a homogeneous group. Those who cannot work and those for whom there are no suitable work opportunities need to be provided for.

NOTES

1. The gross reproduction rate is based on the average number of female children who would be born to a cohort of 1000 women in their lifetime if they were to experience the age-specific birth rates that prevail in the given year and were to survive for the entire period. This number is expressed as a ratio to the original cohort of 1000.

2. Ansley J. Coale, "Increases in Expectation of Life and Population Growth." International Population Conference. Vienna, 1958. Vienna: Im Selbstverlag, 1959, pp. 36-41. Cited in Robert L. Clark and Joseph J. Spengler, *The Economics of Individual and Population Aging.* Cambridge: Cambridge University Press, 1980, p. 14.

3. Clark and Spengler, *op. cit.,* pp. 16, 25.

4. For an interpretation of the development of the institution, see Robert C. Atchley, "Retirement As a Social Institution," *Annual Review of Sociology,* 1982, pp. 263-287.

5. Report of the Panel on Social Security Financing to the Committee on Finance, United States Senate. Washington: Government Printing Office, 1975, p. 5. Cited in Alicia H. Munnell, *The Future of Social Security.* Washington: The Brookings Institution, 1977, p. 102.

6. Richard A. Easterlin, *Birth and Fortune: The Impact of Numbers on Personal Welfare.* New York: Basic Books, 1980, pp. 146-7.

7. *Ibid.,* pp. 148, 150.

8. James A. Sweet, review of *Birth and Fortune: The Impact of Numbers on Personal Welfare. Contemporary Sociology,* November 1982, Vol. 11, No. 6, pp. 766-7.

9. Herbert S. Parnes, Lawrence Less and Gilbert Nestel, *Work and Retirement Data: National Longitudinal Surveys of Middle-Aged and Older Men, 1966-1976.* Columbus: Ohio State University Center for Human Resource Research, 1980, p. 138.

10. Herbert S. Parnes, "Inflation and Early Retirement: Recent Longitudinal Findings," *Monthly Labor Review,* July 1981, pp. 27-30.

11. National Council on the Aging, "Is Inflation Slowing Retirement," Press Release (Washington: mimeo, August 17, 1981).

12. "Why Do People Retire from Work Early?" *Social Security Bulletin,* September 1982, p. 10. For a marshalling of the evidence that Myers questions, see Eric R. Kingson, "The Health of Very Early Retirees," *loc. cit.,* pp. 3-9.

13. James H. Schulz, *Economics of Aging;* Herbert S. Parnes and Gilbert Nestel, "The Retirement Experience," Chapter 6 in Parnes, et al., *Work and Retirement: A Longitudinal Study of Men* (Cambridge: MIT Press, 1981).

14. See Eveline M. Burns, *Social Security and Public Policy* (New York: McGraw-Hill Book Company, 1956), p. 4.

15. Michael Taussig has pointed out to me that the analogy is not perfect. In the case of public education, taxpayers can "vote with their feet" by moving out of high-tax areas. Moreover, liberal expenditures for education may redound to the advantage of property owners by enhancing the attractiveness of their communities and hence the values of their property.

16. The data have been collected as part of the National Longitudinal Surveys of Labor Market Experience, which have been the responsibility of the Center for Human Resource Research at The Ohio State University under a contract with the Employment and Training Administration of the United States Department of Labor. For a detailed description of the surveys and a bibliography of research based on them, see *The National Longitudinal Surveys Handbook* (Columbus: Ohio State University Center for Human Resource Research, 1982).

17. For a list, see *ibid.*

18. The following paragraphs draw heavily on Parnes, *Work and Retirement,* which is based on data collected between 1966 and 1976. This material is supplemented by the findings of as yet unpublished research based on data through 1980. The 1981 data have not yet become available.

19. Herbert S. Parnes, *Unemployment Experience of Individuals Over a Decade: Variation by Sex, Race, and Age.* Kalamazoo: The W. E. Upjohn Institute for Employment Research, 1982, pp. 6, 9.

Chapter 2
Life Without Work: Does It Make Sense?

Eli Ginzberg*

This introductory chapter sets the stage for the contributions that follow. It deals sequentially with four themes: cullings from a half century of work and research on work about the role of older persons in the workforce; some analytic distinctions about the nature of work; placing work within the larger context of life's experiences; and a few modest suggestions as to policy with respect to older workers.

Some Observations on Aging and Work

When I entered Columbia College in 1927, Nicholas Murray Butler, the president, had been at the helm of the institution for two decades during which time he had transformed it from a mediocre into a top-rated university. But Butler remained at the helm for another seventeen years during which he declined in health and energy, and in the process the university was greatly weakened.

For those concerned with the rise and fall of institutions, none offers more detail than the Catholic Church, which has survived for close to two millennia. I was impressed when the Pope acted some years ago to establish a new policy replacing Cardinals who could no longer perform their duties because of their advanced age. That is my first observation.

---

*I wish to acknowledge the assistance of Dr. Dean Morse in helping me transform my oral remarks into written form.

Secondly, I was much struck by the very different ways in which my parents aged. My father was always in mediocre health and in his latter years (he died at eighty) was performing at a much reduced level of output. My mother, on the other hand, slowed up only in her ninety-fourth year.

The next point has to do with health. I spend most of my time currently in research in health economics. There are many arguments as to whether modern medicine pays off. We know that medicine has relatively little to do with longevity. It would be wrong to say that it has nothing to do with longevity but its major contribution lies elsewhere in its adding to the quality of life, particularly the quality of life of older people. Only a few years ago, for example, if you broke your hip you would probably be confined for the rest of your days to bed. There was nothing that could be done in the days before new surgical techniques were perfected. The question is not solely or primarily longevity, but rather the improved quality of a person's later years. This is critical for some of the issues to be addressed at this Conference, for many older persons now entering their later years in good health are capable of and interested in remaining at work.

Another important trend points to the way in which the work and life patterns of women are getting closer and closer to those of men. As more women enter and remain in the workforce, there has been a parallel devaluation of voluntary activity. In the past, voluntary service had much to do with the way in which older persons related to the world. While many older persons are still concerned about their church or hospital, the role of the volunteer has been devalued, which in turn has affected the role and status of many older persons.

Next, career-oriented persons with strong ambitions who enter corporate enterprise will know by the time they are 35 years old or so whether their rate of progress will enable them to achieve or approximate their career goals. By 35, a person will have feedback from his organization as to whether he is on the fast track or the slow track. Many people in large organizations have plateaued by their mid-thirties. If one's career plateaus in the mid-thirties and that person keeps on doing the same type of work year in and year out, he may decide that early retirement is not such a bad idea after all.

A correlative of the foregoing is that for the few who continue to compete for the top jobs, their only chance of winning is for the old-timers who are up at the top to get out of the way. Since there are only a few jobs up at the top, those who hold these jobs must keep moving out with some regularity if others who are qualified are to have their chance. Professionals who are self-employed or who are members of a partnership or a small corporate group have an easier time of adjusting their workday and workweek as they reach their sixties or seventies. They can shift from full- to part-time activity and most do just that.

When it comes to the rank and file worker, I have been impressed with how many, as they near the end of their working life, look forward to spending more time on avocational or leisure activities such as moving out of the city to their "cabin in the Catskills." They no longer will have to limit themselves to a two or three week stay. They can, when they retire, spend all or most of their time there.

The last observation relates to the more affluent, those who look forward to dividing their "golden years" between pitching horseshoes in Florida and traveling to Europe. This is a typical American, not a European, approach to the later years. Many Americans put a high value on being able to escape from work permanently and to start doing new and different things. If one has never been out of the country, the first trip abroad is usually exciting. But the pleasure diminishes with the fifth or surely the tenth trip. This observation is a useful reminder that attitudes and behavior toward work and retirement must always be assessed within both economic and cultural contexts which in turn are not stable.

The Multifaceted Nature of Work

My second theme takes off from the premise that work is a multidimensional phenomenon. In a recent article that I wrote on Social Security which appeared in the *Scientific American* (January 1982), I presented a table showing that the group that was best off with respect to income in old age were those who were still working. For this group, work accounted for about 55 percent of their total income. Most people, if they want to be comfortable in the latter years, need income from work. Only the rich can afford not to keep on working.

Secondly, in the United States we have always tended to place a person—first men but now also women—by asking "What do you do?" If we learn about the work that a person performs we can rank the individual. The work-status relationship is critical.

In analyzing the satisfaction that people derive from work it is well to distinguish among intrinsic satisfactions, extrinsic satisfactions and concomitant satisfactions (see my *Occupational Choice,* 1951). For some, surely a minority, intrinsic satisfactions from work are critical. However, one of the consequences of aging is the diminution of one's mental and physical powers, which affect work performance. A lawyer friend is one of the nation's great litigators. But now that he is in his early eighties he does not accept certain cases because he can no longer remember all of the details in a trial that might run ninety days or even longer. Similarly, a surgeon may still be a very good diagnostician as he gets into his seventies, but few of us would want to be operated on by him. In the case of many appellate judges, age does not seem to matter very much. Irrespective of age, they continue to write good or bad opinions. Great musical instrumentalists and conductors are a group apart. Many are able to perform at high levels into their seventies and even into their eighties.

Work has great importance for many persons because of its concomitant social satisfactions, the companionship that it provides. This was first brought home to me in our studies of the long term unemployed in New York City in the late 1930s (*The Unemployed,* 1943). What the men missed most was the daily interaction with their fellow workers on the job and sharing a beer after work. The loss of these social ties took a heavy toll. The vice president of AT&T recently made an interesting point at a Columbia University seminar. He reported that they found there were still some women in their middle seventies working the night shift in the Bell Telephone System in New York City who had to use the subways to get to their jobs. They won't stop because of the pleasure they get from meeting and interacting with their friends at work.

Work also provides a structure for the use of time. If one spends eight hours a day at work, what to do with the rest of one's time represents less of a burden. But to make effective use of 24 hours in a day, day after day, without the routine of work can prove burdensome.

The Several Contexts of Work

These then are the five dimensions of work: income, status, personal achievement, social relations and the structure of time. A complementary approach is to consider briefly the different parties that are or may be involved in the structuring of work. The first point of reference is the individual. Whether an individual needs income, whether he has a drive for intrinsic work satisfaction, whether he's concerned about social interactions on the job, in all these respects the individual is the center.

Most of us continue to live in family structures. Hence the importance of relating work to the family. We are in the midst of a major revolution in which the majority of families now have two wage earners. Moreover, an increasing number of mothers of even very young children are in the labor force. And many fathers are caught up in a career that allows them to spend very little time with their children. In short, the interface of work and family is a critical dimension.

We know that a disproportionately large sector of our families living in poverty consist of families with only one wage earner. There are very few families in the United States trapped in poverty where both husband and wife are more or less regularly employed. The reports from Europe suggest that a strong force that is contributing to the expansion of flextime comes from the desires of married people who work to spend more time together and with their child or children.

The employing organization offers still another context in which to consider work. Among the more dynamic factors operating in a market economy are the decisions that firms make as to where to locate, expand, and relocate, the basis for which are often rooted in estimations of the competence and pliability of the workforce. When a long established plant is closed down, especially in a one-industry town, the toll of human suffering is often very great.

The community offers still another vantage point from which to assess the role of work. Consider the differences in the socialization in northern cities of the earlier immigrants and the more recent black migrants. Most Americans have failed to appreciate the differences in the infrastructure available to the two groups. The Italians and the Irish who came to New York had the Catholic Church and Tammany Hall to assist them. The Jews had support from their co-religionists who had come earlier and had put into place an elaborate system of social institutions from schools to hospitals. In contrast, blacks as they moved North have not had the advantage of such self-help structures. I submit that the lack of such infrastructure explains many of the difficulties that blacks have encountered in their efforts to secure a place in urban society.

The final vantage is societal. Does our society need the work that older persons are able to contribute; will it create the opportunities they need to continue to work; and if not, will it provide them adequate income if they do not work? This provides the bridge to a few observations about policy.

Some Policy Questions

The first observation relates to the changing perspectives from a life that is spent working to not working. Currently a college graduate starts to work in his early twenties and ends in his early sixties, a work life of approximately forty years. But the average additional years of life for a man who reaches 62 is 16 years, for a woman it is 21. This points up that at present a person will spend only half of his life at work. The question that must be asked and answered is whether even an affluent society can afford to provide income for half of the population that at any time is not working. I doubt it.

But even if we could afford it, the question must be raised anew: does it make sense? Again, I doubt it. In the penultimate chapter of *The Human Economy* (1976) I postulated that the overriding criterion for measuring societal progress was the broadening of options. Using that criterion, I would argue that many persons in their sixties and seventies and even a few in their eighties would prefer to keep on working and a society that enabled them to do so would be better off. I am not arguing that they should work, only that they have the option to work if they so prefer. But there is another side to the coin. Some workers become enfeebled or disabled in their late fifties and lose their jobs. I see considerable merit in a transition program, such as the French have put into place, that would carry such persons over until they qualify for Social Security. Moreover, I would consider broadening such a program to include persons who, although in good health, are the victims of plant closures and whose prospects for reemployment are minimal in years when the unemployment rate hangs high.

Although I wrote a recent piece on "The Social Security System" I do not pretend to expertise. However, I see merit in slowly raising the retirement age from 65 to 68; in taxing one-half of the Social Security benefit; in correcting the over-indexation for inflation and introducing still other modifications to shore up the financial foundations of the system. In the absence of such reforms, a conflict between the generations, with all its ugliness, is likely.

There is no point of pushing the elderly to the wall and faulty policies that resulted in such pressure could have serious repercussions. We saw a counterculture of the young in the 1960s that had little to commend it. I submit that inciting the elderly to take to the political ramparts could prove more destructive. There is nothing outrageous or impossible in the demands that their leadership has advanced: a protection of the benefits that have been written into the law and an opportunity for the elderly, if they so desire, to work past seventy. The elderly understand that the value of their benefits are linked to the fiscal integrity of the federal government. They do not stand adamant against all modifications. But they will fight hard to protect the systems that are in place, and so they should. I have long believed that the quality of a people is to be measured by how it deals with children, women and the elderly. On that criterion the United States gets a passing mark. Our aim should be to improve, not lower it.

Chapter 3
Aging, Health, and Work

Leon F. Koyl

Introduction

Man's life span has not changed significantly, but individuals are moving closer to achieving the potential number of years in that span. As people live longer they face the problem of sustaining themselves, which raises the question whether more years should be spent at work. However, this choice between work and leisure remains free only if man's physical condition at an advanced age allows work. The overwhelming majority of persons are able to work beyond the conventional retirement age. Increases in work life are entirely feasible provided we react intelligently to the types of ailments that are associated with aging and recognize that work adjustments may be needed throughout working life to maximize the potential inherent in the labor force.

Life Span and Life Expectancy

Evidence for a fixed life span is strong and comes from the diverse fields of anthropology, demography, physiology, cell biology, subcellular biology, and biochemistry as well as from medicine. No social, medical, or public health measure should be expected to modify the intrinsic life span of the human being. There is no good evidence for the existence of an extremely long-lived population. Age 113 ± 2 seems to be the limit to date.[1]

Modern medicine has succeeded in changing the life expectancy of human beings.[2] Health measures, especially sanitation, have reduced premature mortality and morbidity and have thus increased life expectancy. Early acute deaths have been partly exchanged for slower later deaths; as man lives longer, a larger percentage of the life span may be spent in poor health. Consequently, it becomes necessary to reduce the risks of obstructive lung disease, emphysema, lung cancer, stroke, myocardial infarction, and cirrhosis, to name some important ones. Reducing the risks of thes diseases becomes a practical method of improving the quality of life whether or not it adds years to life expectancy.

It is well to recognize the epidemiological importance of psycho-social factors on longevity. For example, it has been shown that socioeconomic status essentially explains away most of the ethnic differences in aging; black-white differences in age-oriented behavior are minimized if differences in socioeconomic status are taken into account.[3]

At any rate, the expectation of life in the United States is at a new high.[4] It reached 73.8 years in 1979, an increase of a half year over 1978 and of 3.1 years since 1970 as compared with a gain of only 0.8 years in the 1960s. These figures are the average of both whites and nonwhites and of males and females. Women have longer expectation of life than men; whites do better than blacks, although the gap is being closed. To the present, almost all of the improvement in life expectancy has been produced by prevention of infant mortality, although in the last few years noticeable improvements have been made in the control of risk factors for chronic diseases, thus improving expectancy of life at older ages.

Physiological Aspects of Aging

With increasing life expectancy and the consequent increase in the number of older persons in the population, considerable attention has been given to the physiological aspects of aging. Blood pressure is a good example of the rapid change both in our knowledge and in our attitudes. In 1940, it was "known" that normal systolic blood pressure increased 1 mg. of mercury for each year over age 25. We now believe that healthy 70 year olds should have the same blood pressure they had at 25. As long as fit people continue age-adjusted exercise and remain fit, their pulse and blood pressure patterns will remain constant. In 1940, blood pressures under 170 systolic and 120 diastolic were seldom treated. Now it has become recognized that statistically significant improvements in mortality are gained if pressures above 140 systolic and 90 diastolic are treated.

Data Problems

Almost all people deteriorate and eventually die from disease, but usually people withdraw from the labor force prior to the onset of these illnesses. Thus if the general population is used as the population base, age standardized mortality ratios (SMRs) will understate the total mortality experience of the *employed* population.[5] The latter is composed of individuals who are necessarily healthy enough to be at work and therefore have a lower mortality risk. The "healthy worker effect" is due not only to the initial selection of healthy workers, but also to the fact that only the healthy cohort remains at work. The phenomenon also depends on the length of time the population has been followed.[6] For example, the mortality rate within five years of entry to a group exposed to vinyl chloride monomer was shown in one study to be as low as 37 percent of expected. However, there was a progressive increase in the SMR with the length of time since entry, so that the healthy worker effect had almost disappeared after 15 years. By classifying men who had survived 15 years after entering the industry according to whether or not they were still with the industry, the survival effect could be separated from the selection effect: The standardized mortality ratio of those who left the industry was some 50 percent higher than that of workers still employed in the industry. Similar patterns were found among workers of all ages between 25 and 74 and for all causes studied.

It is difficult to find competent epidemiological evidence about aging. The Framingham Disability Study is a new addition to the well-known heart disease epidemiological study in Framingham, Massachusetts.[7] From September 1976 to November 1978, 2,654 surviving individuals age 55 to 84 years from the original Framingham cohort (nearly 30 years of data collection) were interviewed. This is one of the few good studies of the noninstitutionalized elderly. It demonstrates that life after 60 is not a period inexorably marked by massive physical deterioration. On the contrary, the majority of the Framingham elders retained substantial physical ability in their later years. It is true that advancing age is accompanied by increased risk of physical disability. Women seem to have higher physical disability rates than men, and this is not an artifact produced by the higher proportion of women who live into old old-age.

Atherosclerosis

Cardiovascular disease is the most common cause of death in the elderly.[8] In fact 72 percent of cardiovascular deaths in the United States occur in persons 65 years of age or older. The vast majority of these deaths are due to coronary artery disease, either sudden death or myocardial failure. The Western Collaborative Study Group has found that the incidence of coronary heart disease is significantly associated with parental coronary heart disease history; blood pressure; reported diabetes; serum levels of cholesterol, triglycerides, B lipoproteins; schooling; smoking habits; and overt behavior pattern.[9]

A Type A behavior pattern was strongly related to coronary heart disease incidence and this association could not be explained by any single predictive risk factor or any combination of them.[10] Type A persons are hard driving, competitive, striving to accomplish more and more in less and less time. They exhibit chronic impatience with people and situations they perceive as thwarting their attempts to maintain high levels of achievement. Type B individuals are relatively relaxed and easygoing, although they may be goal-oriented.

An interesting concept that has been advanced recently is that there may be Type A and B organizations as well as Type A and B people. Type A organizations are those where the work atmostphere may be described best as hard-driving and competitive. Type B organizations, on the other hand, are relaxed and easy-going. Type B people in Type B organizations report the fewest symptoms that correlate with stress-produced or stress-aggravated loss of health homeostasis with the environment. Type A people in Type A organizations report the most symptoms. Type B people in Type A organizations and Type A people in Type B organizations report an intermediate level of symptoms.[11] These findings, while tentative, tend to correspond with the experience of the author in doing comprehensive medical examinations of executives from approximately 100 corporations. Exercise programs seem prophylactic for stressed senior corporate staff.

Even after myocardial infarction,[12] in persons 30-64 years of age controlled exercise will produce a significant difference in mortality (4.6 percent vs. 7.3 percent in controls) and morbidity (5.3 percent vs. 7.0 percent re-infarction in controls) during a 3-year follow-up period. The fact that such patients have been motivated to help themselves also reduces the percentage of persons going on long term disability insurance and salvages a large pool of professional knowledge for the patients' organization.

44

Cancer

There are many known carcinogenic substances in the environment, although there is no reason to suppose that any new hazards have been introduced in the last few decades, especially in North America, except the unexplained increase in melanoma and the now well-recognized hazard of cigarette smoking which has spread from men to women.[13] There have been many estimates of the proportion of cancer deaths attributed to the environment and to occupations, some of which have been politically motivated and lack scientific merit. Perhaps the most useful estimates are those of Doll and Peto who attribute 4 percent of cancer deaths to occupational factors, 2 percent to pollution, 1 percent to industrial products, and 3 percent to geophysical factors, in contrast to 30 percent to tobacco and 35 percent to diet.[14] One of the hopeful things about occupational cancers is that they are preventable, if not curable.[15] Most discoveries along these lines have been helped by special situations—serendipity and luck. For instance, clustering of cases of a rare disease in the catchment area of one hospital led to the discovery of nasal cancer of furniture workers and of shoe workers. When only a few cases of an unusual cancer occur in a large metropolitan area, their significance may be missed. Many occupational carcinogens produce unusual cancers such as mesothelioma of the pleura and angiosarcoma of the liver, or in unusual places, such as scrotal cancer in chimny sweeps and millwrights who use penetrating oils.

Lung Disease

Diseases which produce scarring of the lungs are important causes of disability. However, most of the industries with a pulmonary hazard are policed so that early signs of danger cause compulsory withdrawal from the workplace. Most of the allergenic and irritative submicroscopic dusts and solvents cause discomfort and shortness of breath to the

15 percent or more of the working population who are sensitive, and they tend to withdraw from the workforce. The main problem involves disease with a long latency so that the middle-aged and older employees become ill from exposures which date back 10 or 30 years. Common examples are silicosis, berylliosis, and asbestosis.

Neuropsychiatric Problems at Work

Some working people will have episodes of psychiatric illness, which may be acute and temporary or chronic. The acute evanescent episodes can be handled in the same way that an acute somatic illness is handled. Whether the illness is of the psyche or the soma, it will involve a time away from work, perhaps a period of convalescence and a return to work. Provided the work environment was not the stressing agent, no job modifictions are likely to be necessary. The same attitude can be taken to the psychoses. When the treating psychiatrist feels that the patient is ready to return to the working environment, the patient's problem should be studied by the company medical and personnel staff. Laymen should not be asked to provide psychiatric support during rehabilitation, but should be able to understand that a treated paranoid schizophrenic may remain a bit suspicious and withdrawn on return to work. They can accept this, as they accept that persons who have had a below-knee amputation and a successful prosthesis may limp after return to work.

A loss of efficiency in an employee requires careful study. If employees have begun to have repeated Monday absences, supervision should refer them for a medical opinion in the hope that the medical department can find a remediable disability. A few such referred employees will be found to have always been inept and will have to be handled as ordinary personnel problems. A few will have a dementing process that may be advancing in steps, perhaps coincident with strokes, or may be advancing remorselessly. At this stage the resources of modern neurological science departments are needed to define the problem. In the early stages of vascular brain disease, employees may be fit to return to their own jobs after rehabilitation from a cerebrovascular accident. Later, dementia may supervene. Nutritional disease such as advanced irreversible vitamin B or K deprivation or Korsakoff's psychosis are good examples. Pick's lobar dementia and Alzheimer's dementia are functionally the same and require withdrawal from the job market.

Modern noninvasive diagnostic tests such as Electroencephalograms, CT scans, Ultra sound scans and Doppler scans of carotid arteries are most helpful. It is unusual[16] for any one test procedure to be diagnostic by itself; several carefully chosen methods of investigation may have to be used.

Psychological Aspects of Aging

As to the psychological aspects of aging, there is evidence to indicate that age *per se* is not a deterrent to good communication.[17] In fact, communication may improve with age, because the aged person has a lifetime of talking and listening experience, a lifetime of living and career experience from which to draw conversational material. Data from numerous psychometric studies support the colloquial belief that aging results in reduced memory function, but also indicate that impairments are neither uniform nor extensive. Normal elderly have little difficulty with immediate or remote recall, but often do worse than younger persons on tests of recent memory.

Normal elderly adults also perform as well as young adults on tests of vocabulary and general information. They have a high accuracy of recall of historical events or famous personalities of their youth. Older adults typically remember fewer items on verbal free recall, paired associate memory and tests of memory for designs. Older professionals in their 80s will retain about half as much as young professionals of this class of materials.

However, several studies have shown that older adults may fail to recall because they never really learned the item in the first place. This problem can be helped by using mnemonics, by allowing more time to respond, and by minimizing anxieties. One of the key diagnostic features distinguishing the recent memory failures of normal elderly people from those patients with amnestic or dementing features is a sensitivity to remediation of the benign form.[18]

Under experimental conditions, there are no significant differences between older and younger individuals in accuracy of performance on a visual monitoring task.[19] There are significant differences, however, in the pace at which they elect to perform the tasks, and preference for a given pace is significantly related to information processing ability. But the lessons are the same here as in the other experiments. The test must be appropriate to the person in light of his or her physical abilities, but if allowed some freedom in choosing work pace, the older person will perform at the same level as younger workers. Other experimental work suggests that age affects all stages of information processing.[20] The important point is that memory performance of older adults is modifiable.[21] An efficient performance is obtained when instructional training is aimed at the processes that are crucial to the task performance. Effective training procedures have to be based on an analysis of the task, so that the optimum strategies and processes involved in the task are known.

What emerges from an analysis of the training processes is that it is possible to teach people some of the elemental skills of learning; once it is recognized that adults continue to have the basic ability to learn, a great deal can be accomplished.

Belbin, in Great Britain ten years ago, demonstrated in an immensely practical fashion that a large number of persons age 20-64 could be upgraded in important skills. Unskilled laborers became bricklayers; 80 uneducated freight handlers were trained to run a computerized airport freight handling system with no failures; 1,000 London bus conductors were retrained to be bus drivers with only 15 percent failure. The message is clear: once we begin to apply some of the newer technologies of teaching and recognize older people's ability to participate in these activities, impressive results can be achieved.

Work and the Older Worker

But as we look at the evidence on the incidence of illness and the problems that are posed by the environment and the usual degenerative diseases, the fact remains that there are changes as people get older and that these changes may well affect their work status. I turn now to a discussion of these changes and also the problem of work accidents.

Loss of Strength

There is some apparent physiological loss of muscle power which begins to affect athletes in competitive sports in the third decade. For those who earn a living in more ordinary ways, very few jobs in urban areas are so physically demanding that this gradual deterioration in motor power affects their work life. However, some jobs do involve hard physical work. Among urban job holders who do heavy labor are bedside nurses, butchers, steelriggers and furnacemen in steel plants. In smaller communities, hard-rock mining, railway construction or repair, logging, farming, highway construction and maintenance also require heavy labor. This category of jobs may be so demanding that a significant percentage of workers can no longer function in the sixth and seventh decade.

In this group of jobs we must not forget the armed forces. There are few battle-worthy persons over age 45. There are few divisional, brigade and battalion commanders able to command in battle over the age of 40. Cumulative fatigue and emotional drain can paralyze effective action, thought, and decisionmaking in battle. Under such extreme conditions a relatively small decrease in stress tolerance becomes significant.

The steady attrition in the workforce can be seen to parallel and slightly precede the employee mortality experience described earlier. The survivors are mostly healthy. Not more than 10 percent of them develop disease sufficient to force them out of the job market prematurely.

To summarize, most survivors to age 60, 65, 70, and even 75 are fit and able to work. Those that are not fit can be identified by standard medical procedures. It is recognized that this statement is only statistically true and will not include the occasional person with a rare or obscure disease. However, insuring companies and employing companies can balance their books with a statistically valid method of measuring fitness to work.

Fitness to Work

Almost all workers surviving to any given age are physically and mentally fit to work, and many are desirous of remaining in the work situation. Older workers themselves and several organizations supporting them have succeeded in extending their protection under the Age Discrimination in Employment Act and its amendments in the U.S.A. and under the Human Rights Legislation in Canada. Employers and occupational physicians cannot presume that an employee or an applicant for employment is physically or psychologically unable to perform the duties of a job.[22]

The question of fitness for employability must be resolved by a physician, whereas the decision to employ or not to employ (i.e., whether the prospective employee fits the requirements of the desired job), is a personnel function. The handicapped employee must be given an opportunity to demonstrate how the job can be modified to suit the handicap without reducing the quantity, quality, or speed of the job. Generalizations or presumptions must be avoided. For an already employed worker who develops a handicap, it is probably good sense in 1982 to see what the science of ergonomics can do with the man-machine or man-office interface.

Ergonomics is concerned with optimizing the role of man within the man-machine and environment system. This includes the controls whereby energy is passed between man and machine. The science of ergonomics thus is a valuable source of information and practical know-how about designing tools suitable for humans to work with, and environments in which to work. It is particularly helpful with aging employees because the science helps to exploit the distinct advantages older people have in knowledge, judgment, reliability and patience, and to minimize their occasional deficits. Modern machines are very complex, but it has been noted in recent years that ergonomics has been used in machine design. Many semi-skilled jobs can be done using computerized equipment, with the operator basically monitoring the equipment for errors or failures. Older people do this type of job very well. The engineering department and the medical department with industrial hygiene knowledge, can usually do optimum remediation of machines and environment. It is easier to lengthen the legs on a chair than shorten the legs of an employee.

With the advent of legal protection for the disadvantaged employee, employers have to consider the problems of any worker who is physically or psychologically unable to do the whole job. Objective criteria for assessing fitness must be used. Similar criteria must be used to assess the job so that there is a true job match. In industry, remediation of a job mismatch may require only posting the employee to the same job in subassembly as was formerly done on final assembly. The next stage, which may require some minor loss of salary for the employee, is to use his bumping rights to obtain a more suitable job. At management levels an over-stressed manager can be posted laterally out of line management into a consultant job.

One mature and successful method of matching people to jobs has been developed by the author and his colleagues.[23] The error in job placement with this method is predictably less than 2 percent per annum, including positive and negative errors. The original research was targeted on the older worker but the method has proven to be equally useful and practical for all age groups and all varieties of disadvantaged.

The most sensitive diagnostic instrument and prognostic tool the health sciences have yet developed, or are likely to develop, is the trained intelligence and special senses of the examiner. After the examiner has defined the problem, modern diagnostic instruments can refine the solution. It is essential that the tests given be relevant to the proposed job or they are potentially discriminatory in many jurisdictions. If a test is not relevant to general employability or to the specific job, the test should not be given.

Accidents at Work Among Older Workers

Age and injury-frequency profiles for males and females have been found to be similar when controlled for sex differences in the occupational distribution of employment. Younger workers have many accidents per employee-hour, but the accidents are less severe than those that older workers experience. Cost experience data is needed to combine with injury rate experience.

From a practical point of view, experienced semi-skilled and skilled workmen in a craft factory rarely have an injury. Almost all workplace injuries occur during the first 24 months of employment. There are, of course, exceptions to this generalization. In one case, for example, in order to speed up assembly of a rush order, it was decided to move subassembled parts out of the parts stores and onto the floor around the aircraft being assembled. Senior men who were accustomed to a set position for every obstruction around the final assembly area had a rash of minor to severe accidents, mostly from falling backward over stockpiled parts.

Most industrial accidents involve a moment of inattention as an immediate trigger. The results bear no relation to the cause or length of the inattention. As employees get older, the inattention may be the onset of angina pectoris, a myocardial infarct, a cerebro-vascular accident, or many of the organic diseases common in the old-old but beginning to appear in middle age and increasing thereafter. If the problem can be anticipated, the older employee can be posted to a safer job. If he or she refuses, we do not force the issue. The employee's life is his/her own to live. However if there is a public health problem, management will act. For example, a cardiologist allowed a patient to return to work one month after a myocardial infarct. The company medical officer told the cardiologist we could not let his patient work on the wing of an aircraft 30 feet above the ground. The cardiologist became quite irate, insisting he had to believe his patient, who claimed he could do the job, rather than the company medical department. Exactly the right note was struck when we told the cardiologist that our concern was not merely that his patient might fall and break his neck; that there were other men working with him and under him and that we could not allow the cardiologist's patient to kill any of them when he fell! Public health at its best!

As tools and machines have increased in complexity, man has been straining to use his adaptive ability to use machines that are beyond his capacity. As knowledge has become more complex, it has tended to become compartmentalized. The areas of expertise of the various physical scientists have become separated from each other and from the various compartments of the biological sciences.

By World War II the performance capability of military aircraft was outstripping the human capacity for control. Systems began to fail. This led to the concept that man and machines are not independent entities. One cannot design a machine for human use without considering the limitations and capacities of those who are going to operate and maintain it. When one of the components of a system is a human being, then we have a man-machine system. The components of a system are dynamic and interact. A man-machine system exists within an environment. All three interact. Man's activities and requirements define the machine. The machine in turn modifies or determines man's activities. Both change the environment, as the environment changes both the machine and man by influencing each of them and their interaction.

Summary and Conclusion

About 90 percent of surviving older workers remain fit through their work life. Another small percentage, perhaps 5 percent require posting to physically or mentally less demanding jobs during the last few years of their working life. About 30 percent die during their work life, about 5 percent retire on disability pension and about 5 percent require reposting within the workforce to survive.

Healthy older people retain the ability to learn and to remember new learning. This ability is partly a learned skill and can be improved with specific training. Older people do best in self-paced activities as compared to assembly line activities. If allowed to set their own pace, their productivity and accuracy increases.

Healthy older people may be very competent at handling stress as their experience in doing so is very broad. They tend to prefer an administrative rather than an executive approach to problem solving and demand more facts than the very young.

Modern industry and commerce needs the older age group. Equipment is being modified in the optimum direction to suit older persons with their learned skills of patience, attention to detail and reliability. The science of ergonomics is able to assist materially in making the interface between older employees, the machinery they use, and the environment they work in less fatiguing, safer, more comfortable, with more efficient results.

NOTES

1. Life Expectancy Increases but the Life Span is Fixed. James F. Fries, M.D. Letters to the Editor. Amer. J. Public Health. Vol. 72, No. 1, p. 91. Jan. 1982.

2. Aging, Natural Death and the Compression of Morbidity. James F. Fries, M.D. N. Engl. J. Med. Vol. 303, No. 3, pp. 130-135. July 17, 1980.

3. The Epidemiologic Importance of Psychosocial Factors in Longevity. Judith Blackfield Cohen and Jacob A. Brody. American J. of Epidemiology. Vol. 114, No. 4, pp. 451-461. Oct. 1981.

4. Expectation of Life in the United States at a New High. Statistical Bulletin. Vol. 61, No. 4. Metropolitan Life Insurance Company. Oct.-Dec. 1980.

5. Standardized Mortality Ratios and the "Healthy Worker Effect": Scratching Beneath the Surface. A. J. McMichael, M.D., Ph.D. Journal of Occupational Medicine. Vol. 18, No. 3, pp. 165-168. March 1976.

6. Low Mortality Rates in Industrial Cohort Studies Due to Selection for Work and Survival in Industry. A. J. Fox and P. F. Collier. Brit. J. Preventive and Social Medicine. Vol. 30, pp. 225-230. 1976.

7. The Framingham Disability Study: II. Physical Disability Among the Aging. Alan M. Jette, PT, Ph.D. and Laurence G. Branch. Ph.D. American Journal of Public Health. Vol. 71, No. 11, pp. 1211-1216. Nov. 1981.

8. Coronary Artery Disease. Donald A. Rothbaum, M.D. Cardiovascular Clinics. Vol. 12, No. 1, Geriatric Cardiology, pp. 105-118.

9. Coronary Heart Disease in the Western Collaborative Study Group—Final Follow-up Experience of eight and one-half years. Roy H. Roseman, M.D., Richard J. Brand, Ph.D., C. David Jenkins, Ph. D., Meyer Friedman, M.D., Reuben Strauss, M.D., Moses Wurm, M.D., Journal American Medical Association. Vol. 233, No. 8, pp. 872-877. 1975.

10. For additional evidence, see also the relationship of psychosocial factors to coronary heart disease in the Framingham Study III. Eight year incidence of coronary heart disease. Susan G. Haynes, Manning Feinleib and Wm. B. Kannel. American Journal of Epidemiology. Vol. III, No. 1, pp. 37-58. 1980.

11. Type A and Type B Behavior Patterns and Self-Reported Health Symptoms and Stress: Examining Individual and Organizational Fit. Michael T. Matheson, Ph.D. and John M. Ivancevich, D.B.A. Journal of Occupational Medicine. Vol. 24, No. 8, pp. 585-589. August 1982.

12. Effects of a Prescribed Supervised Exercise Program on Mortality and Cardiovascular Morbidity in Patients after a Myocardial Infarction. The National Exercise and Heart Disease Project. Lawrence W. Shaw reporting for the staff. American Journal of Cardiology. Vol. 48, No. 1, pp. 39-46. July 1981.

13. For one list, see The Causes of Cancer: Quantitative Estimates of Avoidable Risks of Cancer in the United States Today. Richard Doll and Richard Peto. Journal of the National Cancer Institute. Vol. 66, No. 6, pp. 1191-1308. June 1981.

14. *Ibid.,* table 20.

15. Towards a Strategy for the Detection of Industrial Carcinogens. E. D. Acheson. British Journal of Cancer. Vol. 44, p. 321. 1981.

56

16. Computerized Axial Tomograms and Dementia in Elderly Patients. Charles V. Ford, M.D. and James Winter, M.D., Ph.D. Journal of Gerontology. Vol. 36, No. 2, pp. 164-169. March 1981.

17. Communicative Aspects of Aging. Daniel R. Boon, Ph.D., Kathryn A. Bayles, Ph.D. and Charles F. Koopman Jr., M.D., F.A.C.S. Symposium on Geriatric Otolaryngology: Otolaryngologic Clinics of North America. Vol. 15, No. 2. May 1982.

18. Odor Identification in Young and Elderly Persons: Sensory and Cognitive Limitations. Thomas Schemper, B.A., Scott Voss, B.A., and William S. Cain, Ph.D. Journal of Gerontology. Vol. 36, No. 4, pp. 446-452. July 1981.

19. Age and Self-selected Performance Pace on a Visual Monitoring Inspection Task. Paul E. Panek, Gerald V. Barrett, Ralph A. Alexander and Harvey L. Sterns. Aging and Work. Vol. 2, No. 1, pp. 183-190. Summer 1979.

20. Isolating the Age Deficit in Speeded Performance. Timothy A. Salthouse, Ph.D. and Benjamin Somberg, Ph.D. Journal of Gerontology. Vol. 37, No. 1, pp. 159-163. 1982.

21. Training Older Adult Free Recall Strategies. Frederick A. Schmitt, Ph.D., Martin D. Murphy, Ph.D. and Raymond R. Saunders, Ph.D. Journal of Gerontology. Vol. 36, No. 3, pp. 329-337. May 1981.

22. Accommodating Equal Employment and Occupational Health Obligations. Nina G. Stillman, J.P. Journal of Occupational Medicine. Vol. 21, No. 9, pp. 595-606. Sept. 1979.

23. Employing the Older Worker: Matching the Employee to the Job. Leon F. Koyl, M.D., Mary Hackney, Ph.D., and R. D. Holloway, B.A. Second Edition published in 1974 by the National Council on the Aging, Inc., Washington, DC.

Chapter 4
Health and Retirement, Retirement and Health: Background and Future Directions

Carl Eisdorfer
and
Donna Cohen

Introduction

Contrary to what might be supposed, the relationship between health and retirement lends itself to no easy description. At the outset, it is important to recognize that health changes may be a cause as well as a result of retirement, that age of retirement is more flexible than often suspected, and that beliefs about health may be more important to functioning than are objective indices of health.

Age of retirement, often identified as the year of an individual's 65th birthday, has been changing dramatically. At the turn of the century, retirement as we know it, did not exist in the United States. Two out of three men aged 65 and older worked compared to one in five by 1980. In 1950, almost one-half of men aged 65 and older were in the labor force. Private pensions and social security benefits had made retirement possible for most people. Moreover, a long period of relatively stables prices and increased levels of post-retirement support under the Social Security Act and broader pension plan provisions began to encourage the exit of working people at age 65 and earlier. In the period 1950 to 1980, labor force participation of men 65 or older dropped from 45 percent to 19.1 percent. From 1960 to 1980, labor force participation of men 55-64 dropped from 86.9 percent to 72.3 percent. For women the reverse trend has been occurring, with participation of those aged 55-64 rising from 37 percent to 43 percent during 1960-70.[1]

This trend for women leveled off in the 1970s, and in 1980, 42 percent of women 55-64 were in the labor force. If current trends continue it is estimated that four out of every ten older men and two out of every ten older women will be in the labor force.[2]

For much of the past decade it has been a case of more and more workers retiring at a younger age although the trend in favor of much earlier retirement has levelled out since 1979.[3] In 1978, 66 percent of male and female retirements occurred prior to age 65, but since 1977 the proportion of people retiring early has declined, reaching 64 percent by 1980.[4] It remains to be seen whether this is a reversal of the early retirement trend.

The significance of these data to the subject under consideration is simply that as the retirement age changes, either up or down, there is a relative shift in the importance of health as a co-variable. It is of some interest to note that in 1900, when the life expectancy of men was 48.2 years, two-thirds of the entire lifespan was spent at work, with retirement accounting for only 6.5 percent of total life expectancy. In 1980, with a life expectancy of 68.3 years for men, only 57 percent of total life expectancy was spent at work while 16.8 percent was spent in retirement. Thus, in 1980 the average man spent 11.5 years in retirement in contrast to approximately three years for the average male in 1900. Obviously, the data are distorted by the fact that proportionately fewer men reached retirement age in 1900. They nevertheless clearly indicate the impact on the total community of increased longevity and the consequent increase in years of retirement. It should also be noted, that these trends are expected to continue. Life expectancy of males is projected to be 68.5 years by 1990, at which time 55.8 percent of the average male's life will be spent at work and 17.2 percent in retirement.[5]

Since advancing age, especially beyond 75 years, is itself a predictor of health status, any modification in age of retirement may have a powerful influence upon the statistical relationship between retirement and health. With a longer work life, more workers will retire for health reasons; conversely, as work life becomes shorter, the number of workers who retire for health related reasons will diminish. Alternatively, since future cohorts of the aged are predicted to be healthier, health may be a less significant factor in retirement for the young-old (60-74 years). It is possible that workers who retire earlier than age 65 are likely to have higher rates of illness, while those who work beyond such an age will be healthier, other considerations relatively constant.

The continued competence and productivity of the individual with advancing age, and the limitations imposed on performance by health problems prior and subsequent to retirement are perennial issues in policy deliberations relating to the retirement and health of older workers. Much of the debate, however, has paid inadequate attention to research findings. The title assigned for this paper was "Health and Retirement; Retirement and Health." This topic clearly emphasizes some complex interrelationships, and implies at least two major questions:

- To what extent does health or functional disability influence retirement decisions?
- What is the impact of retirement upon health?

Before reviewing the empirical data on these issues, it is well to emphasize an important methodological point. The results of most studies in gerontology are based upon persons of specific ages at a specific point in time. The aged of the future, according to current projections, will be better educated, will have received better health care, and thus will maintain their competence and health longer than the current generation of middle-aged and older workers. Furthermore, job-related competence of the middle-aged and older worker is a function of motivation, type of job, experience and training, as well as health.

Health in an abstract sense may or may not be relevant to an individual's occupation. The specific nature of a person's ill health, i.e., disease or dysfunction, is part of a complex of adaptive capacities relatable to the needs of the occupation as well as the symbiosis as it influences the future state of the employee. Clearly we have learned a powerful lesson in the employment of the handicapped. It is one's abilities rather than disabilities that are—or at least should be—at issue in judging the effect of health and disease upon propensity to retire.

Impact of Health on Retirement

How many people retire from various occupations because they are required to do so for reasons of health or functional disability? This question has at least two components: (1) certain occupations require medical examinations and/or proficiency evaluations intended to detect functional changes and disorders that have a negative impact on job performance; and (2) in other situations, the individual makes a personal and voluntary decision to retire because of perceived and/or objective health status.

Occupations Affecting Public Safety

Certain occupations affecting public safety require regular health certification, e.g., commercial airline pilots, flight officers, and FBI agents. On the basis of these regular physical examinations, the workers may be deemed unqualified for their job, and a change in job status or retirement may result. The basis for the disqualification may be a demonstrable loss and inability to function, or it may be a more subjective opinion of the employer that the worker has suffered a limitation on occupational capacity.

Under the Age Discrimination in Employment Act, courts have sometimes considered age to be a bona fide occupational requirement (BFOQ). Age restrictions in a variety of settings are under challenge, and there is increasing controversy concerning the value and validity of age restrictions in employment. Historical arguments that advancing age is accompanied by progressive declines in physical and mental functions have unfortunately led to BFOQ decisions or arbitrary retirement restrictions in the absence of any empirical documentation that older workers are impaired on the job.

Certain occupations affecting public safety raise important concerns about the impact of specific health problems on decisions to retire. The commercial airline industry has required regular medical and proficiency examinations that successfully identify and ground those individuals who should not continue to fly an aircraft. In a study of more than 2,000 pilots employed by a major airline, 103 were found to have retired between 1938 and 1980 for medical problems occurring between age 45 and 60.[6] In a major analysis of more than 5,000 pilots in another major airline, 0.2 percent were grounded each year from 1938-1981 for medical reasons.[7]

The report on "Aging and Pilot Safety" of the Institute of Medicine (IOM) indicates that incapacitation and impairment were identified as causes of only 1.7 percent of general aviation accidents in 1978. Alcohol was identified as the most frequent physiological/psychological cause, accounting for about two-thirds of all accidents. These data do not apply to commercial pilots, but give a sense of the limited impact of health on this complex activity.

Statistics are available on health-related retirement decisions of uniformed state and municipal personnel, i.e., police officers and firefighters,[8] but to date there have been no carefully designed empirical investigations of health and retirement linkages for this group. It is interesting to note, however, that in a number of federal agencies where employees must pass specific endurance tests or certifying physical examinations, a substantial number of older workers remain employed. As of May 1976, 235 (14 percent) of the 1,650 Postal Inspectors were aged 50 or older. Only about six inspectors are assigned to desk jobs per year as the result of findings on the physical exam. In 1976, 1,578 (18 percent) of 8,521 FBI Agents were aged 50 or older, with only 100 agents of all ages assigned to limited duty on the basis of physical examinations. Of 35,943 workers in the Justice and Treasury Departments, as well as in the Postal and Forestry Services in 1976, 5,906 (16 percent) were aged 50 or older, had 30 or more years of service, and were still on the job.

Voluntary Decisions by Workers

The second view of the issue of health as a basis for retirement focuses on employee self-selection. These are cases in which individuals voluntarily withdraw from the labor force either because they believe themselves to be too sick to work or to perform the job, or because they have simply decided that the job is too difficult for them.

Retirement research in the 1950s and early 1960s established that poor health was the most prevalent reason for early voluntary retirement. A 1963 national survey of employment patterns of men aged 65 and older[9] showed that when wage and salary workers retired voluntarily, 35 percent cited poor health compared to only 6 percent in those cases where employers made the decision. Self-employed workers cited poor health more frequently than other factors in explaining their retirement. Fifty-three percent mentioned poor health, compared with 29 percent who said they wanted more leisure time, 5 percent who cited business problems, and 13 percent who specified other reasons. Most investigators agree that the poor retirement benefits of that period created pressures against early retirement that only poor health could overcome.[10]

In a sample of 725 automobile workers who retired early in 1965, 25 percent identified poor health as the reason for early retirement, while 50 percent reported that they retired early because their retirement income was adequate, and 20 percent said they wanted more leisure time.[11] The remaining 5 percent explained their retirement in terms of dissatisfaction with their job.

The Social Security Administration's Longitudinal Retirement History Study initiated in 1969 has provided observations about the health and labor market activity of older Americans during the 1970s.[12]

The original sample included 11,153 individuals who were 58-63 in 1969. They were subsequently interviewed at 2-year intervals through 1979, by which time most of the people in the sample were retired.

Analysis of the baseline data showed a relationship between health and nonwork status. Of the 17 percent of the men and 41 percent of the women in the sample who were not working in 1969, 65 percent of the men and 38 percent of the women listed health as the reason for leaving their last job. Most of the nonworkers had not been employed for several years, but 10 percent of the nonworking men had terminated work as recently as the year before the survey. Of those persons still in the labor force who were working less than 35 hours per week, 14 percent indicated that poor health was the reason for their part-time status. Furthermore, of persons who had turned down job offers in the preceding two years, 21 percent cited poor health.

Despite these relationships between work and health, most individuals in the 58-63 year old group were approaching retirement with a conviction that they were as healthy or healthier than others their own age. Two-fifths considered their health to be about the same as others their age and 35 percent rated their health as better. Men who were living with their spouses and women who were not living with husbands had similar responses: 35 percent of each group described their health as better than that of their peers while 20 percent described it as worse. Of men without wives or living away from them, 28 percent felt healthier than their peers and 27 percent felt less healthy.

A majority of the people in the 1969 sample described themselves as having no limitations or handicaps affecting their mobility or capacity for work, but 35 percent reported work limitations. Over half the disabled reported that their disability had begun five or more years earlier; only 11 percent had become disabled in the year before the interview. Most of the disabled had continued working; two-thirds of the disabled married men considered themselves able to work, as compared with only 54 percent of the men without wives. This commitment to work by the disabled is consistent with a body of recent research, which documents that a considerable proportion of disabled individuals work despite severe disabilities. Among the disabled, age and severity of health problems predict who work part time compared to full time.[13]

One or more contacts with the health care system were reported by 90 percent of the sample. This included physician care (67 percent), prescription drugs (67 percent), hospital care (14 percent), dental care (40 percent), and other miscellaneous services (39 percent). Four-fifths of single men reported getting one or more health services compared to 90 percent of men with wives and of women without husbands.

All respondents were asked whether there was some kind of health care need that they were postponing. Single women with the lowest incomes were the most frequent postponers of care. Dental treatment was the care most often postponed (39 percent) followed by diseases of the nervous system and sense organs (22 percent). The major reasons given for delaying health care were the cost of the care and fear.

In summary, about 75 percent of the baseline sample considered themselves at least as healthy as their peers. Three-fifths were free of disabling health conditions. Nine out of ten encountered the medical world and 25 percent were postponing medical care they felt they needed. A complete analysis of the cohort changes over the 10 years will provide valuable descriptive information, but analyses of interim data on selective problems have already proven to be useful. In 1980, Quinn examined the retirement patterns of self-employed workers in the 1969 interviews of the Social Security Study.[14] The self-employed workers were less likely than wage and salary workers to opt for early retirement, had more flexible work schedules, and were influenced in their retirement decisions by the same factors that influence everyone else, e.g., pension benefits, social security eligibility, and health.

Several other studies have identified the impact of poor health on participation in the workforce.[15] However, few studies have the complex interactions between the behavioral and social factors that affect both health status and retirement. Whereas the 1969-1979 Social Security Study will identify the effects of health on retirement in this cohort over a 10-year period, different generations of workers will "age" differently.

Continued investigations are needed to evaluate new factors that may affect future generations in the labor force. For example, studies of the occupational consequences of coronary bypass operations have yielded some fascinating statistical results.[16] An analysis of 1,165 patients under 60 years of age for periods up to 77 months after coronary bypass surgery revealed that 76 percent had returned to work. Preoperative unemployment, a preoperative job requiring strenuous effort, and low educational attainment respectively, were the strongest predictors of unemployment after the operation.[17] With future advances in medical technology, such as transplants and coronary operations, return to the workforce after serious illnesses should become more common.

Effects of Retirement on Health

The second major concern of this paper is the impact of retirement upon health. Little can be said with confidence on this subject.[18] The loss of the work role is a major event in anyone's life, and it can have powerful effects upon many factors, including interpersonal relationships, economic comfort, life satisfaction, and, of course, health. The health consequences of retirement may be physical or emotional and may compromise the individual's functional effectiveness. These changes may be major or minor as they affect daily activiies, life events, exercise and so on. However, the changes are not exclusively, nor indeed principally, negative, and changes in different factors are not necessarily in the same direction.

Retirement may affect health in different ways. In the classic study of Thompson and Streib, blue-collar workers reported improvement in health after retirement.[19] Since poor health is a reason for early retirement (although income levels may mediate that decision), it is clear that many individuals might welcome retirement as a relief. On the other hand, Ellison has observed that retirees might perceive themselves to be in poorer health as a mechanism to deal with their new and less acceptable role in society.[20] Changing attitudes toward work, aging, and retirement may clearly alter such perceptions, although particular individuals are always exempt from group trends. Interestingly, Ostfeld's careful evaluation of older persons in Chicago indicated that the "older poor" report fewer serious medical problems than were disclosed by their physical exams, revealing that older persons often attribute functional incapacity to age rather than disease.[21]

In Ryser and Sheldon's study of 500 retirees between the ages of 60 and 70, 25 percent reported health improvement after retirement while only 10 percent reported a decline in health.[22] A substantial majority (85 percent) reported very good health, despite reports by 32 percent indicating some functional limitation as a consequence of a physical disorder. Mutran and Reitzes examined retirement and well-being as a result of what they refer to as the realignment of role relationships.[23] What is particularly interesting about this study of over 4,000 persons (conducted by the NCOA in 1974) is that retirement has a powerful but indirect effect upon a number of important factors related to psychological well-being. For example, whereas there is no significant relationship between health and well-being among working men, the relationship is strong in the case of retirees. A younger self-identity is associated with well-being in working men, while for most retired men such feelings of youthfulness are often irrelevant. Occupational prestige makes an important contribution to the well-being of workers; the prestige of an individual's former occupation is not as consequential. Thus, for men over age 55, employment has the advantage of maintaining a total involvement with the community along with age, health and friendship. While retirement *per se* does not lower a person's self-esteem, subsequent involvement in community activities and the social environment may play a powerful role in how people perceive themselves after retirement. This once again emphasizes the importance of the old maxim that it matters less what you retire *from* than what you retire *to*.

New attitudes toward work and the relative decline of onerous physical labor have been operating to increase the probability that people will opt to continue to work if they can, part time or full time, after they reach normal retirement age. A survey of the attitudes of older Americans by Lou Harris (1981) indicates that four-fifths of workers between 55 and 64 years of age are opposed to stopping work completely when they retire.[24] Most wanted at least part-time paid work, and many wanted to continue in full-time employment. A report to the House Committee on Aging, indicates that 30 percent of retirees aged 62-67 are not healthy enough to work at all, 20 percent could work only part time, 14 percent are healthy but not interested in further work and 30 percent are potentially available for work (with 12 percent very interested and needing employment).[25]

The psychological impact of retirement has been described as a crisis, but the data on the incidence or prevalence of this crisis are lacking. Certain forms of psychopathology occur with increasing frequency in the aged, most of whom are not employed. Suicide and alcohol consumption increase with age. The aged account for 25 percent of all suicides in the United States; at the highest risk are white males over age 65 who live alone and consume moderate amounts of alcohol. Alcoholism shows a bimodal age distribution, with an early peak at age 45-54 and a second lower peak at ages 65-74.[26] The causes of this pattern of psychopathology are unclear. It has been proposed that much of the psychological impact of retirement is the consequence of modified life-style rather than in the event itself, and that retirement may actually ameliorate pre-retirement anxiety for some who find suitable activities in their post-retirement life.[27]

For certain individuals retirement can be devastating, if they adversely identify themselves with their position and have no alternative life-style to move toward. At least one study has described the military forced retirement of officers who failed promotion to higher rank. This was preceded by a pre-retirement crisis of about two years duration in which alcohol abuse and gastrointestinal complaints emerged among this group of unhappy and angry officers. Thus, retirement may be seen as a failure rather than a reward.[28] With the aging of our population and the resulting intense competition between younger and older adults for jobs in the workplace, careful analysis of the unmet goals and aspirations of certain professionals and employees should lead to the implementation of flexible job and retirement options.

Qualitative as well as quantitative changes in the family support system and social networks after retirement may have a significant impact on an individual's mental health. Most evidence suggests that family members provide the strongest emotional support. Gore demonstrated that unemployed men who had supportive spouses had fewer physical and psychiatric problems than did unemployed men without supportive wives.[29] Whether support is derived from a spouse or a friend, a confidante is essential. As early as 1968 Lowenthal and Haven stated that older persons with confidants were able to adapt to gradual losses in social interaction as well as the more significant changes of death and retirement.[30] For most individuals, the social support systems that provide both emotional and instrumental support are described as concentric circles moving from the nuclear family in the center to relatives and friends in the middle circles, to work associates in the outer circumference.[31] Different parts of the network play various roles throughout the life span.

Women are more likely than men to have confidants. Therefore, significant life changes such as retirement may have a greater impact on health status and functional effectiveness of men than of women. Holahan surveyed 352 women in the Berkeley study of the gifted and reported that women who had had careers as well as those who ran households had greater life satisfaction and better health than women who had a history of working solely for income.

The Future

From a policy perspective, a number of issues face us. New cohorts of aging persons will be healthier, better educated, and more likely to be in jobs with less strenuous physical requirements. They will also be living longer. What is an appropriate employment policy? Do we face the challenge of creating new careers, flexible career patterns, a lattice career trajectory, or voluntary sabbaticals throughout the lifetime? Perhaps retirement should be delayed or perhaps retirement should be discouraged so we can die with our boots on at our desk at the computer terminal, that is to say, terminate at the terminal!

The economic impact of increasing the retiree population will not only pressure us to address the needs of the older worker, but also force us to attend to a number of other issues raised. What happens to options for the young within an aging workforce? Does management or do unions have a continued responsibility for the worker past retirement? If the private sector does not do it, will the government?

In summary, the two questions we asked at the outset require answers:

1) How does health influence retirement decisions?
Answer: It depends upon the individual's income, previous work experience, the demands of the present job, and the nature and severity of any health problems. The aged are

generally physically able and willing to work and interested in working if retirement income is not sufficient. Many older people indeed prefer a part-time occupation.

2) Does retirement influence health?
Answer: Yes, but the data are sketchy. For some there may be a crisis, for others an improvement in life satisfaction. Life-style at work and after retirement are key variables in predicting success during retirement and/or the impact of loss of work. Activity, both physical and social, is a key. The effect of part-time work on health has not been adequately assessed.

NOTES

1. Kieffer, J. A. So much for the great American dream of retiring early. *Generations.* Summer 1982, 7; Morrison, M. (Ed.) *Economics of Aging: The Future of Retirement.* New York: Van Nostrand Reinhold, 1982.

2. White House Conference on Aging. *Chartbook on Aging in America.* Washington, DC, 1981.

3. Robinson, P. K. Research update: The older workers. *Generations.* Summer 1982, 52.

4. White House Conference on Aging. *Chartbook on Aging in America.* Washington, DC, 1981.

5. Best, F. *Work sharing: Issues, policy options, and prospects.* Kalamazoo, MI: W. E. Upjohn Institute for Employment Research, 1981.

6. Oxford, R. R. and Carter, E. T. Pre-employment and periodic physical examination of airline pilots at the Mayo Clinic, 1939-1974. *Aviation, Space, and Environmental Medicine. 47*:180-184, 1976.

7. Cohen, D. *Age and Medical Groundings of Pilots and Flight Officers.* 1982.

8. Comptroller General Report to the House Committee on Post Office and Civil Service. *Special Retirement Policy for Federal Law Enforcement and Firefighters Personnel Needs Reevaluation,* 1977.

72

9. Palmore, E. Retirement patterns among aged men: Findings of the 1963 survey of the aged. *Social Security Bulletin.* August 1964, 3-10.

10. Atchley, R. *The Social Forces in Later Life.* Belmont, CA: Wadsworth, 1972.

11. Pollman, A. W. Early retirement: A comparison of poor health and other retirement factors. *Journal of Gerontology.* 1971, *26*:41-45.

12. Irelan, L. and Bond, K. Retirees of the 1970s. In C. Kert and B. Manard (Eds.), *Aging in America.* Alfred Publishers, 1976.

13. Schechter, E. Commitment to work and the self-perception of disability. *Social Security Bulletin. 44*:22-30, 1981; Schechter, E. Employment and work adjustments of the disabled: 1972 survey of disabled and non-disabled adults. *Social Security Bulletin. 40*:3-15, 1977.

14. Quinn, J. F. Labor force participation patterns of older self-employed workers. *Social Security Bulletin. 43*:17-28, 1980.

15. See for example, Holtzman, J. M., Berman, H. and Ham, R. The decision to retire early. *Journal of the American Geriatrics Society. 28*:23-28, 1980.

16. Love, J. W. Employment status after coronary bypass operations and some cost considerations. *Journal of Thoracic and Cardiovascular Surgery. 80*:68-72, 1980.

17. Danchin, N., David, P., Bourassa, M. G., Robert, P., and Chaitman, B. R. Factors predicting work status after aortocoronary bypass surgery. *Canadian Medical Association Journal. 126*:255-260, 1982.

18. Minkler, M. Research on the health effects of retirement: An uncertain legacy. *Journal of Health and Social Behavior. 22*:117-130, 1981; Somers, A. R. Social, economic, and health aspects of mandatory retirement. *Journal of Health, Politics, Policy and Law. 6*:542-557, 1981.

19. Thomson, W. E. and Streib, G. Situational determinants: health and economic deprivation in retirement. *Journal of Social Issues. 14:2* 18-34, 1958.

20. Ellison, D. L. Work, retirement and the sick role. *Gerontologist. 8*:189-92, 1968.

21. Ostfeld, A. Frequency and nature of health problems of retired persons, pp. 83-96 in F. M. Carp (Ed.), *The Retirement Process.* Public Health Service Publ. No. 1778, Washington, DC: Dept. of HEW.

22. Ryser, C. and Sheldon, A. Retirement and health. *Journal of the American Geriatrics Society. 17*:180-190, 1969.

23. Mutran, E. and Reitzes, D. Retirement, identity and well-being: Realignment of role relationships. *Journal of Gerontology. 36*:733-740, 1981.

24. Harris, Louis and Associates. *Aging in the Eighties: America in Transition.* Washington, DC: National Council on Aging, 1981.

25. Select Committee on Aging, U.S. House of Representatives. *Retirement: The Broken Promise.* Comm. Pub. No. 96-267. December 1980.

26. Atkinson, S. and Schuckitt, M. Alcoholism and over-the-counter and prescription drug misuse in the elderly. In: Eisdorfer, C. (Ed.), *Annual Review of Gerontology and Geriatrics.* New York: Springer, 1981.

27. Eisdorfer, C. Adaptation to loss of work. In: F. Cerp (Ed.), *Retirement Behavioral Publications.* New York, 1972.

28. Berkey, B. R. and Stoebner, J. B. The retirement syndrome: A previously unreported variant. *Military Medicine. 133*:5-8, 1968.

29. Gore, S. The effect of social support in moderating the health consequences of unemployment. *Journal of Health and Social Behavior. 19*:157-165, 1978.

30. Lowenthal, M. F. and Haven, C. Interaction and adaptation: Intimacy as a crucial variable. *American Sociological Review. 33*:20-30, 1968.

31. Greenblatt, M., Becerra, R. and Serafetinides, E. Social networks and mental health: An overview. *American Journal of Psychiatry. 139*:977-984, 1982.

Introduction

My comments will only indirectly relate to the two principal papers, because I believe that the employability and adaptability of the healthy older worker has been clearly and firmly established. Older workers can perform and do perform almost any job in a productive manner. The problem is not the health status or work potential of the older worker, nor is it the current Social Security design; rather, the basic issues relate to the economy and job availability.

A Profile of a Union, Its Workers and Retirees

"If we think that 76 is old, let's look at Rose Macaluso, who has actually been on the job that long." That statement was part of a tribute to garment worker Rose Macaluso by the late Lowell Thomas in a national broadcast a few days before his death. Rose Macaluso was born on August 6, 1887 in Palermo, Sicily. She came to Middletown, New York in 1911. After a 76-year work history, including a 56 year stint with one employer, lasting through 3 relocations, 20 foremen and 3 managers, she retired on her doctor's instructions in December 1981, at age 94. At retirement she announced that she was planning to go back to setting coat pockets as soon as her health returned. In the interim, she would make new drapes for the house and work on a quilt. Unfortunately, she succumbed to her illness six months later.

75

Dressmaker Celia Orlansky was born in Poland in 1891. She arrived in New York City in 1906 and commenced a lifetime of work at a sewing machine. Her retirement in July of 1981, at age 90, came as a shock. An April 1980 feature story in Justice, the ILGWU newspaper, entitled "Celia Orlansky—Still Going Strong At 90," portrayed this nimble ILGer as likely to sew throughout the 1980s. She worked a full day, commuting daily by subway to Eighth Avenue, Manhattan from her home in the Bronx; (her only concession to age being the half fare privilege accorded senior citizens). Her hands were still strong and sure, guiding fabric against needle in the same manner as when she started work some 75 years ago. However, during the last year, her shop closed. She found work at another shop, but it was slow. When her new employer took in pants for work, Celia Orlansky finally announced her retirement. It was dressmaking or nothing. What will she do in her retirement? "There is a limit to how many times I can clean my house in one week without going crazy," she joked. "I would love to work with children. I need advice on how to get started." If there were still dresses to be made, Celia would certainly be found working at her sewing machine.

It surely can be said that these profiles are atypical, representing two unique individual older workers. Perhaps such is the case. Yet these two remarkable women, while somewhat older, are but a few among the many thousands of garment workers who work beyond the normal retirement age of 65. Of the 111, 836 workers who retired with benefits from the ILGWU National Retirement Fund from January 1965 through September 1982, more than 13.5 percent, or 15,163 men and women, retired at age 70 or older; 3 percent or 3,265 workers, retired at age 75 or older, of whom 766 were at least 80. This experience covers almost an 18 year period; the more recent retirements would probably show a definite trend toward later retirements. Moreover, absent the lingering recession, sharp import penetration, and the growth of non-union competition fostered by an underclass of undocumented workers, the statistics of delayed retirements no doubt would have been swelled by large numbers of older workers who have been compelled to retire earlier because of the lack of work opportunities.

What is the industrial and labor relations environment in which this experience takes place? The ILGWU represents workers producing ladies' and children's apparel in some 38 states and Puerto Rico. Eighty-five percent of its shrinking membership is composed of women. Most of the production in this labor intensive industry is based on a piece work system. Average earnings are $5.50 per hour exclusive of fringes. The average shop has some 40 machines and requires low capitalization. The application of technological changes is minimal. Work is generally seasonal with intense pressures to meet orders during peak periods. There is a high employer turnover and great worker mobility from shop to shop. Under the collective bargaining agreements, the basic work week is 35 hours. Usually there are no seniority provisions, as the principle of sharing of work prevails. There are no provisions for mandatory retirement.

The work force is covered by health benefit programs which typically include hospital, surgical, major medical, sick pay, prescription and eye glass benefits. The mail service prescription program fills almost two million prescriptions annually. Although retirees represent one-fourth of the eligible population they use more than one-half of the prescriptions. For active workers over age 65 Medicare supplements are provided. These benefits all end on retirement except for the prescription program and, in some cases, eye glass benefits. Workers and retirees in the New York area are covered for disagnostic procedures and ambulatory care at the Union Health Center first established in 1914. This institution serves 800 to 900 patients daily.

Retirement benefits are provided through a national multiemployer pension fund. The normal retirement age is 65 and the plan provides reduced benefits at age 62. Disability retirement is available at any age after 20 years of service. There are now more than 112,000 living retirees receiving monthly pension benefits. The worker-to-retiree ratio is just under 3-to-1 and is declining each year. Some 10 years ago, the ratio was 8 to 1. The current basic benefit is a modest $120 per month, ranging up to a maximum of $150 per month for higher wage earners. The Plan's benefits are not integrated with, but supplement, Social Security payments. For retirees who return to work in the industry, benefits are suspended in accordance with ERISA regulations.

The ILGWU maintains a Retiree Service Department staffed by social workers and part time retirees. Included among its activities are social work services, a visiting program, and cultural, education and travel programs, as well as a network of retiree clubs. A pre-retirement counseling program is operated in conjunction with the union's social service and education departments.

I believe that the ILGWU, through its collective bargaining agreements, health benefit programs, and pension plan design, has created an essentially age-neutral environment. This environment enables older workers to make their retirement decision based primarily on health, job characteristics, employment prospects, and retirement income, with age playing a secondary role. The only options absent from this picture are availability of jobs and training and employment programs for those older workers whose jobs have disappeared or who are unable to continue work because of the physical demands of their regular jobs. In the garment industry, as in other manufacturing jobs, "room at the top" is a nonissue!

Policy Considerations

Why at a conference on policy issues in work and retirement have I opened this presentation with a profile of a particular industry and its work force? Why this approach in a session on "Aging, Health and Work Performance," at which the major papers essentially deal with health issues? I do so because I believe that the ability and productivity of the older workers has been clearly established. I do so because I am concerned that the growing acceptance of the worthwhile goal of extending the labor force participation of the older worker has brought with it a host of proposed policies which are not as worthy as the goal they seek to achieve.

Given that the health of older workers is constantly improving, given that more older workers are capable and desirous of working additional years, given that our society can ill afford to waste the vast resources of skill and experience that reside in older workers, the work and retirement problems confronting older workers can be adequately addressed only through policies that lead to the expansion and revitalization of the national economy and to programs that provide full employment for all able-bodied citizens as well as economic security for those who can no longer work.

As workers become older, duration of unemployment rises sharply, and large numbers unwillingly withdraw from the labor force. On October 7, 1982, the House Select Committee on Aging reported that unemployment among workers over age 65 had risen 24 percent since January, contrasted to an overall increase of 16 percent. The disastrous rise in this unemployment level to 10.1 percent in September and 10.4 percent in October were not yet reflected in these figures. While age-neutral practices and policies, job-sharing, part-time work, job redesign, work incentives, and training and education programs all can extend the working lives of older workers, the availability of jobs is a prerequisite to these policies. Older workers cannot be placed in jobs that do not exist; and the goal of extending the working years of older workers must not be achieved at the expense of other groups in and out of the work force.

In today's economy, characterized by a severely declining industrial base and low productivity growth, the false nostrums of increasing the retirement age, easing or eliminating the Social Security earnings test, and providing general tax credits to employers who hire older workers cannot be considered to be sound public policies. The employment problems of older workers are inseparable from the national problem of unemployment.

Increasing the Normal Retirement Age

In addition to altering the labor supply and affecting capital formation, raising the normal retirement age unnecessarily punishes older workers who are laid off for economic reasons or unable to work because of poor health or lack of job opportunities or skills. Raising the retirement age would merely be a form of benefit reduction for older workers. It is a policy which will do no more to create jobs than would the establishment of a sub-minimum age for young workers. A policy of raising the retirement age incorrectly assumes homogeneity of the older population. Despite increasing life expectancy, at age 65, there has not been a comparable improvement in health status. While a healthy older worker could possibly continue at work until retirement at full benefits at a later age, studies clearly show that a significant portion of early retirements are involuntary and relate to poor health, job conditions, chronic unemployment, or all of these. With higher rates of morbidity for blacks and other minorities as well as for older women, a policy of delaying full benefits would unfairly add to the burden of ill and disadvantaged workers. More positive policies would include programs for economic growth and expansion, as well as work incentives and training for that group of older workers who can continue to work after age 65. The adoption of economic policies consistent with a commitment to full employment would result not only in more income for the Social Security trust funds but in more older workers remaining in or re-entering the labor force voluntarily rather than by virtue of economic necessity. Programs providing for options are necessary; however raising the retirement age would eliminate an existing option for a large number of workers.

Eliminating the Earnings Test

The elimination or liberalization of the earnings test is too costly a policy to delay retirement and increase labor force participation of older workers. From its inception, the Social Security program was intended to be an insurance program. It provides protection against the loss of income from work due to old age, death, or disability. Also, private pension plans are generally designed to provide income to non-working retirees. The purpose of these programs is not to pay benefits to full time workers. Past studies indicate that the elimination of the earnings test would result in little or no change in hours worked by males, currently receiving Social Security pensions, but would cause a substantial increase in benefit payments directed to men who currently choose to work full time, generally a group with above-average earnings. Thus, the removal of the earnings test would benefit primarily those who need the help least. The additional benefits that would be paid to the small percentage of retirees earnings more than $6,000 a year would be better spent for programs which encourage later retirement among lower wage earners.

General Tax Credits

Proposals for general tax credits to employers who hire older workers, which on the surface appear to be a reasonable approach, contain several serious drawbacks. In the first place many employers would receive windfalls for complying—as they are already required to do—with the Age Discrimination in Employment Act. Scarce federal revenues would be unnecessarily diverted from other important programs. Secondly, any policy of subsidized employment devoid of specific targets and controls could very well lead to the displacement of other groups of workers without the creation of a single new job. Targeted federal grants should be made available for limited periods of time only in those specific instances where an employer experiences demonstrable higher costs due to the employment or training of older workers. If general tax credits were ever implemented, pressures undoubtedly would build to expand the concept to encompass employment of other categories of workers experiencing similar employment problems (e.g., youth, minorities, displaced, disabled, etc.). If so, this approach would unfairly shift the burden of unemployment to those remaining groups not eligibile for subsidized jobs.

Conclusion

Serious tampering with the existing Social Security benefit scheme or granting general subsidies to employers are undesirable approaches to broadening work opportunities for older workers. The creation of a full employment economy is a mandatory first step in developing an environment for meaningful policies and programs which would enable older workers to continue working. Labor, industry and government must find a common ground in pursuit of this goal.

Chapters 3 & 4
Discussion

Anne Foner

As a sociologist, I should like to put forward a perspective for thinking about the issues before us. Over the last few decades there has been a good deal of research on age and aging in many different fields. As research has accumulated, certain principles have emerged as important for a full understanding of the complex issues related to age and aging, no matter what the field.[1] I shall focus on a few of these principles that I believe are particularly relevant for interpreting data about aging, health, and work performance.

Consider the fact that much of the work on aging and health focuses on old people only. These studies make a contribution and many are appropriate for particular research goals. But they do not tell us whether the pattern of behavior or attitudes observed is unique to old people. To understand whether or not we are dealing with an "Old People" problem, we need to compare older people with younger adults. When such comparisons *are* made, we learn that older people do not always do more poorly than younger adults. Even when the average performance of older persons is inferior to that of younger people, the differences are often small. Moreover, there is wide variability within the older population; there are some older persons who outperform some younger persons.

The general principle here is that older people are part of the whole age structure of a society. To fully comprehend the position and capabilities of the old in society, the old must be viewed against the background of all other age strata.

Another aspect of this general principle is that older people coexist with younger people. Their interactions and relations with the young and the middle aged are part of their everyday living and can affect the way older people function. We know that there is an exchange of emotional and instrumental support between the old and their adult offspring in the family. But we know less about conflicts between the old and their children. And we know even less about the nature of the relations between young and older workers in the work place. As in the family, there may be reciprocity between old and young workers. But it is also likely that relations between young and old at work may give rise to stress—an occupational hazard somewhat different from the type mentioned in Dr. Eisdorfer's paper. There may be subtle or not-so-subtle pressures from younger co-workers or younger supervisors that create tensions among older workers affecting the older workers' health. Thus, it is not only the physical environment on the job that affects the way older workers function but the social environment, including the attitudes and behavior of younger workers.

A second set of principles for interpreting data on age and aging has to do with the aging process. I shall start off with several negative statements, suggesting what aging is not. It is not a process that begins only in the later years; it is not all downhill; and it is not only a physiological process. Put positively, aging is a process that begins at birth and ends with death. It involves accumulations and accretions as well as decrements. And in addition to biological changes and physical alterations, it involves social transformations such as changes in the individual's social roles, social status, and relations with age peers and age dissimilars. Moreover, the physiological, psychological, and social aging processes interact and affect each other.

Let me suggest a few implications of this perspective for the issues at hand. For one thing, the way people grow old is affected by the way they grew up and matured. We are only beginning to find out, for example, that exposure to environmental hazards in the work place and elsewhere when they were younger has damaged the health of many older workers. We have learned, too, that earlier patterns of nutrition and exercise can affect physical well-being in the later years. Let us not forget that the individual's social biography can also play a role.

A ten-year longitudinal study of men in the United States by Melvin L. Kohn and Carmi Schooler illustrates this last point.[2] Kohn and Schooler found a reciprocal relationship between people's occupational conditions and their psychological functioning. More specifically, intellectual flexibility affected the course of men's careers—leading to jobs with substance complexity. At the same time, the substantive complexity of the men's work affected their intellectual flexibility: being in a job with substantive complexity enhanced intellectual alertness and flexibility. In short, conditions of the jobs themselves affect the capacities of the individual.

It is not only the social environment of the family or work that has an impact on the way the individual ages. The larger social environment also plays a role. For example, we have been considering here a key life course transition—retirement from the labor force. We know that the older person's reaction to the loss of the work role is affected by such individual factors as his or her health and income. Important as these factors are, the societal context in which retirement takes place should not be disregarded. Societal attitudes that define retirement as a well-earned rest and as a reward for a lifetime of work, as well as the sheer number of fellow retirees—a sign that everyone else is doing it—serve to validate the retirement role. The stamp of public approval of the retirement role helps to assure the retiree that he or she is doing the right thing.

As for aging being viewed as inevitable decline, research has demonstrated that such a view is an exaggeration. On some abilities there are minimal or no decrements for many years past age 65, on the average. One psychologist, K. Warner Schaie, claims that reliable decrements on all mental abilities for all individuals are not evident until advanced old age—the late 80s.[3] Other research indicates that the predominant trend for many characteristics is stability until the very later years. And, as Dr. Koyl suggests, certain abilities—like communication abilities—may actually improve with age.

The third principle I shall put forward is that aging, inevitable though it is, is not an immutable process. The way people grow up and grow older has changed historically. The cohort of people born before the turn of this century have had different experiences, have been exposed to a different social and physical environment as they aged, than people born decades later. Certainly the way the aged of the future will have grown older will not duplicate the way today's older population has aged. We already know some characteristics of the future aged—say the aged of the year 2020—that can affect the way they will function then. They will probably live longer, on the average, than earlier cohorts of the old. They will probably be healthier—not only because science has learned how to prevent some diseases, but also because there have been advances in learning how to prolong people's ability to function "normally." The old of the next century will be better educated than today's old. More of them will have been in jobs that involve substantive complexity. And more of the women will have been in the labor force for most of their adult lives.

In short, the early experiences of tomorrow's older population would seem to provide a solid basis for their continued ability to make contributions to societal activities in their later years. At the same time, there may be factors that work in an opposite direction. For example, more of the old of the next century will have experienced marital disruption because of divorce. We do not fully understand the effects of such disruption on people's ability to function. Nor do we now know about the possible deleterious effects of all the new chemicals being introduced. This cautionary note suggests the difficulties facing those who wish to shape social policies affecting the old of the next several decades. The future old will face old age in a different social and physical environment than the old of today. And they will have had different lifetime experiences, the effects of which we cannot now evaluate.

The fact that no two cohorts age in exactly the same way leads to my last point: definitions of old age and what are considered to be the problems related to old age are largely social phenomena. As Dr. Koyl notes, not too long ago a worker was considered old at age 40. Now in the United States age 60 or 65 is the magic number, a criterion of old age influenced by Social Security regulations. The very issues we are discussing arise from the unique circumstances of the advanced countries—an unprecedented number of older people in the population and retirement at around age 65 as the practice of the vast majority of older workers.

In earlier times in the United States and elsewhere, and even in many developing countries today, the work potential of the elderly was not an issue. It was assumed that older people would continue productive activity as long as they possibly could. Moreover, older people were thought to have special contributions they could make. Even in the relatively short time that retirement has been institutionalized in the United States, different concerns have come to the fore. Not too long ago people were concerned about mandatory retirement because they thought that workers were being forced to retire—contrary to the workers' wishes. Recent studies indicate that only a small proportion of older workers retire because of the operation of mandatory retirement rules.[4] In the recent period most retirees have been retiring "early," that is, before age 65. And most retirees report satisfaction with retired life.

A major reason the work potential of old people is now of interest is undoubtedly the concern about the economic burden the country faces in supporting large numbers of retirees. However, in our eagerness to assess the "real" potential of older workers, we may well be building a new orthodoxy—that older workers *should* remain in the labor force well past age 65. Such a policy could have unfortunate and unforeseen consequences for both younger and older people. It could foreclose job openings and promotions for younger and middle-aged workers, and thereby exacerbate tensions between young and old. It would be unfair to the many older people who would not be fully capable of continuing to work. And it would be unfair to the many others—a large proportion of whom are blue-collar workers who started working before age 20—who have worked forty or more years in jobs that are unpleasant, monotonous, unhealthy, and physically demanding and who look forward to retirement as an earned right. In our concerns about easing one type of burden on the working population, we risk undertaking social policies that will put new burdens on both young and old.

NOTES

1. For a detailed discussion of these principles see, Matilda White Riley, Marilyn Johnson, Anne Foner. 1972. *Aging and Society. Volume 3. A Sociology of Age Stratification.* New York: Russell Sage.

2. Kohn, Melvin L. and Carmi Schooler. 1979. "The Reciprocal Effects of the Substantive Complexity of Work and Intellectual Flexibility: A Longitudinal Assessment." Pp. 47-75 in Matilda White Riley (ed), *Aging from Birth to Death: Interdisciplinary Perspectives.* Boulder, Colorado: Westview Press.

3. Schaie, K. Warner. 1979. "The Primary Mental Abilities in Adulthood: An Exploration in the Development of Psychometric Intelligence." Pp. 68-115 in Paul B. Baltes and Orville G. Brim, Jr., (eds.), *Life Span Development and Behavior.* Volume 2. New York: Academic Press.

4. Parnes, Herbert S. and Gilbert Nestel. 1979. "The Retirement Experience." Pp. 167-255 in H.S. Parnes, G. Nestel, T.H. Chirikos, T.N. Daymont, F.L. Mott, D.O. Parsons and Associates, *From the Middle to the Later Years: Longitudinal Studies of the Preretirement and Postretirement Experiences of Men.* Columbus, Ohio: Center for Human Resources, Ohio State University.

Chapters 3 & 4
Discussion

Elliot Liebow*

Dr. Koyl has given us a picture of older workers and the aging process that is at once comprehensive and marvelously detailed. Some of his assertions, however, are surprising. Is it really true, for example, that "there is no reason to suppose that any new cancer hazards have been introduced [into the environment] in the last few decades"; or that only 4 percent of all cancer deaths are work-related; or that, by implication, high estimates of work-related cancer are "politically motivated," while low estimates are scientific? These and other issues of fact and substance need to be dealt with, but for this discussion I want to focus instead on Dr. Koyl's approach to the problem of the work potential of the elderly and the relationship of the worker to the job.

The first point I want to make is that one cannot assess the work potential of the elderly by looking only at the elderly. To properly assess the work potential of the elderly or any other group, one must look equally hard at work itself and the organization of work, the politics and economics of work, and the social values that attach to it. To ignore these things and to assume that work potential resides wholly within the individual is to take the first big step toward blaming the victim. Less benignly, perhaps, this is precisely what we do when we make judgments about the work potential of low income, central city, black youth by looking only at the youths themselves, and their attitudes and values about

---

*The opinions expressed here are those of the author and do not necessarily reflect those of the National Institute of Mental Health.

work, without bothering to look at the other side of the equation, at their opportunities and rewards for work, and at what they have learned from their own work experiences and the experiences of those around them.

The point here, then, is that Dr. Koyl's carefully argued and unambiguous conclusion—that "most survivors to age 60, 65, 70, and even 75 are fit and able to work"—addresses an important factor, but only one factor, in the complex equation that describes the work potential of the elderly.

At the risk of faulting Dr. Koyl for not writing a different paper, I would argue that his conceptualization and presentation of the problem leads not only to locating the work potential of the elderly wholly within the elderly themselves, but to other problems as well. In this paper, the workforce is presented in all its rich and ever-changing variety of age, sex, race, health status, personal habits, personality types, varying physical and mental capacities, and so forth. Jobs, in contrast, are presented as a more or less static array of holes or job slots, each with its own particular shape. The problem, then, as Dr. Koyl seems to present it—except for a brief discussion of the potential contribution of ergonomics—is that of fitting a heterogeneous collection of ever-changing individuals to a fixed and finite set of holes or, more simply, to match the people to the jobs.

Such a model of work has profound implications for how we go about the business of organizing people for production. What should be done, for example, with the worker who doesn't fit a particular hold? Dr. Koyl would try to retailor the worker so that he does fit or, failing that, move him out and bring in another worker. Is the job a high-stress job? Exercise is a stress prophylactic. If the worker is still overstressed, he can use his bumping rights to move to a more suitable job, with perhaps a minor loss of salary. The overstressed manager can be "posted laterally out of line management into a consultant job."

What if the job slots are in industries that pose, say, a pulmonary hazard to their employees? Dr. Koyl suggests there is little need for concern because most such industries "are policed so that early signs of danger cause compulsory withdrawal from the workplace." And for those who escape early compulsory withdrawal, there is yet another line of defense: "most of the allergenic and irritative . . . dusts and solvents cause nose discomforts and shortness of breath to the 15 percent or more of the working population who are sensitive, and they withdraw from the workplace."

When we move from hazards to accidents, we find that here, too, many workers are simply not adaptable to the demands of the job. The "immediate trigger" for most industrial accidents, Koyl says, is the failure of the worker to pay sufficient attention to what he's doing. In older workers this inattention may signal the onset of disease, and such workers can then be posted to a safer job. Dr. Koyl does not tell us what to do about workers who have no such excuse, perhaps because inattention in a dangerous work environment sort of takes care of itself.

Once again, this model of fitting people to jobs has brought us back to blaming the victim. Is it really so—or rather, do we, as a society, want to make it so—that the primary responsibility for maintaining worker health and sanity in stressful and dangerous workplaces lies solely with the individual worker? Or that the employer's responsibility goes no further than propping up the employee in place or replacing him with the next person in line to face the exact same threats and difficulties? Is it always and only the worker who must change or move out and never the jobs or the work environment that need changing?

Dr. Koyl, I'm certain, would be the first to disavow such a position, but this is indeed the logic of his paper, and it is indeed the kind of thinking that is often found among managers and personnel people, and all too often among labor economists and policy makers and even workers themselves as well. But even from the perspective of those who hold such a view, it is terribly short-sighted because it is so wasteful of the very people who do the jobs that need doing.

Moreover, if one states the problem narrowly in terms of matching people to a fixed and finite set of jobs, one is likely to overlook the intimate and powerful interaction between workers and jobs. In an important sense, our factories and offices produce not only particular goods and services but particular kinds of people as well. That is, workers are as much a product of the workplace as are goods and services. Quite apart from making it possible to support ourselves and our dependents, the workplace is an important crucible of personal identity and self-esteem, and our work experiences importantly determine our health, our skills, our values and attitudes, and even our personalities.

Despite the centrality of jobs to individual, family, and community well-being, however, we continue to stockpile the unemployed, and continue to face the problem of choosing who will have jobs and who will not. Dr. Koyl has given us hard and persuasive evidence that the elderly are able and willing to work. But so are young workers and middle-age workers, and so are whites and blacks and men and women and the skilled and unskilled. Given the importance of jobs to survival and self-hood, there is no moral basis on which to choose among them. Until we acknowledge the unconditional right to a job of every person able and willing to work, jobs will continue to go to those groups which can muster the political and social power to get them and an ever larger number of people will increasingly go without.

My comments on the paper by Eisdorfer and Cohen, "Health and Retirement, Retirement and Health," will be especially brief and general because I have not yet seen the final version of the paper.

From a policy perspective, a major contribution of this paper is that it documents the complexity of the relationship between retirement and health and identifies the many different factors and influences that must be taken into account. Given this complexity, it is no wonder that the research in this area is often ambiguous and sometimes contradictory.

A major problem is that it is not simply the relationship itself that is complex; the central constructs, especially "retirement," are also complex. Retirement—whether viewed as an event, a status, or a process—involves different kinds of people in radically different circumstances, with different personal, social, and health histories, and equally different futures. The profound social, psychological, and economic changes often occasioned by retirement argue strongly for a powerful connection between retirement and health. But these powerful connections—good for Jones' health but bad for Smith's—will probably continue to wash out into ambiguity until we take a much closer look at Jones and Smith through the progressive disaggregation and specification of populations, occupations, circumstances, and histories.

Some things are already clear, however, and one of them is that money is important. Eisdorfer and Cohen tell us that, in the 1950s and 1960s, "poor health was the most prevalent reason for early voluntary retirement," and that "poor retirement benefits of that period created pressures against early retirement that only poor health could overcome." Here, and in most other research as well, money is deeply implicated in the relationship of health and retirement and retirement and health. Stanislav Kasl, for example, summarizes his excellent review and evaluation of the retirement and health literature with the conclusion that "Financial considerations dominate the entire picture."[1] Although the arguments of Eisdorfer and Cohen are consistent with this view, one might wish that they make more use of money as a possible explanatory variable. For them, the fact that "a considerable proportion of disabled individuals work despite severe disabilities" is evidence of commitment to work. One wonders to what extent this commitment to work on the part of the disabled may be another way of saying they simply cannot afford to give up their jobs.

In addition to money, workplace safety and health are also central to the health outcomes of retirement. For most people, however, "money" in this context means "Social Security benefits" and "workplace safety and health" is largely a matter of standards and enforcement. In an important sense, then, the relationship between retirement and health is fundamentally political, and precisely because it is political, the consensus cited by the authors that future generations of the older workers will "maintain their competence and health longer than the current generation" is by no means a certainty. Quite apart from the larger issues of immigration, unemployment, recession, inflation, and health care, imminent changes in Social Security and recent changes in safety and health standards and practices in the workplace suggest that older and retired workers are headed for poorer health, not better.

Given the terms of discourse, for example, the current debate on Social Security must end up with reduced retirement income for the present generation of recipients, or the next two or three generations, or all of them. Similarly, recent political decisions around workplace safety and health have compromised the safety and health of all workers,

---

1. Kasl, Stanislav V., "The Impact of Retirement on Health and Well-being." Prepared for the National Institute on Aging, NIH, Order No. 263-78-M-2062, January 1978.

among whom the older workers are perhaps the most vulnerable. And to this one might add the unseemly tightening of the rules governing disability and the associated appeals process.

We can hope that Eisdorfer and Cohen are right about the future of retirement and health; we cannot count on it.

Chapter 5
Keeping Older Workers on the Job: Methods and Inducements
Daniel E. Knowles

I'm very pleased to have the opportunity to speak on the subject of the middle-aged and older worker. When I became 39 years of age I developed an interest in this subject because I finally became a member of one of the quasi-protected groups—a group that, God willing, we all get to belong to. Since then I've spent considerable time going around the country giving talks on the subject to anyone who would listen to me. On many occasions I've run down to a House or Senate committee to testify before committees looking into the Age Discrimination in Employment Act (ADEA) or similar legislation. Probably the reason I've had so many invitations to speak, testify, do magazine and newspaper interviews, and write papers is not because I'm so good at it, but rather because there are so few people in industry or the business sector who are at all interested in the middle-aged and older worker—the largest and most neglected segment in the workforce today. Not only has industry in general ignored the middle-aged and older worker, but government, specifically the Congress and Department of Labor, has likewise viewed and treated this backbone of our society with benign neglect.

My very first thought when considering the title of the paper I was being asked to write was that the problem is not keeping older workers on the job (that's almost a mechanical question) but rather how one creates an environment in the workplace that is conducive to the middle-aged and older worker's either being able to or wanting to stay on the job. My second thought was to examine my own feeling on keeping the middle-aged and older worker on the job, and I had to recognize that although I want to see them staying on the job collectively, I don't want to see a single older worker staying on the job if he or she doesn't want to. I think it's time we viewed the subject from a more behavorial perspective. Retirement is moving in two directions at the same time. There is, on the one hand, a trend toward earlier retirement and, on the other, a strong manifestation of a desire to be free to work as long as one wishes. What this really signifies is that people want more to say about their own destiny; they want society and industry to offer more freedom for individual choice rather than to attempt to manipulate older workers in order to achieve other objectives. From this point of view, it is equally objectionable to try to get rid of older workers to make room for younger people as to try to keep them on the job in order to salvage the Social Security system.

With that statement of values out of the way, let me now address the topic that has been assigned me. Starting in the 1960s, considerable federal legislation has been enacted that has required affirmative action to combat discrimination against minorities, women, the handicapped and veterans. Legislation and executive orders, such as Executive Order 11246, the Civil Rights Act of 1964, the Equal Pay Law of 1967, the Rehabilitation Act of 1973, and the Vietnam Era Veteran Readjustment Assistance Act of 1974, have provided the full weight of the federal government to ensure that these protected groups got a fair shake. Is it any wonder that annual audits by the Office of Federal Contract Compliance of the Department of Labor have caused the quality of life in general to improve for these groups covered by affirmative action programs? Affirmative action programs are big business within big business today. Millions of dollars, if not billions, are spent each year by government and business to ensure compliance with the law.

No one with a sensitive conscience can deny the importance and righteousness of affirmative action for these groups. My quarrel is not with government and its concern with these groups, but rather with the benign neglect the government has demonstrated towards the middle-aged and older workers, the forgotten Americans who represent the largest of the so-called protected groups.

In 1967, Congress passed the Age Discrimination in Employment Act. While its motivation is obscure, it nevertheless focused attention on the question of discrimination. The message to industry and business 15 years following the enactment of the Act is still obscure. The message, in short, has been "Do not *overtly* discriminate against the middle-aged and older worker, especially by policies that affect *groups* of such employees." The ADEA's impact on industry has been minimal. As compared with the action-oriented positive thrust of affirmative action programs for other groups, the ADEA has constituted little more than an occasional irritant. While the impact on industry has been minimal, the impact on the middle-aged and older worker has been significant. The discrimination against the elderly is the most insidious type of labor market discrimination taking place today. For one thing, a good part of the discrimination is subconscious and subtle (people discriminating against the older worker are often not aware they are discriminating). For another, age discrimination is insidious because it is being perpetrated not by younger workers but by other older workers who are in the management positions to do the discriminating. Finally, since the middle-aged and older workers are the largest of the so-called protected groups, there is greater potential for discrimination against them.

I find it ironic that the legislation itself, ADEA, is discriminatory because of its exclusion of executives from the prohibition of mandatory retirement below age 70. If an employee is key and is guaranteed a certain pension, he or she can be involuntarily retired as early as age 65. If the pension is below the specified amount, on the other hand, the company cannot involuntarily retire the person until age 70.

If Congress accepts the fact that ADEA has not kept pace with other legislation in the area of discrimination, it should enact further revisions of the Act to require, as a minimum, that:

1. The Department of Labor promote education programs in industry pertaining to the middle-aged and older worker.
2. The Department of Labor support research relating to middle-aged and older workers and disseminate its findings to industry.
3. Industry be provided with detailed demographic information by skills and age so that companies can better understand how the composition of their workforces compares with the availability of older workers.

It should be the goal of Congress, through such legislation, to require the Department of Labor to institute a meaningful program of voluntary action that will accord a "fair shake" to this group. Industry cannot and will not meet the needs of these people unless Congress directs the Department of Labor to provide industry with the tools to do so. If business, given the necessary tools by the Department of Labor, fails to comply voluntarily with the principles of fairness and fails to enact a voluntary affirmative action approach to the older worker, it will have no one to blame but itself if Congress enacts further legislation requiring an annual formal affirmative action plan similar to that required for the other protected groups.

The Department of Labor should institute an ad hoc committee to prepare a "How To Do It" booklet that would include an awareness section depicting the plight of the middle-aged and older worker; a section devoted to exploding such myths about older workers, as "you can't teach an old dog new tricks"; information on the demographic composition of the workforce; and a demonstration of how a company should undertake a self-analysis of its workforce by age. Failure by the Department of Labor to take such positive steps will only convince American industry of the government's indifference toward this important segment of our workforce.

Industry is similar to Congress and the Department of Labor in at least one respect: all three are pragmatists. Each group, at its leisure, can pay lip service to the dignity of all mankind, of all Americans, and even of all of the heterogeneous groups that make up the national workforce. Yet industry, in general, is quick to respond to the pressures of running a business. These pressures can take the form of production, quality, costs, schedules, sales and, yes, even affirmative action programs. Failure to comply means sanctions; consequently, affirmative action programs have been industry priorities or "must jobs," while concern for the middle-aged and older worker has been at best a "should" or "like to do" job and, at worst, has been completely unknown to a major segment of industry. If the average company were asked it if discriminates against the older worker, I am sure it would reply indignantly that it does not. But I submit that probably not one company in ten thousand has ever examined its own organization's age structure in comparison with the limited workforce availability statistics provided by the Department of Labor. We are all caught up in the youth cult and are its victims. When in need of additional personnel, what manager of a department isn't looking for a 26 year old college graduate with ten years of experience? The entire society seems to be living according to the advertising messages in all the media: "If you're not part of the Pepsi generation you should be put out to pasture."

Older workers, in most cases, are being discriminated against by companies that are unaware that they are discriminating and, what is worse, employees are unaware that they are being discriminated against because of the subtleties.

Although there is an increasing awareness of age discrimination on the part of individuals and companies, the awareness is momentary; that is, when an allegation of discrimination is made by an individual, the company gives it the same attention as a leak in a factory window. Fix the leak and back to business as usual. Little thought is given to reviewing the causes of the alleged discrimination. Most employers are more likely to attribute allegations of age discrimination to paranoia.

An industry mentality that young is good and older is bad results in a self-fulfilling prophecy. As older workers perceive an expectation by management that their value and ability will diminish, they sometimes behave in ways that contribute to the myths.

Basically pragmatic by nature, industry will respond to the needs of the older worker if it can be convinced that it is good business to do so. Let me summarize a minimum agenda for industry before we turn our attention to specific programs. With a commitment from top management, a company should:

1. Promulgate a positive policy of ensuring a "fair shake" for employees between the ages of 40 and 70.

2. Make the policy statement known to all employees and require the subject to be included in all supervisory development programs in the company.

3. Review company personnel policies, practices and benefits to determine if there are built-in prejudices not consistent with fair treatment. At a minimum, the review should include hiring, promotion, career counseling, performance appraisal, training, compensation, termination, retirement, pension, long-term disability, life insurance and other benefit programs and recreational and social programs.

4. Perform an analysis of workforce composition based on minimal available demographic data provided by the Department of Labor. For example, according to the Bureau of Labor Statistics' Employment and Earnings of June 1981, 41 percent of the national workforce is over age 40 and 31 percent is over age 45. The age composition of the company's total workforce should be measured against these standards. Comparable analyses should be made by broad categories of employees—e.g., officials and managers, professional, clerical, and blue-collar workers—as well as by specific skills.

5. Set up a mechanism within the company to ensure that an employee who alleges age discrimination can have his or her case reviewed objectively and that a fair solution is provided.

In the final analysis, if a company is clearly perceived to have a positive philosophy and set of attitudes toward the middle-aged and older worker, there is relatively little need for special programs; unfortunately, the converse may also be true, i.e., that special programs for "keeping the older worker on the job" may be present in organizations that are either discriminating against or underutilizing middle-aged and older workers. I submit that there are not significant differences between older and younger workers and that the belief that there is, is the biggest myth of all about the older worker. For example, younger people have just as much absenteeism as older workers; they take time off for different reasons. In one study of a large manufacturing company that laid people off on the basis of performance rather than seniority, a layoff of 13,000 persons resulted in a rise in the average age of the remaining workforce from 37 to 45. In that case there appeared to be a positive correlation between age and performance.

The key to the need for special programs is through an analysis of your company's activities. If your training, promotion, recreational activities, etc., fairly represent the middle-aged and older worker in proportion to the company workforce as well as the national workforce, nothing special should be necessary. It is only if there is an imbalance that corrective action through special programs should be instituted. In general, the solutions to specific problems are obvious. If older employees are underrepresented in the company's recreational and social programs, an analysis may indicate that there is too much emphasis on sports and not enough on clubs; if older workers are not proportionately represented in company-sponsored training programs, the selection procedure can be reviewed and the imbalance corrected. If older workers are overrepresented in layoffs or terminations for other reasons, the reasons and solutions may not be as obvious but should be thoroughly investigated so that whatever corrective action is warranted may be taken. "Keeping older workers on the job" should only be considered in response to a demonstrable problem. In other words, "if it isn't broke, don't fix it." Older workers should be free to leave an organization to start a second career or to go into retirement or to stay on the job without having government, industry, or gerontologists manipulating them through programs. At best I'd consider a phased retirement program to assist the older worker who can't decide between full employment and retirement. But it is important that such a program be mutually agreeable to both parties and that it not be used as a tool to get rid of older workers. Another program that I think has great value to both industry and retirees is a part-time, temporary, or on-call workforce made up of retirees who are interested in participating. Maintaining a skills bank of retirees can be a significant program of mutual benefit to a company and its retirees. Companies can also advertise the availability of the skills of their retired employees to other companies in the community as another method of maximizing post-retirement labor market opportunities. The best technique of ensuring the welfare of retirees is for companies to sponsor and support an active Retirees' Club to act an an adjunct to the company in supporting the needs of its retirees.

In summary, if the climate is right within an organization, there is little need for programs to induce older workers to remain on the job; older workers really are just like other workers, some good, some bad, some leaders, some followers. Such programs are needed only to the extent that there have been demonstrable injustices to older workers in the past, and can be successful only if the sources of such injustices are eliminated.

Such programs are at the end of the journey at best. The work is just beginning to form a partnership between the Congress, the Department of Labor, and industry to develop an environment that replaces benign neglect with concerned respect for middle-aged and older workers and accords them the recognition they deserve as the largest segment of the national workforce. Hopefully, within our lifetime the follow-

ing poem will no longer be applicable in summing up
society's attitude towards the older worker:

> "In savage tribes where skulls are thick,
>   And primal passions rage,
> They have a system sure and quick
>   To cure the blight of age.
> For when a native's youth has fled,
>   And years have sapped his vim,
> They simply knock him in the head
>   And put an end to him.
> But we, in this enlightened age,
>   Are built of noble stuff.
> And so we look with righteous rage
>   On deeds so harsh and rough.
> For when a man grows old and grey,
>   And weak and short of breath,
> We simply take his job away
>   And let him starve to death."

Chapter 6
Maximizing Post-Retirement
Labor Market Opportunities

Anna Marie Buchmann

Although it is a privilege to participate in this conference, I hope we can stop meeting like this. Let me explain. I share the view that "Society's goal must be to eliminate the need for special issues or conferences on the 'older worker'. . . . The *individual* will be the basic unit of future society, not groups grasping to find a false basis of commonality like age."[1]

As we approach the twenty-first century, we need to assure that public policy is based on age-neutral or age-irrelevant factors, that one's access to a job is not limited by the years he or she has lived but rather by ability to perform. Indeed, we need to entertain the idea of making the concept of retirement obsolete.

As the foregoing makes clear, I have become increasingly uncomfortable with the title that has been assigned to this paper, since I believe that we must stop thinking of "post-retirement" opportunities and recognize that work fits into the continuous growth process of persons of all ages. We can no longer compartmentalize play, school, leisure, and work but must recognize that each of these enriches our lives and should not be limited to prescribed years. Life is a continuous process of growth and enrichment.[2]

In the 1980s and 1990s demographic changes will necessitate changes in public policies. We must make certain that policies affecting the work place as well as other sectors of our society are based on sound principles and on facts that are already available to us. We know, for example, that older persons are becoming a larger part of the population, and that younger workers will be in shorter supply. It should be equally clear that the decreasing proportion of active workers to retirees will place a heavy, if not unsupportable, strain on current retirement and benefit practices. Under these circumstances, encouraging older people to work utilizes this willing, available and experienced national resource and is surely sound social policy.

Managers in corporations that make a practice of hiring older workers point to their reliability and experience, the pride they take in their work, the high value they place in their jobs, their devotion to corporate goals, and the paucity of "convenient" absences. They speak of cost savings and efficiency resulting from low turnover, and of the absence of significant additional expenses compared to the employment of all other workers taken as a group. A concise summary of data concerning performance abilities of older workers published by the Andrus Gerontology Center helps to refute common myths concerning this group. Specifically, it cautions against facile generalizations about the relationship between age and productivity, decisionmaking ability, intellectual functioning, memory, learning ability, general health status, and accident experience, and points out that along some of these dimensions older workers appear to have a better record than their younger counterparts.[3]

Louis Harris,[4] as well as others, has found that fear of inflation, uncertainty about the future and lack of knowledge concerning options are key factors affecting retirement decisions. As employers and as a society we need to pay more attention to providing adequate information concerning later adulthood—not only as it affects work options, but all factors of an individual's life. To a considerable extent this can be accomplished through company sponsored pre-retirement education programs.

Pre-Retirement Programs

The 1981 White House Conference on Aging urged "businesses and other organizations comprising the private sector to offer a full range of pre-retirement services to their employees."[5] A sound pre-retirement counseling program assures that the prospective retiree will be well-equipped to make an informed choice at that critical, often traumatic point.

A 1981 American Management Association survey, conducted by Robert Jud, examined how managers felt about retirement and their companies' retirement practices and the manner in which they personally were preparing for retirement. The study indicated that retirement policies and retirement education programs fall short of expectations and concluded that individuals must do more personal planning.[6]

We at Bankers Life and Casualty Company maintain that retirement planning is life-long and that it should begin early in one's career. Our program, "Planning For Your Future," is open to employees of all ages. We also believe that whether sessions are conducted in small groups or one-on-one, there is merit in including a spouse or "significant other" in discussions, since retirement involves the family unit as well as the retiree.

There is wide agreement on the elements of good pre-retirement counseling. There should be discussions of:

1) company benefits, such as pension plans and health and life insurance coverage;
2) other income sources, such as Social Security and personal savings;
3) complete financial planning and budgeting;

4) housing and living arrangements;
5) personal and property safety;
6) physical and mental health aspects of aging;
7) social relations and use of leisure time;
8) post-retirement options.

The AMA study admonishes pre-retirement educators to place greater emphasis on job retraining, outplacement services and guidance in part-time employment. Most of the respondents fully expected to continue working after retirement, but on a part-time basis or at a "reduced level of intensity." More than 40 percent of those respondents age 50 indicated an intention to work past 65, and 18 percent said they would like to keep working until 70 or older. The author of the study concluded that ". . .American managers are becoming open to new, more flexible ways of retiring. Often this means drawing a less rigid line between working years and retirement years."[7]

Pre-retirement planning programs are a relatively low cost benefit and provide an immediate intangible payoff in employee good will. More importantly, a well founded program will equip older workers to gain control over their future, which may include paid work, volunteer work, or education. For many, it is a combination of all three. While many corporations prefer to develop their own pre-retirement counseling programs, packaged programs are available through a number of reputable organizations including AIM and NCOA.

Alternate Work Patterns

Alternate work patterns open new and creative possibilities in scheduling work and job duties. Many of these lend themselves well to the expressed desire of retirees for less than full-time employment. The Work in America Institute predicts that by the end of this decade over half the workforce will be on alternate work schedules. San Francisco's New Ways to Work, an advocate of work options, has selected four industries as especially appropriate for innovations of this kind: banking, data processing, health care, and telecommunications.[8] Testimony before the House Select Committee on Aging provided case studies of alternative work patterns in the fast food, high technology and banking/financial/insurance industries.[9]

The experience of my own organization has been well documented. From its founding, Bankers Life and Casualty has never had a mandatory retirement age. We have traditionally hired persons over the age of 65 who have been mandatorily retired from other organizations, and have more recently instituted a part-time pool of employees from our own retiree group. In addition to my own company, the insurance industry in general has tended to respond positively. Connecticut General, Mutual of Omaha and Travelers Insurance are among those exploring pre- and post-retirement options. In testimonies presented to the U.S. House of Representatives in October of 1981, a number of industry representatives presented their own corporation's view concerning the value of retaining and rehiring older workers. Programs specifically geared to retired workers include full- or part-time options, temporary work and semi-retirement. For some, these are aids in adjustment to final complete retirement.

Phased Retirement

Through this option, employees nearing retirement gradually decrease their hours and responsibilities over a period as long as several years. It is an aid to retaining skilled executives and professionals who might otherwise elect to retire early. It is also perceived as a means of providing promotional opportunities by freeing up positions held by these persons. The study by Jud referred to earlier found that higher-paid managers (those earning $60,000 or more per year) were the most likely to choose to continue to work on a reduced schedule and at less intensity.[10]

Gail Rosenberg, President of the National Council for Alternative Work Patterns, maintains that phased retirement is a key issue of the 1980s. She notes that the apparent interest of older persons in reduced work hours, as well as the favorable experience of companies which have initiated phased retirement programs, may result in increased use of such programs.[11]

Variations on the phased retirement theme include rehearsal retirement, tapering off, sabbaticals and job reassignments. Each of these will be described briefly in turn.

Rehearsal Retirement

At Polaroid Corporation, employees may take an unpaid leave of absence to "test the waters" of retirement without losing their jobs. At the end of this time, the employee may either return to the job or retire. Average length of "rehearsal retirement" is three months. About 50 percent of employees who have tried this return to full-time work. When an employee returns, seniority date credit for frozen benefits is resumed.[12]

Sabbatical

This concept is fairly new to industry, but a tradition of the academic world. It permits time away from the job and usual responsibilities to pursue education, public service, avocational and other interests. The Executive-on-Loan program sponsored by many companies is a variation.

Job Reassignment

Employees are reassigned to different jobs with similar responsibilities and compensation as in lateral transfers or job rotation or to positions of less responsibility, stress, pay and status. Xerox Corporation's "strategic repositioning" is an example of the latter. Through this program, employees who are at least 55 with 15 years of company service or 50 with 20 years of service have special rights to "bid downward" on jobs they are capable of performing.[13]

Contrary to popular belief, there is evidence that sizable groups of older workers prefer demotions to early or forced retirement. Jud found this to be true of a "slight majority" of his respondents, and sees this as eventually a common retirement alternative.[14] A 1978 Danish study of 150 largest corporations also found that a significant number of older managers preferred to step down to jobs of less responsibility and status. However, informal conversations with labor market experts in this country have suggested that it may be easier for an older employee to accept a position of less status with a company other than the one in which he or she has spent most of a career.

Additional Alternatives to Conventional Work Pattern

In addition to phased retirement and its variants, there are other alternative work patterns which may appeal to workers of all ages and that thus provide new options for older workers and retirees:

Flextime. Employees may choose their starting and stopping times, but must be present during a core period of the day and work a previously agreed on number of hours.

Part-time Work. Employees have a reduced work schedule on either a permanent or temporary basis. Options may include: part-day, part-week, part-year or alternating days, weeks or months.

Job Sharing. An agreement in which two people have responsibilities for one full-time position. A detailed study of the appeal of this program is found in the January 1982 issue of *Stakeholder Issues and Strategies* published by the Human Resources Network. In the Jud study, this type of program appealed to 70 percent of his respondents.[15]

Job Redesign. Component tasks of the job may be redistributed or the work environment may be adjusted to meet worker needs.

Compressed Work Week. Work is compressed to less than the traditional 5-day week.

Skills/Job Banks. Retirees fill in for permanent workers who are on leave of absence or vacation or are called in for temporary assignments as needed. One recent study indicated that of 30,000 employees surveyed nationally, 55 percent had employers who have established retiree skills banks. In general, only a small fraction of retirees participate.[16]

Cottage Industry. Job assignments can be completed at one's home rather than at a traditional work site. While this appeals to some, we have found that most of our retirees prefer to come into the office, since it gives them an opportunity to socialize with old friends and former co-workers.

Regardless of the format, each of these alternative work patterns aids the individual in a gradual rather than abrupt transition to full-time leisure. We are all aware of the index of psychological stresses which places loss of a job almost as high as loss of a spouse. If the older worker is provided support through this period, the adjustment will be physically and psychologically healthier and may open new avenues of growth.

Second Careers

Some persons approaching retirement age prefer to move on to another full-time career. There are many well known examples of individuals who have continued to make their mark well beyond the "normal" retirement age. For instance on April 28, 1982, the National Council on the Aging announced that Dr. Arthur Flemming, 77, had been elected its President. Flemming's career, the announcement says, "spans several disciplines and service on numerous commissions and advisory councils." He served as HEW Secretary from 1958 through 1961. He chaired the White House Conference on Aging in 1971, was U.S. Commissioner of Aging from 1973 to 1978, and was chairman of the U.S. Commission on Civil Rights from 1974 to 1982. He is an excellent example of an individual with multiple careers during one very productive lifetime.

Gerald Maguire, one of my company's former executives, provides another example of a successful second career option. At age 55 he took the company's liberal retirement program and began a second career with another organization, which, like ours, has never had mandatory retirement. The U.S. Chamber of Commerce, in a recent news release, announced that the Chamber's regional manager, Bob Van Ausdall would take early retirement to become chairman of the Chicago Institute for Management Studies. His seventeen years at the Chamber was not Van Ausdall's only executive position. The position of vice president of the Council on Financial Aid to Higher Education is a second career for Robert Jordan, who had retired after a successful career as executive vice president of Bankers Trust Company in New York. Harry Johns, a Sears executive, now provides outplacement counseling to others as a key staff member of Jannotta & Bray Associates.

Testifying before the House Select Committee on Aging, Max Urlich, president and chief executive officer of Ward Howell International, an executive search firm, stated that

> Some companies bring in older executives to help prepare the next generation of management. One of our client companies sought a leader who could develop its young managers, none of whom was ready to succeed the retiring chief executive. The winning candidate—a 58 year old former chief executive of a much larger company, who had taken early retirement.[17]

These people have done it on their own, but others need more assistance. For them, a growing number of resources are available to aid in identifying job opportunities.

Older Worker Job Agencies

An example of such a resource is Operation ABLE, a Chicago based advocacy group that offers training, consultation, technical assistance, direction, and coordination in all aspects of senior adult employment. The agency was founded in 1977 with the goal of creating employment opportunities for adults 55 and older. ABLE (Ability Based on Long Experience), attempts to convince business people that a maturing American workforce is a growing resource for business. One of ABLE's arms, APT (The Older Experienced Temporary APT to Fit Your Needs), appeals to employees who want to work on a temporary basis. Recently the organization filled its largest job order, 100 part-time clerical positions with the Continental Bank of Chicago.[18] The success of ABLE has enabled it to enlist the support of numerous agencies in the Chicago area as well as the media. Because of its track record, ABLE has become a model that is available for implementation elsewhere. One adaptation of the model has begun in Los Angeles.

Los Angeles also has its Second Careers Program, through which a retiree is offered:

1) choice of full-time or part-time, temporary or permanent, paid positions geared to the individual's skill level and experience.
2) placement and counseling tailored to the individual's needs.
3) access to a variety of volunteer opportunities.
4) informational resources.

In Milwaukee, Retiree Work Search helps retirees find part-time employment. Yet another example of this type of service is provided by NAOWES NEWS (The National Association of Older Worker Employment Service), operated by the National Council on the Aging.

Educational Opportunities

Whether the goal is to prepare for labor market access or to pursue knowledge for the individual's current job, or to open other new vistas, "returning students" are becoming very much at home on the college campus. Educational opportunities have become increasingly available for older adults. Some corporations, like IBM, will pay educational costs for older employees who want to prepare for second careers.

On a recent college tour of New England, I was pleased to find that most of the colleges and universities my teenage daughters and I visited were participants in the Elder Hostel Program. Combining the best tradition of education and hosteling, the program is designed to satisfy older citizens' needs for intellectual stimulation and physical adventure. Elder Hostel, which celebrated its seventh anniversary in 1982, includes 500 colleges and universities, independent schools, folk schools and other institutions in all of the 50 states, Canada, Great Britain, Denmark, Sweden, Finland and Norway.[19]

The Academy of Life Long Learning was established at the University of Delaware in 1980. Open to anyone over age 50, the Academy is modeled in part on the Institute for Retired Professionals at the New School in New York City. An "intellectual cooperative," the Academy draws on the expertise of its members, many of whom are retired executives. The leading force in this program, Edwin C. Busbaun, 79, retired after 35 years with DuPont to devote time to his interest in anthropology. An emeritus professor at Delaware, he sees the Academy as the first in a national organization of such institutions. To its credit, the Academy was one of the eight winners of the Innovative Awards in Continuing Education Program sponsored by the American College Testing and the National University Continuing Education Association.[20]

In Chicago, The Education Network for Older Adults, established in 1977, is flourishing. The Network acts as a resource center and a clearinghouse with 48 colleges, universities and human resource communities. With its thrust toward helping retirees reenter the labor market, the staff attempts to learn about successful programs in older adult education. Bernard Schwartz, Executive Director, believes that both age-segregated and intergenerational educational experiences are useful. The Network serves as Education Information Center for the State of Illinois for older adults and is an official center of the Illinois State Scholarship Commission, with information on state scholarships, grants and loans for older persons.

Many of the vocationally based education programs for older persons build on the students' previously acquired knowledge of the liberal arts. This approach to education is based on the premise that we can no longer plan for one career, but must rather prepare for many careers during the course of a lifetime. Schwartz points out that 80 percent of the jobs that exist today did not exist ten years ago. Older persons, if they have time to enroll in training programs of 3 to 6 months, can be on the cutting edge of such emerging new fields as computer technology, electronics and biogenetics.

Though not limited to older adults, one California program is anticipating the need for qualified persons in electronics. The American Electronics Association projects a need for 113,000 technical professionals and 140,000 technical paraprofessionals by 1985. Local institutions and colleges are working together to develop technicians for the Silicon Valley. The California Worksite Education and Training Act (CWETA), is a model that enlisted the participants of 14 companies including Hewlett-Packard, Litton Industries, Apple, Watkins-Johnson, Siltec and Savin.[21]

A further example of an ideal match between human resources and job needs is provided by the WAVE III Corporation. This systems software development company has trained retirees as programmers. Retirees who successfully completed the short training program were hired on a contractual basis at prevailing market rates for work on systems designed by the parent company.

The WAVE III program, developed in response to a severe shortage of computer programmers in the U.S. is a prototype for such programs. Unfortunately, ACS America is bankrupt. In a recent conversation, John Jacobsen, vice president for corporate planning of WAVE III, told me that a feasibility study has been completed for a possible reorganization or restructuring of the program through Travelers Insurance.[22]

Volunteerism

For some older adults, the opportunity exists to pass on their knowledge through volunteerism. The Volunteer Development Corps (VDC) is a nonprofit organization that assigns retired executives to function as "corporate ambassadors" abroad. Expenses are split between the U.S. State Department, which sponsors the program, and the host country. Each year approximately 50 executives are assigned to advise overseas companies.[23]

The International Executive Service Corp (IESC) is a second group of American executives whose "post-retirement" activities include volunteering their services to foreign governments and enterprises. Initiated by David Rockefeller seventeen years ago while he was chairman and chief executive of Chase Manhattan, its goal was to offer an "old-hand" instead of a "hand-out."

> Since Rockefeller's proposal in 1963 and the first assignment for volunteers to Panama and Taiwan in 1965, the International Service Corporation has sent more than 8,000 retired or on-leave executives to 70 countries. Collectively, these volunteers have spent more than 25,000 months transferring their knowledge to struggling businesses in Latin America, the Middle East, Southeastern Europe, Africa, South and East Asia, and the Iberian Peninsula.[24]

The nonprofit organization, based in New York, is a partnership between the U.S. government and business. It is run entirely by business executives, most of whom are retired. The government provides half the budget; business people who are involved raise the rest. A cadre of volunteer recruiters has developed a "skills bank" containing a file of more than 7,500 names of executives and their specific areas of expertise. Recruiters are retired executives. About a third of the assignments are in agriculture and food, construction and housing, textiles and clothing. Although the volunteers are paid no salary, the IESC provides travel and living expenses.

The IESC is headed by Frank Pace, Jr., who has formerly served as Secretary of the Army, director of the Bureau of the Budget, and chairman of General Dynamics Corporation. This group, like many others, demonstrates that age does not determine usefulness. The average age of executive volunteers is 65, with an average of 40 to 50 years of experience.

The success of IESC's overseas activities has fostered analogous domestic programs. One of these, the National Executive Service Corps (NESC), was initiated four years ago to serve as consultants to nonprofit organizations.[25] Two other volunteer organizations that capitalize on the highly prized skills of retired executives are SCORE (Service Corp of Retired Executives) and RSVP (Retired Senior Volunteer Program).

A corporate model of retiree volunteerism is exemplified by the Veterans' Club of Pacific Power and Light Company. Founded in 1979, the organization has 3 objectives:

. . .to promote the physical, economic and social well-being of its members;
. . .to assist the company in the pursuit of its corporate responsibilities and in the maintenance of its economic well-being; and
. . .to encourage its members in civic action and community service in the many fields in which their experience and expert knowledge can be of significant value.[26]

Outlook for the Future

Although I am optimistic about the long term future opportunities for older workers and retirees, the short term prospects sometimes appear to be bleak. Title V of the Older Americans Act, with its Senior Community Service Employment Program, has been vetoed. Many poor and near-poor unemployed elderly relied on this program for jobs, training, and liaison with their communities. It's demise will also seriously affect such organizations as the National Council on the Aging, a long time advocate of senior adult needs. The prestigious Institute of Gerontology at Michigan State University recently cancelled a series of scheduled seminars. High unemployment rates in the state led the planners to believe that the problems of older workers and retirees would not be a high priority when so many others were out of work. Undoubtedly they were correct.[27]

On the other hand, there are also some encouraging signs. For example, when workforce reductions were recently required at the Polaroid Corporation, all employees with 10 years or more of service were eligible for benefits under a voluntary severance plan. Employees over 55 were granted one month pay for each year of service, while those under 45 were given one month for every two years. "A smooth incline plane" was used to graduate benefits for those between 45 and 55. Severance packages were granted to over 1,000 persons, of whom 584 were 55 or older. Most of this group were over 65 with service ranging between 20 and 30 years.

The company has written into its pension plan that part-time pay will be annualized when computing final retirement benefits. This was done after negotiations with the Social Security Administration and the Labor Department assured that these moneys would be considered "retirement income" rather than wages, and therefore not subject to FICA. Furthermore, a company spokesman stated that the climate is better than it ever was for the rehearsal retirement and tapering off programs.[28]

Elsewhere there are reports of needs for older workers to fill labor shortages. For example, the Federal Aviation Administration has recently asked the government to drop the entry age limit (30 years of age) for certain control tower specialists who want to become air traffic controllers, in order to rebuild the system faster.[29] It is also reported that the Texas Refinery Corporation began a serious effort to recruit older employees when 1981 data showed that three of their top sales people were over 65. As one 73 year old salesman said, "It seems the grayer the hair, the more they'll take your recommendations."[30]

As another example, the Lawrence Livermore National Laboratory has recently undertaken a survey to assess the desirability of establishing a skills/job bank for retirees. Among its highly skilled retirees are Ph.D. physicists, chemists, and engineers as well as technicians and craft workers. The Laboratory has needs for temporary employees to fill peak workload demands and vacation needs and also for consultant services of persons with technical expertise. I am convinced that the Laboratory's current survey of companies that have successfully rehired their own employees will demonstrate the wisdom of this approach.[31]

Another call for data on retiree/older worker programs comes from a joint effort of the Institute of Gerontology at the University of Michigan and the Administration on Aging. The planned computerized information system, the National Older Worker Information System (NOWIS) is designed to provide employers with examples of corporate practice that maximizes productive use of older workers both inside and outside companies.[32]

While developments of these kinds are encouraging, the important question is "Where do we go from here?" As keynote speaker to the Committee on Implications for the Economy of an Aging Population at the 1981 White House Conference on Aging, James Schulz recommended that there be more research and demonstration to help employers understand the feasibility and profitability of flexibility in work environments; that mandatory retirement be completely abolished; and that the Social Security retirement test be significantly liberalized.[33] A research thrust recently announced by the National Commission for Employment Policy and the Labor Department will address these issues.[34]

In their comprehensive paper on "The Future of the ADEA," Edwards and McConnell speak to a number of the issues under consideration at this conference. They remind us that maintaining and attracting older workers is not only good politics, but economically sound. They recommend that tax credits be provided to employers who hire older workers, pointing out that a feasible increase in labor market participation among older workers would add ten billion dollars annually to the Social Security fund. They believe that enlightened treatment of older workers is a nonpartisan issue. There should be no disagreement about the desirability of increasing national productivity and lessening the strain on the Social Security and private pension systems.[35]

While our focus has been on the American older worker, we must remember that the integration of aging workers is an issue of increasing concern universally. The International Federation on Aging outlines a number of actions which can be taken to integrate the aging into their various societies. Not surprisingly, their recommendations parallel those that have been discussed here.

Our goal of partnership among older persons, other age groups, and the private and public sectors should result in a climate, nationally and internationally, in which the aging person can enjoy a sense of acceptance, renewal, and integrity. Life's final years have the potential for being most personally fulfilling; living life to its fullest is the finest way to prepare for its end.

NOTES

1. Hank Koehn and Roger Selbert, "Older Worker: Integral to the Future," in *The Older Worker: Employment and Retirement,* ed., Virginia Boyack, *Generations,* Vol. E., No. 4, WGS (Summer 1982).

2. For an eloquent exposition of this view, see the June 1981 testimony of Anna M. Rappaport before the Senate Committee on Aging; Anna M. Rappaport, "Retirement Ages, Issues, and Trends," mimeographed (Chicago: William M. Mercer, Inc.).

3. "Performance Capabilities of Older Workers," Fact Sheet of the National Policy Center on Employment and Retirement (Los Angeles: University of Southern California, April 1981).

4. Louis Harris and Associates, "Aging in the Eighties: America in Transition," survey for the National Council on the Aging (1981).

5. White House Conference on Aging, 1981, "Committee Recommendations from the White House Conference on Aging" (Washington, DC, 1981).

6. Robert Jud, "The Retirement Decision: How American Managers View Their Prospects," an AMA Survey Report (1981).

7. *Ibid.,* p. 19-24.

8. Human Resources Network, "Job Sharing: Stakeholder Issues and Strategies," January 1981.

9. U.S. Congress, House, Select Committee on Aging, *New Business Perspectives on the Older Worker,* 97th Cong., 1st sess., 28 October 1981.

10. Jud, op. cit., p. 30.

11. Gail S. Rosenberg, Personal Communication.

12. An alternative "tapering off" program offered by Polaroid permits employees to gradually reduce the number of hours worked during a given time period. The schedule of hours worked is gradually lessened

128

until eventual retirement. Plans are flexible and are made to concur with departmental needs. Joseph Perkins, Personal Communication.

13. Pauline K. Robinson, Roger W. Ervin, and Philip Hodges, "Retraining and Creative Downgrading: Solutions for Some Older Workers," in Boyack, *The Older Worker,* p. 40.

14. Jud, op. cit., p. 25.

15. *Ibid.*

16. *Compflash,* No. 82-9, September 1982, pp. 5-6.

17. Op. cit., pp. 89-90.

18. Operation ABLE, *Networking,* December 1981.

19. *Elderhostel Catalog,* Summer 1982.

20. Jane Brooks, "A Campus Where All Students are Seniors," *New York Times Summer Survey of Education,* 22 August 1982, p. 7.

21. American Society for Personnel Administration, "College-Industry Alliance Builds Jobs: Unemployed Regain Hope, Train for New Jobs in Electronics," *Resource,* August 1982, p. 2.

22. John A. Jacobsen, Personal Communication.

23. Lad Kuzela, "Life After the Executive Suite," *Industry Week,* 3 May 1982, p. 51.

24. Ceil Cleveland Waldrip, "Their Retiring Ways Help Others," *American Way,* March 1982, p. 66.

25. Kuzela, op. cit.

26. "Pacific Power and Light's Retired Employees Get New Start," *Response,* May 1982, p. 12.

27. Justine Bykowski, Personal Communication.

28. Joseph Perkins, Personal Communication.

29. *Wall Street Journal,* Labor Letter Column, 24 August 1982, p. 1.

30. Maria T. Padiela, "Firm Recruits Older People as Salesmen," *Wall Street Journal,* 19 April 1982, p. 1.

31. Victoria Kaminski, Personal Communication and Survey.

32. Laurence Root, Personal Communication.

33. James H. Schulz, "Aging Policies: Inflation, Savings and Employment," (Keynote address to the Committee on Implications for the Economy of an Aging Population, 1981 White House Conference on Aging, November 1981) mimeographed (Washington, DC, 1981), p. 9.

34. U.S. Congress, House, Select Committee on Aging, *Productive Americans: A Quarterly Report on Aging and Employment for Business Executives,* 97th Cong., 2nd sess., May 1982, p. 4.

35. Charles H. Edwards and Stephen R. McConnell, "The Future of the ADEA: Pressure Builds to Abolish Mandatory Retirement," mimeographed, p. 24.

Chapters 5 & 6
Discussion

E. Douglas Kuhns

Dan Knowles' suggestion that retirement is moving in two directions at the same time is an appropriate point of departure for me. Union efforts to improve collectively bargained pension plans since the ADEA amendments of 1978 have been characterized by apparently contradictory efforts: simultaneously, to obtain pension credit for work after age 65—which current regulations do not require—so that people will be induced to work after age 65; and to secure earlier retirement rights so that workers may retire earlier. The resolution of this apparent contradiction is simple when it is recognized that people have different needs and desires and that both choices should therefore be available.

Both of these improvements in pension coverage would have the effect of increasing costs. However, lifting the mandatory retirement age under a pension plan *reduces* its cost; indeed, if the average age of retirement under a plan were to become 68 instead of a previous compulsory age of 65, the saving could be sufficient to cover the cost of both improvements described above.

While I agree fully with Knowles' assertion that many instances of age discrimination go undetected, and with his view that the Labor Department should do a great deal more than it is currently doing about it, what I face across the bargaining table on these issues is an industry ambivalence that Knowles does not explain. It is, of course, true that industry resists both of the pension improvements I have referred to because they would cost more money; but companies frequently resist them even in circumstances in which they might not cost very much at all.

Many companies insist that they resist earlier retirement (generally regarded as taking place between ages 55 and 65), because of a number of hidden costs that have nothing to do with pensions: the cost of losing highly productive workers in their most productive years, and the cost of training replacements. In these discussions it appears that most companies badly want their employees between ages 50 and 65; but then, paradoxically, at age 65 they want them gone! And this pattern seems to persist, except that I have noticed that some companies *do* like to keep their *executives* on after age 65, despite the exemption allowed by ADEA, which Knowles laments.

I agree with Knowles that industry will do what it considers to be good business; but regarding older workers in general, it wants its freedom to pick and choose. Industry wants a *laissez faire* attitude towards the workforce in general. The right to pick and choose at the predilection of the one doing the choosing is the essence of discrimination. We know all about this in the trade union movement; we have been fighting it for years by establishing seniority rules and contract provisions regulating hiring, promotions and layoffs. The discrimination we worry about most these days is discrimination against union workers of any age.

Actually, our seniority systems probably are the best protection we now have against discrimination against older workers—where there is a union. But, we are constantly told that these rules impede productivity and reduce management's flexibility. As long as this is the case, while I can easily subscribe to the minimum agenda for industry that Knowles suggests, I must be forgiven if I remain a little skeptical. Also, it is hard for me to believe that, under present conditions, comparing the age composition of a company workforce to that of the national labor force can offer much of a guide for action. With current levels of unemployment, enforcement of seniority rules in union shops has so effectively denuded them of younger workers that such an analysis would suggest that there has been discrimination against the young. What we really need most, of course, is a vigorous policy of promoting *full* employment of all workers, now.

More seriously, I do have some reservations about the emphasis on the age composition of a company in relation to the total labor force as a measure of age discrimination. This approach exemplifies what I would call "the fallacy of symmetry." I doubt that one should expect that all jobs should be proportionately staffed by older workers. Should any older workers at all, for example, be employed in mining (although, of course, they are)? I am called upon to help in negotiations over the Durez Plastics Pension Plan (Hooker Chemical, of Love Canal fame, for the uninitiated). I am appalled by the disaster list they refer to as the pension roll. Perhaps even younger workers should not be employed in that enterprise.

But, I do applaud Knowles' recognition that older workers should have options available, and his plug for phased retirement. It is to be expected that eventually some sanity will return to government policy in matters of these kinds, and when it does, these problems should be given careful review.

Dr. Buchmann's paper is directed at a review of policies, governmental and otherwise, looking toward promotion of post-retirement job opportunities. Of course, if they materialize, retirement is really put off. While I might agree that retirement at age 65 as a concept may be outmoded, I am reminded that the concept emerged with the passage of the Social Security Act during the Great Depression—in part, at least, as a means of inducing older workers to leave the labor force in order to increase opportunities for younger persons. It is true that younger workers will be in shorter supply in the future, but whether or not that portends overall labor shortages depends upon the total level of demand for labor services; it is not at all clear at this point that the economic policies that are likely to be followed in the near future will generate an increased demand for any workers, let alone older workers. Indeed, assuming a continuation of our present course, I can envision an economy that leaves 20 to 25 percent of the potential participants "out in the cold." That, of course, might very well lead to a certain amount of social disorganization; historically, when comparable economic malfunctions have injured substantial portions of the middle class—particularly the equivalent of the "hard hat" components of our society—it has sometimes precipitated a move to the barricades. (Following the serious recession of 1974-1975, a very conservative executive of a very conservative company was quoted in probably our most conservative business magazine as saying that had it not been for SUB plans, unemployment insurance and welfare, we would most assuredly have had people "in the streets"—and he was not talking about the "street people.")

Ultimately, the success of the various forms of alternate work patterns that Buchmann has described will depend upon the pursuit of full employment policies that are antithetical to the philosophy of the Reagan administration—and even, I hasten to add, to the political proclivities of their disloyal opposition. It is to be noted that the most extensive experimentation with phased retirement currently takes place in socialist-democratic Sweden.

I will admit that a resurgence of cottage industry is a much more likely, albeit less desirable, alternative. There was a regression to this mode of production that was forced upon us during the course of the Great Depression, but I doubt that this is an example we should want to emulate. Of course, it can be objected that I am giving the idea a prejudicial historic context; I do recognize that the computer age is making such arrangements more possible. However, I rather doubt that the current managerial mentality would contemplate their development with equanimity. In fact, the disposition of managers to "manage" seems to me to militate against acceptance of a wide range of these potential alternative work patterns.

I am all in favor of second careers—I'm a prime example—but I would advise people not to wait until retirement. There is something about formal retirement that is antithetical to further employment. Indeed, until ERISA made such denials illegal, many pension plans attempted to deny benefits to individuals who continued employment of any sort. But the principal impediment of retirement to the successful pursuit of a second career is the mentality and approach of the "professional manager," i.e., the business school type of manager who is not expert in any particular industrial technology, but who has been trained simply to "manage." I have observed that managers with this "broad" background, appear to become disoriented when they discover that some of their subordinates have alternative sources of income, presumably because such individuals can less readily be brought "under the thumb." How can a manager "own" such a person? Most retired people are assumed to have some source of independent income and, therefore, to be more difficult to be brought to "heel."

It is generally true that the best jobs are best in all ways, and it is therefore no accident that second or part-time careers for retirees have largely been restricted to the executive class as Buchmann's examples suggest. Admittedly there are numerous examples, and Buchmann has noted some of the more successful ones. But, while there appear to be labor shortages that provide opportunities for retirees in a number of relatively technical fields, there is certainly no general labor shortage, and pressures to use older workers or part-time workers cannot be expected in an economy with an unemployment rate of 10 to 15 percent.

Clearly, retraining and re-education opportunities and resources are vitally necessary if second careers are to be a significant option for retirees. Moreover, I certainly agree with Buchmann that education should be regarded as a continuing lifelong process. But in this respect I am outdone by those with a vested interest in the educational process—the professional educators—who, distressed by declining adolescent enrollments, have rediscovered "the worker."

What re-education for second careers really requires is the design of job-oriented curricula that are not loaded with the trappings of the conventional educational establishment. To be more specific, it may be difficult to re-educate an auto mechanic for work in computer programming if, at the same time, he has to surmount a course in freshman composition.

But again, while appropriate retraining and re-education programs are greatly needed, the required funding in the immediate future does not appear to be likely. The federal administration says it is not necessary, local administrations cannot afford it, and private investment will not undertake it because potential returns are too small and cover too long a period of time.

And, so we come to volunteerism, which probably is limited to those who can afford it! My intention is not to belittle any of the efforts that are described in the Buchmann paper, for they all have good intentions. I merely question their capacity to have a significant impact in the current environment characterized by serious unemployment and an apparent unwillingness of government to pursue policies that have a chance of correcting it.

For my own part, I do not wish to imply that the concept of retirement by age 65 has been cast in stone. It developed at least in part as an historical accident reflecting the economic problems of the thirties and the policy responses to them. But, I believe that the real pressure these days for postponed retirement comes from inflation and not from increased life expectancy, which has not been dramatic at least in the case of men. Over the past 20 years, the remaining life expectancy of men at age 65 has risen by little more than one year. The increase for women has been much more substantial—in the neighborhood of three years. It is this latter statistic and its implications that I find truly appalling—particularly because a disproportionate number of the current group of older women as compared with women who will be retiring in later decades, are on survivors or dependents benefits rather than receiving larger retirement benefits in their own right. For this group, I would accept cottage industry, or almost anything else.

The fact of the matter is that this group of older women contains a larger proportion of individuals than any other age group, male or female, who would be regarded by most employers as unemployable. In addition to the high rates of disability among them—and particularly among those over 75—as representative survivors of an older generation, many never were part of the workforce and therefore lack marketable skills. The medical costs of maintaining this group and their male counterparts will continue to be astronomical and will constitute a major burden for the nation's workforce as time goes on. As a result of their needs, nursing homes will continue to proliferate, which, incidentally, suggests some partial solutions. Nursing homes could be reorganized as communes. They are currently organized "not-for-profit" in many cases, but private administrations simply passively pass on increasing costs to a passive, and helpless clientele. A number of patients in such facilities could be partially and usefully employed in these enterprises, taking care of each other, so to speak. Many of them would welcome the activity and feel they were continuing to be useful.

The able-bodied groups over age 65, I fear, will continue to have difficulty with employment in an underemployed economy. Unfortunately, I suspect that if Social Security is emasculated by pushing the normal retirement age back to 68, employment or re-employment opportunities for the elderly might, perversely, improve. Retirement at age 68 rather than at 65 might then simply become the norm.

Chapters 5 & 6
Discussion

Karl Price

The two papers in this session, "Keeping Older Workers on the Job" by Daniel Knowles and "Maximizing Post-Retirement Labor Market Opportunities" by Anna Marie Buchmann, are concerned with two separate but related issues. In commenting on the papers, my focus will be on white-collar and professional employees—in large part, a workforce not covered by union contracts—and the protection of seniority clauses.

In the unionized segment of the workforce, partly as a result of the current state of the economy, age discrimination seems to be working in reverse; the average age of employees is going up, so in some cases 20 years of seniority is needed to avoid layoff.

First, I would like to address the issue of post-retirement employment. Buchmann's paper gives an excellent overview of the various alternative work patterns, from phased retirement to second careers, and clearly makes the point that a number of approaches to retirement are not only possible, but are currently being successfully employed. Why is this important? Simply because there is not one pattern of work or retirement that is appropriate to all people.

Figure 1 summarizes the findings of a study that Jim Walker, Doug Kimmel, and I undertook to help us understand how post-retirement activities affect retirement satisfaction. In our analysis, we identified four retirement styles: "Reorganized," "Holding On," "Rocking Chair,"

Figure 1: Four Retirement Styles

Sample of 1341 Retirees	"Reorganizer" 24%	"Holding On" 19%	"Rocking Chair" 44%	"Dissatisfied" 13%
Retirement style	highly active, but in a newly *reorganized* lifestyle (voluntary activities, perhaps also working for pay)	highly active, want to continue *working* indefinitely	reduced life activity, but satisfied with present level of activity	not working and feel it's difficult to keep busy
Preretirement Attitude	just waiting to retire to start a new pattern of activities	most had not thought of retiring; were asked to retire	looked forward to it (relief from work)	many had not thought of it, and were forced to retire; would like to work, but can't
Overall Satisfaction with Retirement	highest satisfaction; view retirement as positive life stage	negative view of retirement; but satisfaction is high since they are working *after retirement*	moderately high overall; but satisfaction reduced by health problems	least positive attitude toward retired life; lowest on all scales of satisfaction
Health	better health	better health	poorer health	poorest health
Retirement Timing and Choice	tend to be on time (62-65); choice usually voluntary, well-planned, and for positive reasons	tend to be early; perceived as involuntary or for negative reasons; more likely to have been unexpected	tend to be on time (62-65); voluntary	tend to be on time (62-65)

Education and Financial Status	usually more educated; higher occupational status and income before retirement	often technical and professional people; low preretirement income	satisfied with present financial situation; average on other characteristics	lowest education, poorest income and financial situation; many in sales or production jobs before retirement
Other	would probably do retirement planning on their own	youngest group; one-third need income; most like working	would probably attend retirement preparation counseling	oldest group; highly dissatisfied; had been retired longest; depressed and frustrated

SOURCE: Walker, James W., Douglas C. Kimmel, and Karl F. Price, "Retirement Style and Retirement Satisfaction: Retirees Aren't All Alike," *International Journal of Aging and Human Development*, Vol. 12, No. 4 (1980-1981), pp. 267-281.

and "Dissatisfied," in three of which retirees were satisfied. Almost half of the sample (44 percent) who were in the "Rocking Chair" group were satisfied even though they were not working either for pay or as volunteers. These people had retired, in large part, to get away from work they didn't like. One-fourth of the retirees (24 percent) had reorganized their lives and were working mainly as volunteers, although some also worked for pay. Another 19 percent continued working for pay, mostly shifting smoothly into second, third, or fourth careers. People in all three of these groups, some working, some not, expressed high levels of retirement satisfaction.

The smallest group, representing 13 percent of the sample, displayed significantly different attitudes toward retirement. Individuals in this group wanted to work, but were unable to find work for any of a number of reasons. As a result, they reported having difficulty keeping busy and were generally dissatisfied with retirement. The message here is that a range of post-retirement employment options, from no work to full-time employment, is needed if we hope to maintain a rich and fulfilling retirement for older Americans.

In his discussion of "Keeping Older Workers on the Job," Knowles focuses on adding more teeth to ADEA as the way to eliminate problems that keep older workers out of the workforce. If we look back at the data in Figure 1, we find that 44 percent of the retirees in the sample saw retirement as a relief from work. If we add to this the growing phenomenon of early retirement (before 65), even in a poor economy, it becomes clear that what we really want to provide are appropriate options. Figure 2 shows a matrix of management options for managing older workers that considers both the employee's and management's attitudes about retirement.

Figure 2: Management Options for Managing Older Employees

Management evaluations	Employee attitudes	
	Inclined to stay on	Inclined to retire
Would like them to stay	Facilitate career planning, accommodate talents, interests (POSITIVE)	Provide special inducements to stay (POSITIVE)
Would like them to leave	Termination or reassign (ADVERSE)	Facilitate "early" retirement (POSITIVE)

The simplest cases are where management's and the employee's attitudes are the same. If the employee wants to stay and management wants that employee to stay, the only issue is how to create a setting that is satisfactory for the employee and productive for the organization. At the opposite extreme are cases where both want the employee to leave. Here the issue is usually financial: how the organization will provide sufficient income to make retirement comfortable.

More difficult is the case where the employee is inclined to retire but the organization would like the individual to stay. The issue is what the employee's leisure—or whatever the individual was going to do in retirement—is worth to the employee. Whether the currency be cash, status, challenge or responsibility, the organization must decide whether it is willing to pay the price to induce the employee to stay.

The most difficult situation, and the one that tends to create ADEA cases, is where the employee is inclined to stay while the organization wants him or her to leave. If performance is not the reason for wishing to move an employee out of the job, the classic discrimination situation is present. If poor performance is the reason, then the issue is one of management doing its job in handling performance problems regardless of age.

Quite simply, an organization's human resource processes should be equitable, nondiscriminatory and flexible enough to respond to a variety of employee needs. Therefore, as Buchmann's paper also makes clear, we see the need for a variety of tools and approaches to deal with different employment and retirement situations. The older American, both in employment and in retirement, is a complex entity, and simplistic monolithic approaches are not appropriate. Our challenge is to find the right tools and the right approaches to improve the quality of life of older Americans.

Chapters 5 & 6
Discussion

Harold L. Sheppard

The two presentations by Dan Knowles and Anna Marie Buchmann are concrete evidence of the level of employer concern about, and interest in, the older worker topic. Over the past decade, such concern and interest fortunately has been on the increase. One reason for this increase obviously is related to the role of the Age Discrimination in Employment Act. Litigation, and the potential for litigation, have prompted greater active attention among employers. Furthermore, the number of filed complaints has been rising at a significant rate, much higher than the rate of increase in discrimination charges on the basis of race or sex. With the current recession producing historically high jobless rates among men—including those 40 and older—this should not be surprising. In the current scene, seniority no longer provides the job security protection that it has provided in "normal" economic times.

A second reason has little to do with cyclical economic or employment trends. It is related to long term secular, demographic, and population changes. Sophisticated employers and managers are increasingly coming to recognize the changing age structure of the labor force—especially the changes that are certain to come during the 1980s and 1990s. We are talking here about the need to learn how to manage and cope with an aging workforce. It is aging not only because of an increase in longevity among middle-aged workers, thanks to progress in biomedical sciences and to changes in personal life habits (e.g., in smoking and nutrition). It is aging also in the sense that the decrease in fertility during the past two decades, and projected to persist in the future, leads to a dramatic decline in the number of young entrants into the labor force. This decline will not be offset sufficiently by a likely increase in labor force participation among women.

From 1969 to 1979, the U.S. labor force increased at an annual average rate of about 2 percent. Since then it has increased at a much lower rate, and during the 1990s the expected rate of increase will be less than 1 percent. This is due primarily to the reduced size of the young working age population. Another factor—and one that, unlike the fertility rate, can be modified—is the early retirement trend. While inflation continued to be of a crisis nature, the rate of increase in retirements generally had been declining. But the current recession has resulted in an increase in "premature" early retirements.

In any event, with a labor force increasing at a rate markedly below the rate of increase in the numbers of nonworking older persons, we face the prospect of labor shortages and the need to find the resources to support a fast-growing older, aged population. The more informed managements and corporations appreciate the need to take another look at their older worker policies, and to find new ways of retaining older men and women on their payrolls. Dr. Buchmann's detailed inventory of what is now being done can serve as a model for other employers to follow and adapt to their own particular requirements. Mr. Knowles' paper reflects the discovery in recent years that productive, useful employees are not synonymous with youth.

More recently, a study by Data Resources, Inc. has concluded that a restoration of the labor force participation rates of older Americans to those of the early 1970s would alleviate much of the expected labor shortage and at the same time produce some "fiscal dividends" such as a higher GNP. Equally important, the increased utilization of older workers would also provide greater resources to provide decent, humane levels of living for our very old fellow citizens (most of them women)—those, say, 80 and older. This group will be increasing in numbers at a rate far in excess of any other age group in our society.

A third reason for the growth of employer interest must be traced to the effects of the dissemination of the results of research on working and aging by gerontologists and others—beyond the worlds of the researchers. Once disseminated, these research findings can, and do influence the thinking and decisionmaking of managers. They have helped to weaken negative stereotypes about older workers, to emphasize that year of birth is not a totally reliable predictor of an *individual's* performance and learning capacity, and to caution that the use of statistical averages about a given age *group* serves to obscure differences among individuals. In part, this latter doctrine is the basis for the Age Discrimination in Employment Act, originally enacted in 1967.

This does not mean, however, that discrimination in the workplace on the basis of age has been eradicated. In the 1981 survey for the National Council on the Aging, by Louis Harris (*Aging in the Eighties*), nearly 80 percent of the respondents in a position to hire or fire employees agreed with the statement that most employers discriminate against older workers, even though they themselves had more positive attitudes about older persons than did the total of all sample members in the labor force.

The coming years will see an even greater level of activity and positive programs among employers. The use of part-time work after "retirement" will characterize much of this development. If the impending "high technology revolution" (including robotics) is going to be as dramatic as some believe, training and continuing training—even among persons 40, 50, and 60—may be necessary. With regard to the popularity and practicality of part-time work, it may be useful here to present some findings from a special analysis I carried out on the data gathered from the 1981 NCOA survey. Among all the workers 55 and older in the sample, I identified those who could be considered as candidates for "post-retirement part-time work" (based on their response to two key question on this topic). More than two-fifths of this group of older workers told us (1) that they would prefer to continue some kind of part-time work when they "retire," instead of retiring completely; and (2) that the availability of part-time work would be of help to them if they wanted to work after "retirement."

The overall average of 43 percent was exceeded, especially among lower-income, less educated workers (including those with no current pension coverage). Hispanics, blacks, and nonmarried women, as might be expected, had the highest rates of candidacy for post-retirement part-time work. But economic necessity, although a major factor, was not the only explanation. For certain types of professional men and women, the psychological desire to continue to be active and useful was also involved.

In connection with the training and retraining issue, the general NCOA study found that the willingness of older workers to learn a new skill for a job different from what they were used to doing is quite high—for example, 58 percent among those 40-54, and 39 percent among those 55-64. It is significant, in my opinion, that in the earlier NCOA survey conducted in 1974, only 47 percent of those 40-54 expressed a similar level of interest in learning new skills. In many ways, this age group (those 40-54) is the most critical target group for employers to be concerned with, since persons in that age range are—comparatively speaking—less definite about retiring at some planned age. In this connection, between 1974 and 1981, the two surveys revealed an increase in the age of planned retirement.

The need for more effective utilization of older workers should now be taken as a given. And so should the degree of interest and willingness to be so utilized be accepted. What is called for now is a more comprehensive and intensive public and private-sector effort and set of programs that will meet both that need and the desires of older workers.

Chapters 5 & 6
Discussion

Barbara L. McIntosh

The dramatic decrease in the labor force participation of older workers is well documented. Over the 25-year period between 1956 and 1980, the labor force participation rate of persons 65 and older dropped by about one-half, from 24.3 percent to 12.6 percent. For males the decline was much more pronounced—from 40.0 percent to 19.3 percent; for women the drop was from 10.6 percent to 8.0 percent.[1]

There are reasons for believing that these trends may not continue into the future, however. For one thing, inflation and the consequent erosion of pensions and savings may force continued work activity on the part of many older workers. For another, the decreasing rate of labor force growth—from 2 percent per year in the 1960s and 1970s to a projected 1.1 percent between 1985 and 1990 may create labor shortages for which increased utilization of the "experienced older population" is the most realistic remedy.[2]

This is the context in which both Knowles and Buchmann have discussed enhancing the opportunities for older workers. The paper by Buchmann in particular focuses on techniques for keeping older workers on the job. It is also critical, however, to look at the older worker in the external labor market. For a variety of reasons some older workers either cannot or do not wish to remain with their current employers, yet they still want or need to be employed. What I should like to emphasize is that in order to maximize the effective utilization of older workers there is a need for a reexamination by employers of their human resource administration policy in the context of recruiting and selecting older workers. Several aspects of government employment and training policy also warrant reevaluation.

Before elaborating this theme, however, it is useful to examine the limited evidence on the extent to which older workers do indeed choose to remain employed, but in different jobs from those which they previously held. Available data do not permit a confident estimate of the proportion of workers 65 years of age and over who shifted into a "second career" after retirement from their "regular job." There are several clues, however, that this proportion is by no means negligible. For one thing, Philip Rones has shown that the industrial distribution of employed men 65 and over differs substantially from that of men who are 60 to 64.[3] Specifically, only 13 percent of the older as compared with 30 percent of the younger group are in manufacturing; on the other hand, 44 percent of the older and 32 percent of the younger men are employed in retail trade and miscellaneous service industries. These differences, plus the fact that there is little difference in these proportions between the 60-to-64 year group and men 25-to-59 years of age, suggest a considerable amount of movement incident to retirement.

As another piece of evidence, Parnes has found that among a representative national sample of men 55 to 69 who had retired at some time between 1966 and 1975, about one-sixth were employed in 1976, and that a majority of these were in different occupations and industries from those of their pre-retirement jobs.[4] More specific quantification of the post-retirement labor mobility of men and women would be very useful, but enough information already exists to suggest that it is substantial; moreover, as has been seen, there are reasons for supposing that it will increase. It is therefore important to point out the ways in which both employers and government can and should facilitate the process.

Aspects of Employer Policy

Hiring

In recruiting and selection, employers should consider special training for recruiters[5] since the biases that tend to exist in this activity are well documented.[6] Also, selection criteria should be clearly defined and should reflect tradeoffs between educational level and years of experience. Signaling may inappropriately eliminate a disproportionate number of older workers from some jobs. Testing as a general selection technique should also be validated for age within an organization.

As has been noted, older workers tend to seek post-retirement jobs outside of manufacturing, and employers in these industries may need to be particularly sensitive to attracting older workers in the future. Likewise, businesses that employ large numbers of skilled craftsmen, operatives and transport workers—occupations in which older workers are underrepresented—may need to make a critical assessment of the impact of future demographic trends on their businesses.

To facilitate matching the skills of older workers with existing needs some firms are currently attempting to establish data banks. Travelers Insurance has experienced success with the job bank established for its own retirees,[7] and Santa Fe Federal in California has had a positive response to RESCUE (Return Employable Senior Citizens to Useful Employment) a broader referral service they helped to organize.[8]

Referral services and data banks can be set up not only by individual companies, but also within local labor markets and/or industries. There may be a number of reasons why the older worker cannot remain with his/her original employer even though this might, in the abstract, be preferable. For example, suitable alternative programs may not exist within the firm or relations with co-workers may not allow for altering authority relationships. Older workers in such situations may nevertheless be excellent employees, and it may therefore, be desirable to establish an exchange pool with other firms in the local labor market or in the industry for sharing these resources. This approach has already proved useful for some industries in controlling labor supply through training.[9] Within a local labor market, such placement networking for older workers could most logically be accomplished through the local personnel director's association.

Creating Openings Through Training

Hiring and retraining older workers depends to a large extent on the structure of the internal labor market. Ports of entry simply may not exist at appropriate levels to recruit experienced older workers.[10] In such situations the employer should explore the possibility of filling more positions through the external labor market as well as stimulating greater internal mobility for current employees through opportunities for training. Short ladder jobs (intermediate next step positions designed to stretch the incumbent and/or serve as the training position for the next level up), rotation and cross training (switching assignments and helping employees learn each other's positions), and temporary assignments on task forces or problem solving committees can all be used for this purpose.[11]

Promotion and Development

To attract and retain older workers in the future, employers will need to be more sensitive to the continuing growth needs of this group. There is evidence of management discrimination against the older worker in providing promotion and/or retraining opportunities because of a perceived resistance to change[12] despite the large body of literature supporting the value of the older worker as an employee.[13] Succession analysis should no longer preclude the older worker simply on the basis of chronological age and/or assumptions about retirement.

Promoting growth and fulfilling individual needs for development are critical to motivation and continuing productivity. "Continuing opportunity is the motivator most people need to keep them working with a high degree of effort and enthusiasm."[14] In one study on age and job facet satisfaction, work itself was the only facet that older workers were satisfied with; they were dissatisfied with supervision, pay, promotion and co-workers.[15] The stronger attachment to the labor force of the older professional/technical workers who have more control over their work content and growth also supports the argument for providing more promotion and development opportunities for workers in all occupational categories.

In addition to opening up more positions, another mechanism for providing growth opportunities and recruiting older workers may be employer sponsored second career programs. There is a growing awareness "that persons over 45 are not adequately served by American educational institutions and are frequently denied opportunities to embark upon second careers in which they can make significant contributions."[16]

One model that has been particularly successful has been the Second Careers program undertaken by the George Washington University School of Medicine and Health Services. The program focused primarily on the exploration of career opportunities and promoting realistic career decisions. This type of program would be particularly important to firms that wish to capture (or recapture) older workers who wish to change occupations and/or industries.

Government Policy

A number of public policies ranging from Social Security to the ADEA, have an impact on retirement/work decisions made by older workers. In terms of improving the utilization of the older worker, increased attention needs to be given to the Employment Service. Older workers make up a larger proportion of all job applicants than of those who are counseled and/or placed. "In 1978, for example, 13.1 percent of all applicants were 45 and older, but only 11.7 percent of all persons counseled and 8.8 percent of all those placed were in this age group. The discrepancy is even greater for those 55 and older."[17] Special training and use of older men and women themselves as older worker placement specialists—programs that already exist in five states—are the types of efforts needed if the Employment Service is going to be able to respond to the employment needs of the older worker. Other types of government programs which might be considered in the future as efforts to place older workers include tax incentives and aid in linkage development. Employment tax credits such as the current Targeted Jobs Tax Credit program may be expanded to include the economically disadvantaged (involuntary) older job seeker. Alternatively, wage subsidies may be provided to offset the higher wages more experienced older workers command.

Finally, the government may be in the best position to facilitate the development of private sector "placement networks" by providing seed money for these efforts. Some state governments have already found this useful in making training and entry level positions for others in the labor market.

NOTES

1. U.S. Department of Labor, U.S. Department of Health and Human Services, and U.S. Department of Education, *Employment and Training Report of the President,* Washington, DC, U.S. Government Printing Office, 1981.

2. Gillespy, R. Thomas, "Labor Force Participation of the Older Population Toward 1990: A Demographic Approach" in Pauline Ragan, ed., *Work and Retirement: Policy Issues.* University of Southern California Press, 1980, pp. 127-139.

3. Rones, Philip L., "Older Men - The Choice Between Work and Retirement," *Monthly Labor Review,* 101, Nov. 1978.

4. Parnes, Herbert S., *Work and Retirement: A Longitudinal Study of Men.* MIT Press, 1981, pp. 169, 174.

5. Heneman, Herbert, III, "The Impact of Interviewer Training and Interview Structure on the Reliability and Validity of the Selection Interview," *Proceedings Academy of Management,* 1975; Schneider, Benjamin, *Staffing Organizations,* Pacific Palisades, CA: Goodyear Publishing Co., 1976.

6. Carlson, R. E., "The Relative Influence of Appearance as Factual Written Information on an Interviewers Final Rating," *Journal of Applied Psychology,* 1967, 51, pp. 461-468; Okanes, Marvin and Harvey Tschirgi, "Impact of the Face to Face Interview on Prior Judgments of a Candidate," *Proceedings Midwest Academy of Management,* April 1977.

7. Billings, Eugene, discussant comments, "Ageism: The Problem of the 80's Conference," December 2, 1982, Edison, NJ.

8. "Referral Service Helps Seniors Find Part-Time Jobs," *Savings and Loan News,* November 1980, pp. 116-117.

9. McIntosh, Barbara and Theodore Settle, "Human Resource Acquisition From Local Labor Markets: An Interorganizational Network Perspective," *Proceedings Southern Management Association,* Atlanta, GA, 1981.

10. Doeringer, Peter and Michael Piore, *Internal Labor Markets and Manpower Analysis.* Lexington, MA: D.C. Heath and Company, 1971.

11. Kanter, Rosabeth Moss and Barry A. Stein, "Ungluing the Starch: Motivating Performance and Productivity Through Expanding Opportunity," *Management Review,* July 1981, pp. 45-49.

158

12. Rosen, Benson and Thomas H. Jerdee, "Too Old or Not Too Old," *Harvard Business Review,* N/D 1977, pp. 87-106.

13. Smith, Mark W., "Older Workers' Efficiency in Jobs of Various Types," *Personnel Journal,* May 1953, pp. 19-23; Aldag, Raymond J., "Age, Work Values and Employee Reactions," *Industrial Gerontology,* Summer 1977, pp. 192-197.

14. Kanter and Stein, *loc. cit.*

15. Muchinsky, Paul M., *"Aging and Job Facet Satisfaction,"* Aging and Work, Summer 1978, pp. 175-179.

16. Boren, N., M. McCally, and R. Goldberg, "A Career Transition Program for Older Persons," *Alternative Higher Education,* 5(1) Fall 1980, pp. 40-56.

17. U.S. Department of Labor, *Socio-Economic Policies and Programs for the Elderly,* May 1979.

Chapter 7
Age Discrimination in Employment
Stephen R. McConnell

Introduction

America is in the midst of a civil war in which the demographic forces of an aging population are pitted against a labor force composed of a declining number of older workers. Today one in nine Americans is age 65 or older and in 50 years that proportion will change to one in five. Along with the growth in the aging population comes, of course, an increased burden on those who are working. Unfortunately, the conflict arises because fewer and fewer of the burgeoning older population are remaining in the labor force to contribute to their own and to the larger society's well-being.

The factors contributing to the demographic trends—lower fertility and mortality—are largely beyond the control of public policy. But, the declining labor force rates of the elderly are in large part a direct result of public policies that have long encouraged early retirement and allowed (even created) obstacles to continued employment. In addition, eight major recessions or depressions since 1948 have wracked the economy, resulting in a dramatic decline in labor force participation rates among older workers.

One reason for the labor force declines among the older population is age discrimination, which creates greater difficulties for older workers as they seek and attempt to retain jobs. Many give up their job search after months of unemployment and then simply drop out of the labor force. They become discouraged because of employment obstacles created by persistent negative attitudes among employees that older workers are less desirable, less productive, and less creative than younger workers.

The challenge for policymakers is to find ways of stemming the labor force exit of older workers. One option is to eradicate the age discrimination that older workers face. This paper examines the extent and nature of age discrimination and concludes with a review of recent legislative attempts to strengthen the federal statute barring age discrimination in employment.

I. The Extent of Age Discrimination

Age discrimination in employment is widespread. There is no agreement on the exact nature of the problem nor is there a consensus on how to solve it. But few would disagree that the problem is real and that it affects the lives of millions of Americans.

Perceptions of the Problem

Public attitudes. Despite federal legislation to ban age discrimination from the workplace, most Americans believe age discrimination remains a serious problem. Two nationwide surveys by Louis Harris and Associates—one in 1974, the other in 1981—found nearly identical results: eight of ten Americans believe that "most employers discriminate against older people and make it difficult for them to find work."[1]

The public is also in agreement that age discrimination should not be tolerated. When asked by Louis Harris in 1981 if age discrimination in the form of forced retirement is justified, nine out of ten Americans said no.[2] Moreover, between 1974 and 1981 the sentiment against forced retirement based on age grew stronger.[3]

Employer attitudes. The perception of widespread age discrimination held by the public is shared by a majority of business leaders. Most employers believe age discrimination exists, according to a 1981 survey of 552 employers nationwide conducted by William M. Mercer, Inc.[4] The following key points summarize the survey's findings:

- 61 percent of employers believe older workers today are discriminated against in the employment marketplace;
- 22 percent claim it is unlikely that, without the present legal constraints, the company would hire someone over age 50 for a position other than senior management;
- 20 percent admit that older workers (other than senior executives) have less of an opportunity for promotions or training; and
- 12 percent admit that older workers' pay raises are not as large as those of younger workers in the same category.

Historical Perspective

A glance into history reveals that age discrimination has existed for a long time. According to historian William Graebner, age discrimination dates back to the last quarter of the 18th century and is a direct product of the industrial revolution.[5] Industrialization brought with it increased market competition, advanced technology and demands for greater speed on the job. These forces, in combination with the increasing popularity of the shorter workday, placed a greater strain on the older worker to keep up. Older workers also had difficulty keeping abreast of the new and changing technologies. The real culprit, though, was the theory of scientific management which dominated American business shortly after the turn of the century. Scientific management demanded efficiency and flexibility, both qualities that were considered lacking in the older worker. The result was a direct form of age discrimination that simply wore older workers down and pushed them out of the workforce.

After 1915, age discrimination, which prior to this had been limited to a "management strategy," began to diffuse into the larger society. The "youth cult" of the 1920s and the high unemployment of the depression era turned older workers into a convenient scapegoat. Societal and employer attitudes after 1915 characterized the older worker as dispensable in favor of younger workers, and the myth that productivity automatically declines with age gained a solid foothold in American culture. In terms of ability, older and younger workers were perceived to be substantially alike by employers, at least according to a 1938 survey of the National Association of Manufacturers.[6] Nonetheless, a clear preference persisted for the younger worker.

There was one mediating factor in the bias against older workers. Many employers perceived the older worker, with all of his inefficiencies, to be a stable influence on the comparatively younger, more hot-headed workforce. The trade union movement was a source of great concern to most employers during the 1930s, and older workers were seen as a conservative force which could help check the excesses of the fledgling union movement. According to Graebner, "Excessive radicalism, associated in the public mind with youth and immaturity, could be countered with age."[7] Despite this new "attractiveness" of the older workers, age discrimination did not diminish.

The first "official" study. Age discrimination festered just out of sight of the nation's attention until the early 1960s when, in the heat of the Civil Rights movement, the U.S. Congress focused briefly on the issue. Despite amendments offered by Congressman Dowdy of Texas and Senator

Smathers of Florida, age was left out of the 1964 Civil Rights Act, ostensibly because not enough was known about the nature and extent of the problem. Instead, the Department of Labor was instructed to carry out a study of age discrimination and report to Congress its findings by June 30, 1965.[8] The study results were so compelling that Congress enacted the Age Discrimination in Employment Act in 1967.

The Labor Department study examined four major sources of age discrimination.[9] The first type of discrimination was that arising from dislike or intolerance of older people. The study did not find this to be serious enough to warrant public concern. There was ample evidence of employers choosing youth over age, but the study concluded that this was the result of preferences *for* the younger group, rather than antagonism *against* the old.

The second form of age discrimination was termed "arbitrary" by the Labor Department's analysts, and it involved specific employer policies which excluded people over a certain age for consideration in hiring, without concern for the individual applicant's qualifications. The study found "substantial evidence" of this second type of discrimination. For example, a 1965 survey of employers disclosed that, "approximately half of all job openings which develop in the private economy each year are closed to applicants over 55 years of age, and a quarter of them are closed to applicants over 45."[10]

Forces of circumstance caused by the impersonal factors, such as technological change or lower educational levels, constituted the third form of discrimination examined in the Labor Department study. Here the study concluded that there may or may not be arbitrary discrimination. The lower educational level of the cohort of older workers is a factor that could result in discrimination against most older workers. But, only when such discrimination results from not assessing the individual's educational level and other qualifications for the job would it be considered arbitrary and thereby within the purview of Congressional action, according to the Labor Department study.

The fourth and final cause of age discrimination was considered to be the set of institutional arrangements that indirectly restrict employment of older workers. Employee benefits, seniority rules and personnel policies are included in this group. Here the Labor Department study concluded that age discrimination exists and offered specific ways to overcome it.

The recommendations by the Labor Department included statutory changes to address the arbitrary forms of discrimination, and public and educational efforts to reduce the more subtle forms of discrimination. The result was the Age Discrimination in Employment Act of 1967 (ADEA), which included measures to penalize offending employers as well as instructions to the federal enforcement agency (then the Department of Labor, now the Equal Employment Opportunity Commission) to provide technical assistance to employers and information to the public to break down the myths about older workers.[11] (For a summary of the ADEA, as Amended, see Appendix I.)

Age Discrimination as a Legal Problem

With enactment of the ADEA, the problem of age discrimination moved into clear public view as formal charges were filed by aggrieved individuals and eventual litigation ensued. As yet, there have been few systematic analyses of the characteristics of age discrimination victims who file charges or of the court cases brought under the ADEA. Recent data made available to the House Committee on Aging, however, offer valuable insights into the extent of age discrimination in employment.

Growth in age discrimination charges. According to data provided by the Equal Employment Opportunity Commission (EEOC) and the Department of Labor, the number of age discrimination charges has skyrocketed in recent years. (See Figure 1.) In 1969, two years after the ADEA was enacted, the Labor Department, then charged with enforcement responsibilities, reported 1,031 charges of age discrimination. This number grew through 1975 then leveled off until 1978, at which time the enforcement duties were transferred to the EEOC.[12] The most dramatic increase in age charges came between 1979 and 1981 when the annual number of age discrimination charges rose by 76 percent to 9,479.

This profound increase in age charges may be the result of intensified discriminatory activity by employers sparked by downturns in the economy, but no studies are available to document this. The transfer of enforcement to the EEOC also may have drawn some attention to the ADEA, and thereby increased the number of Americans who are aware of their rights under the Act. Again, however, no studies have been conducted to verify or refute this notion.

One likely explanation for the increased number of age charges may have been the Amendments to the ADEA, championed by Congressman Claude Pepper, chairman of the House Select Committee on Aging, and enacted with great public fanfare in 1978. The 1978 Amendments were widely debated and publicized, largely because they were to alter the institution of retirement, moving the permissible mandatory retirement age upward to 70 from 65. The public discussion of mandatory retirement issues served to increase the nation's awareness of age discrimination as a problem, while at the same time heightening older workers' knowledge of their rights under the ADEA. Even so, only two in five Americans are even aware of the ADEA, according to a 1981 nationwide Harris survey.[13] Unless age discrimination is

166

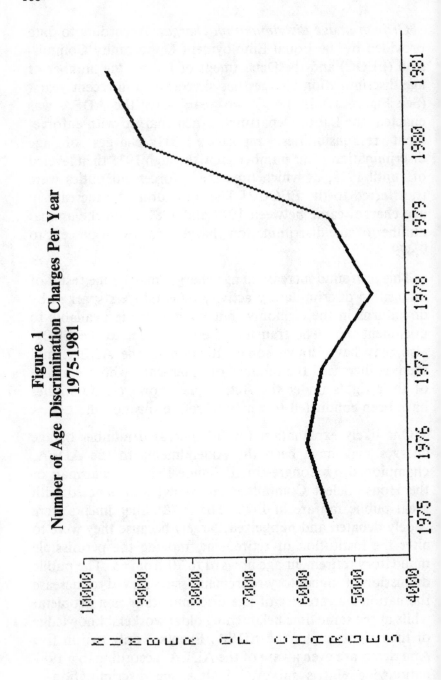

Figure 1
Number of Age Discrimination Charges Per Year
1975-1981

significantly reduced, we will, no doubt, see a further rise in age discrimination charges as awareness of the federal age discrimination statute increases in the future.

Who files a charge of age discrimination? Only since late 1980 has the EEOC begun codifying characteristics of charging parties and making the data computer accessible. Data for FY 1981 provide a glimpse, albeit preliminary, into the typical person who files a charge of age discrimination with the federal enforcement agency.

As Table 1 indicates, the typical charging party is in late middle age and is male. Two-thirds of all age charges are filed by persons age 50-64 (nearly half are age 50-59) and 63 percent are filed by males. Only a small fraction (5 percent) of charges are filed by those over 65. Thus, age discrimination may affect a wide age band, but legal and administrative remedies are sought primarily by middle-aged males.

Table 1
Age Discrimination Charges Filed
with the EEOC in FY 1981, by Age

	Number of charges filed			
Age	Men	Women	Both sexes	Percent of total
40 - 44	663	459	1,122	12
45 - 49	968	626	1,594	18
50 - 54	1,219	786	2,005	22
55 - 59	1,501	808	2,309	25
60 - 64	1,121	477	1,598	18
65 - 69	312	139	451	5
70+	13	7	20	0
Total	5,797	3,302	9,099*	100

*Total is less than 9,479 (the actual total for FY 1981) because of missing data on the sex of the charging party.

A 46 state survey of 550 alleged age discrimination victims conducted by the House Select Committee on Aging found in 1982 that 43 percent of respondents believed that supervisors and managers (especially middle-managers) were most frequently the targets of age discrimination.[14] Non-union workers were also perceived to be targets.

What kinds of charges are typical? The most common basis for filing an age discrimination charge is "forced termination." (See table 2.) Nearly half of all charges filed with the EEOC in FY 1981 involved alleged discrimination in discharge, layoff or involuntary retirement. Hiring discrimination, which is much more difficult to substantiate, was the basis for only 12 percent of all charges. The least frequent charges were for discrimination in training, demotions, and promotions.

Table 2
Types of Age Discrimination Charges
Filed with the EEOC in FY 1981

Type of Charge	Number	Percent
Termination[a]	7,443	49
Hiring[b]	1,915	12
Terms and conditions	1,188	8
Wages/Benefits	1,134	7
Promotion	825	5
Demotion	540	4
Training	136	1
All other	2,130	14
Total	15,311[c]	100

a. Discharge, layoff, involuntary retirement

b. Hiring, recall

c. Total adds to more than 9,479 because charging parties can file more than one type of charge.

The types of charges vary according to the age of the charging party. For example, hiring and training discrimination are more typical among the younger ages, presumably because it is the youngest of the protected individuals who have greater expectations in those areas. On the other hand, older individuals were most likely to allege discrimination in employee benefits, perhaps because benefits packages are more salient and more important to the oldest workers, and, at the same time, are perceived to be more expensive by some employers. Males and females exhibit similar patterns of charges, except that males are more likely to file a charge.

Age discrimination charges by industry. Charges of age discrimination are leveled by employees in every industry, but some industries produce more victims that others. Table 3 displays both the absolute and relative numbers of charges by industry. Public administration has the highest frequency, with 432 charges per 100,000 employees. Second is transportation, followed by mining and manufacturing. Those least likely to file age discrimination charges are employed in the construction industry (55 per 100,000), services (188 per 100,000) and retail trade (199 per 100,000).

One plausible explanation for these patterns of age discrimination charges is the growth (or lack thereof) of the industry in question. Public administration, transportation, mining, and manufacturing, each of which had a large number of age discrimination charges, all are facing major contractions caused by a sluggish economy and a shift in the demand for these goods and services. Moreover, these are declining industries which tend to employ a larger proportion of older workers than do expanding or stable industries. Services and retail trade, both expanding industries, experienced fewer age discrimination charges, in part because they employ larger numbers of younger workers who are not in the protected age category. Also, termination from a job in an expanding industry does not necessarily mean the end

Table 3
Proportion of Age Discrimination Charges by Industry, 1981
(except Agriculture)

Industry	Number of employed persons age 40+ (A)* (000s)	Number of age discrimination charges (B)**	Proportion of age discrimination charges (B - A)	Rank order
Mining	382	124	.000325	3
Construction	2,354	129	.000055	9
Manufacturing	9,314	2,708	.000291	4
Transportation	2,792	946	.000339	2
Wholesale Trade	1,628	341	.000209	6
Retail Trade	5,410	1,076	.000199	7
Finance	2,446	578	.000236	5
Services	11,739	2,208	.000188	8
Public Administration	2,474	1,070	.000432	1
Other/Agriculture	--	868	--	
Total	38,539	10,048		

*Unpublished data from the Current Population Survey, Bureau of Labor Statistics, 1981 Annual Averages.

**Unpublished data, Equal Employment Opportunity Commission, FY 1981.

of one's working life as it might in a declining industry. This may also account for the smaller number of age discrimination charges in the expanding industries. Construction, the least affected by age discrimination charges, may be unique in that it offers no job security to speak of and fluctuates so wildly in terms of its demand for labor that members of that profession have low expectations of job security.

Which charges reach the stage of litigation? There is no reliable source of information regarding litigation activity under the ADEA because only a fraction of all litigation is initiated by the Government[15] and decisions in private lawsuits are not always recorded. Some ADEA litigation, however, is recorded in LEXIS, a computerized information system, which provided the basis of a recent content analysis by Michael Schuster.[16]

The results of Schuster's analysis indicate that lawsuits brought under the ADEA closely parallel the charges filed with the EEOC, as described above. For example, the vast majority of litigants were males (79 percent); nearly half were age 50-59 (48 percent); most were drawn from professional and managerial occupations (52 percent); and the manufacturing industry produced the most lawsuits (48 percent), while the construction industry produced the fewest (2 percent). Termination of employment was the most common basis for litigation (81 percent). It is interesting to note that employers won two out of three cases.[17]

Again, the evidence suggests that the ADEA offers legal remedies that are typically utilized by middle-aged, managerial level males who have been terminated from their jobs, allegedly because of age. While provisions of the Act—such as those pertaining to the permissible mandatory retirement age—directly benefit older individuals of both sexes from a wide variety of occupations, the legal and administrative recourse is most often sought by a narrow group of younger males.

II. The Nature of Age Discrimination

The above analysis of age discrimination charges and litigation activity gives a numerical perspective on the problem but offers very little insight into the complex set of factors which come under the rubric of age discrimination. This section puts a face on the numbers and describes in more detail how age discrimination is justified and how it is practiced.

The Most Obvious Age Discrimination: Mandatory Retirement

The most clear-cut form of age discrimination is that which the Labor Department termed "arbitrary" in the 1965 study cited earlier. According to a more recent Labor Department study, 51 percent of the nation's workforce faced an arbitrary mandatory retirement age in 1980, usually age 70, while 45 percent faced no mandatory retirement age.[18] Mandatory retirement rules are subsiding, but they persist for a variety of reasons.

The most common arguments used by employers to justify a mandatory retirement age have not changed substantially over the years despite evidence refuting most of the stereotypes of aging.[19] The most common negative beliefs about older workers which are used to justify compulsory retirement involve personal characteristics associated with aging.[20] Many employers perceive older workers as a group to be ill-suited for certain jobs because of declining mental and physical capacity, an inability to learn, a lack of creativity, and inflexibility.[21] Vast amounts of research on the abilities of older workers, however, consistently refute these employer-held stereotypes. For example, studies of industrial workers,[22] supervisory personnel,[23] and skilled and unskilled clerical workers,[24] disclosed that age was unrelated to performance appraisal ratings, efficiency and overall productivity. Some studies show partial declines on some production line tasks among the oldest age groups,[25] but other studies show slight increases in productivity with age.[26] Similarly, learning ability does not decline significantly with advancing age and any decline which does appear is often more related to motivation and physiological condition than to learning capacity.[27]

Employers continue to utilize mandatory retirement because of outmoded notions that age is equated with declining abilities. As performance assessment technology improves and more research findings are generated that destroy the negative stereotypes of aging, we are likely to see a reduction in rigid personnel policies that base important decisions on age rather than actual performance.

A favorite argument in support of mandatory retirement is that it provides order and predictability to the retirement decision, and it makes the retirement decision impersonal, thereby relieving the older worker of the burden of being told he or she is no longer productive. When older workers are asked their opinions about this matter they offer a very different story. Take, for example, Sarah Paz, a 69 year old school clerk in Chicago who was within several months of the school district's mandatory retirement age when she testified before the House Select Committee on Aging regarding her feelings about the impersonal nature of mandatory retirement ages:

> The principals I have worked with through the years have marked me as being a superior clerk; I have always put my whole being into my job. . . . As for being sick or tardy I have the best attendance record of any staff member in the school, and this has been true for 27 years. I have been tardy perhaps once a year and have accumulated 135 unused sick days in the past 27 years. When it has

been 60 below zero I have arrived at school on time or ahead of time. . . . Who wants the pittance of Social Security when one is able to contribute to society and the working force. . . . Inaction has killed more people than action. Don't commit us to the death house while we are active and alive.[28]

Mandatory retirement ages are rapidly dying out. Many large corporations (such as ALCOA, ARCO, Levi Strauss & Co., Mattel, Inc., Pepsico, Inc., Digital Equipment Co.) have already eliminated mandatory retirement, as have eight states (California, Florida, Iowa, Maine, New Hampshire, Tennessee, Utah, and Vermont). The federal government is likely to outlaw the practice in the near future. (See Section III.) When mandatory retirement is finally abolished it will be an important step toward the eventual elimination of all other forms of age discrimination in employment.

Subtle Discrimination: Job Harassment

Mandatory retirement may, in the words of Rep. Claude Pepper, ". . . engender dependency, foster ill-health and squander productive potential,"[29] but other more subtle forms of age discrimination can create greater havoc for older workers. Subtle discrimination can take a variety of forms, as summarized (albeit, somewhat tongue-in-cheek) by Michael Korda in a book entitled *Power: How to Get It, How to Use It.*

> . . . the best way to *speed* an executive's retirement is to keep him involved in power decisions which no longer concern him, and can only cause him trouble and aggravation. . . . Other, more subtle, signs can indicate to a man that his time has come. Promoting his secretary is a move that never fails to indicate the erosion of power. It is also possible to produce anxiety by rapidly changing all forms and

procedures of the office, so that everything looks unfamiliar to him, including the labels and letterhead . . . and when all else fails, it is always possible to change everybody's telephone extension number so that he's always dialing the wrong one.

Exaggerated deference and extreme rudeness can both be useful in making a man think about retiring, and it is also possible to make him feel uncomfortable by constantly referring to pop music stars he has never heard of, dances he has never learned and restaurants he has never been to. . . . It is possible to talk in a very low voice in an effort to make him believe he is going deaf, though some prefer to shout in a loud voice as if they were already convinced of the victim's deafness.[30]

The most effective techniques of subtle discrimination are those that demoralize the victim by reducing his or her self-image. Nonmanagement, blue-collar employees are repeatedly reminded, for example, that their age is an impediment, that they aren't what they used to be and that they are overpaid. In the words of one victim:

. . . my supervisors displayed animosity and made derogatory remarks about older employees by stating that they are over the hill, do not earn their pay, and that they take too much time in doing the job.[31]

Older executives are victimized by stripping them of their real sources of power. Very few executives are willing to become figureheads. "It's crazy, but a lot of quite smart guys would rather be kicked out than kicked upstairs," notes Michael Korda.[32] Sometimes more drastic measures are taken to embarrass the executive into retirement. A prominent age discrimination attorney testified before the House Select Committee on Aging that the desk of one of his clients was moved into the hallway by his client's employer as an attempt to humiliate his client and encourage a "voluntary" retirement.[33]

Enforcing the ADEA against these subtle forms of age discrimination is, of course, very difficult. Many victims of such tactics are unaware of their plight. Most victims, as noted earlier, are middle-aged males who never dreamed they would be targets of discrimination. Those who are aware have great difficulty producing evidence substantial enough to convince a judge or a jury that age discrimination was the motive underlying their employer's actions. It is likely that employers will become increasingly sophisticated in these subtle tactics as the more blatant forms of discrimination disappear because of the prospects of high litigation costs.

Early Retirement Incentives: The Newest Discrimination

During periods of economic downturn employers seek ways of reducing the size of their workforces using techniques that will not result in undesirable litigation. A favorite technique for eliminating older workers is the early retirement incentive.

Early retirement options are blossoming during the recession of the 1980s. There are no reliable statistics on the number of firms using such options, but business consultants agree that they have "never seen as many early retirement windows open as in the last 12 months."[34] A recent survey conducted by the House Select Committee on Aging and the Public Broadcasting System's "Nightly Business Report" disclosed that many larger companies—such as Crown Zellerbach, Uniroyal, Continental, Firestone, Metropolitan Life, Mead, Sears, Xerox, Eastman Kodak, Travelers Insurance, Continental Group, IBM, A&P, and American

Can—have recently implemented early retirement options to entice older workers out of the workforce.

Most early retirement plans are not, on their face, discriminatory. Most offer a substantial bonus to employees who retire early, usually at age 55 with a specified number of service years. Most employers offer these benefits as a humane alternative to layoffs. But there are instances of discrimination which can creep into these early retirement plans.

A recent U.S. District Court decision, for example, found that the Chrysler Corporation's early retirement plan was discriminatory because, in the opinion of the court, the workers were coerced into accepting the company's offer under threat of layoff.[35] Sometimes the discrimination is more subtle, as when an employer misrepresents or exaggerates the long term economic benefits of an early retirement option, thus encouraging workers to retire when with better information they may have chosen to remain on the job.

Hiring Discrimination

One of the most important sources of age discrimination is the practice by employers of refusing to hire a person because of his or her age. This is also one of the most difficult forms of discrimination to document, which may account for the relatively small number of such charges filed with the EEOC. (See above.)

Hiring discrimination as expressed in age biased job announcements once was a greater problem than it is today. This is largely due to very stringent guidelines promulgated by the EEOC which place limits on the terms that can be used in job listings. Terms such as "age 25 to 35," "young," "college student," "recent college graduate," "boy," "girl," or similar terms or phrases are considered to be violations of the ADEA.[36]

Hiring discrimination is also fostered by job applications on which the applicant's age or date of birth is requested. The official position of the EEOC on this matter is that such requests do not automatically constitute a violation of the Act, but they will be scrutinized very carefully to assure that the request is for a permissible purpose. Employers can usually protect themselves if they include on the application a statement that reads: "The Age Discrimination in Employment Act of 1967 prohibits discrimination on the basis of age with respect to individuals who are at least 40 but less than 70 years of age."[37]

A consequence of hiring discrimination is the longer period of time older workers require to find a job compared to younger workers. On average, in 1982, an unemployed worker age 55 and over will remain jobless for 19 weeks, which is 23 percent longer than the 15.5 weeks average for all age groups.[38] Also, many older workers become discouraged and give up the job search. Workers 60 and over are three times as likely as all other adults (over 25) to give up and withdraw from the workforce.[39]

Long term unemployment and discouragement are a direct result, though not exclusively so, of age discrimination. An unemployed machinist, age 56, summed it up best in testimony before a hearing of the House Aging Committee when he said:

> During the time the rumors were flying around about the Torrington plant closing I wasn't too concerned. I am a skilled machinist and the feeling among most of the skilled workers in the plant was that we would have no problems finding jobs if we were laid off. I figured it might take a few weeks to

find another job. It never dawned on me that my age might be a problem in the job search.

I'm too young to retire, but apparently some employers think I'm too old to work. All of the younger machinists I know have jobs, but a number of us older guys are still unemployed 6 months after we lost our last job.[40]

From the employers' point of view, older workers are sometimes considered to be less desirable because they have fewer work years remaining and, especially if training is involved, the employer is concerned about recouping his investment. Many older skilled workers, however, require little or no training and their lower rates of turnover often make them more dependable employees than younger workers. Similarly, employer concerns about higher benefit costs associated with older workers are realistic, but in many cases these may be offset by the more efficient work habits, lower turnover and lower absenteeism of older workers.

Salary Discrimination

One of the most complex forms of age discrimination involves salary or wages. It is generally held by the public that older workers are discriminated against because they are too costly and younger workers can replace them for much less money. Supporting this position are numerous stories about older workers who are discharged just a few days before they would have achieved vested rights in their pension, thereby saving the employer thousands of dollars in pension payments. Or, there are examples of older workers who are allegedly discharged and replaced by two younger workers for the same total salary. Certainly these stories are true and illustrate an important source of age discrimination. There is, however, another salary pattern which suggests a quite different view of age discrimination: salary deceleration.

Salary deceleration, in the form of smaller or fewer salary increments, often occurs among older workers. The former vice president of personnel and organization development for Abraham & Strauss, the largest division of the Federated Department Store conglomerate, described the process of salary deceleration at a Congressional hearing:

> Then there is the deceleration process and the phenomenon of "pattern" increases. In salary management, salary increases are frequently decelerated for job holders who are at or above the top of the established salary range for a given job.

> This process of deceleration is designated to relieve relative inequities, like where the subordinate is making more than the supervisor. . . . Unfortunately, this salary management technique has been subverted. In the case of Sam . . . because he was 62 he received an increase of $1,500 every other year, far below the official guidelines of around 7 percent annually for his level of performance. But then the idea is that as age increases, job mobility decreases, and this factor is an invitation to decelerate, crop and deny increases simply because the employee has lost job mobility. The employee can't or won't leave.

> This is especially true of older women, because they tend to have less self-confidence and experience in the job market and fewer possibilities in the job market due, in turn, to the traditional and historical roles of women in our society and because of sex discrimination.[41]

In contrast to the stories of older workers being replaced by less expensive younger workers, the process of salary deceleration described above suggests that it is the younger workers who may be more expensive. Certainly at the executive level this is often true. For example, testimony before the Select Committee on Aging by a former executive using confidential salary and age data on "key executives" of the Abraham & Strauss Department Store chain illustrate this point. Executives under 40 had average salaries in 1976 that were nearly $10,000 higher than executives over 40; by 1979 the discrepancy was nearly $30,000. (See Figure 2.) Thus, it was the younger executives who were more expensive than the older ones. Apparently, the company considered younger executives to be more valuable than the older executives.

Salary discrimination, then, hits older workers in two very different ways. In some cases salaries rise "too high" and the employer replaces the older individual with less expensive younger workers. In contrast, other employers suppress the salary increases for older workers and inflate those of younger less experienced workers, presumably because older workers have less job mobility while younger workers are perceived to be more valuable. The net result is the same: older workers are discriminated against.

Freezing Pension Contributions: Legalized Discrimination

One of the most controversial provisions of the 1978 Amendments to the ADEA permits employers to stop contributing to a worker's pension plan at age 65.[42] Despite evidence that such a policy has no cost justification,[43] nearly half of all employers nationwide freeze pension benefits at age 65.[44] The net result is that many older workers choose to retire by age 65 rather than suffer the loss of benefit accruals associated with a later retirement age.

From a national policy perspective, allowing discontinuance of pension accrual is irrational. To the extent that such a policy discourages continued employment among older workers,[45] it runs counter to the overriding concern of Con-

182

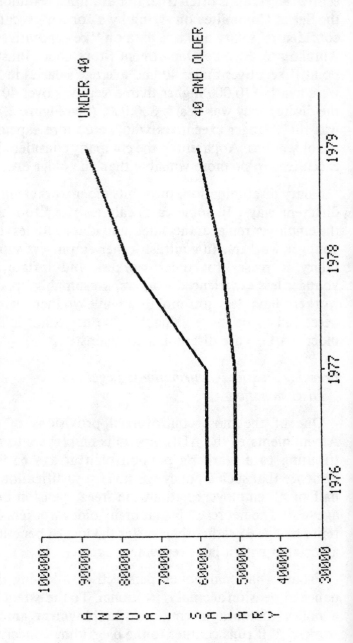

Figure 2
Average Salary for Key Executives Employed Between 1976-1979
A & S Department Stores

gress which is to reduce the costs of retirement programs. Encouraging longer worklives should be the goal of public policy in the face of dramatic demographic trends which portend heavier and heavier financial burdens on young workers to care for the expanding retiree population. Nevertheless, the policy of discouraging employment among the old persists and will not be changed unless Congress specifically mandates it.

III. Recent Efforts to Modify the ADEA

The 97th Congress will be best remembered for its budget cutting activities, its dearth of social legislation and a reluctance to make major modifications in the troubled Social Security system. Buried deep in the dust of that Congress, however, are the remnants of a stillborn attempt to end once and for all the last vestiges of age discrimination in American society. This legislative effort to build on the 1978 ADEA Amendments, although thwarted by a variety of circumstances, reflects a growing awareness by national policymakers that age is a poor indicator of job ability; that the older members of society should be unshackled and allowed, even encouraged, to remain productive as long as possible. The following review of legislation to end age discrimination during the 97th Congress and of attempts by the business community to weaken the current act is not only an interesting lesson in American politics, but also reflects the competing interests, misplaced priorities and dashed hopes of the various actors involved in the debate over extending fundamental civil rights to America's older citizens.

Legislation to Amend the ADEA

Early in the 97th Congress, Rep. Claude Pepper introduced legislation (H.R. 3397) that would, among other things, amend the ADEA by removing the upper age limit of 70 and by closing various loopholes which allowed age discrimination against older members of select occupations. This legislation received a boost when President Reagan announced on April 2, 1982 that he would, ". . . back legislation which eliminates mandatory retirement requirements in government and private industry based solely on age."[46] The President's announcement unleashed a flurry of activity in Congress.

Congressional negotiations. The Labor Department, designated by the Reagan Administration, initiated negotiations with key members of Congress to work out the details of a bill to abolish mandatory retirement and other remaining forms of age discrimination. At the outset there was wide disagreement in Congress about what issues should be included in legislation, but one issue was clear: the best means to end mandatory retirement was simply to remove the upper age limit of 70 from the Age Discrimination in Employment Act (ADEA). Other issues—such as requiring equitable pension treatment for workers over 65, eliminating discrimination against executives and removal of other loopholes in the ADEA—were discussed but eventually set aside by their proponents in exchange for commitments for swift enactment of a bill that would end age discrimination for workers age 70 and over.

Business and labor reactions. Immediately following the President's April 2 statement, major business and labor organizations indicated that they had no problem with the elimination of mandatory retirement. According to an April 13 *Wall Street Journal* article, "Few business groups oppose the bill, and the AFL-CIO says it would 'go along with it.' "[47] Within weeks, however, the major business groups began to reconsider their initial position on this issue and, at the urging of a small group of employers represented by a Washington law firm, they began to raise concerns about several of the protections offered by the ADEA. By early

May, business opposition began to crystalize and, according to a June 3 *Washington Post* article,[48] this opposition was felt in the White House.

Apparent switch in Administration position. On May 17, 1982 Undersecretary of Labor Lovell reported to Rep. Pepper that the Administration was no longer supporting a simple removal of the age 70 limit from the ADEA. According to Lovell, the President could only support extending job protections to workers over 70 who have jobs; those who were seeking jobs or who deserved promotions would be unprotected under the President's proposal. This proposal met with vigorous opposition from all major aging organizations, as well as from key members of Congress, but the Administration stood firm.

Compromise position worked out. A compromise was worked out between the Administration and House Aging Committee Chairman Claude Pepper. The terms of the compromise were that Pepper and other key House and Senate leaders would go along with the Administration's revised position in exchange for direct White House involvement in opposing any amendments (such as those being proposed by the business groups) to weaken the ADEA. Since support for the weakening amendments appeared to be stronger in the Republican controlled Senate, the strategy was to allow the Senate to act first on the legislation, thereby leaving the Democratic controlled House with the option of killing the bill if it contained any harmful or weakening amendments. Unfortunately, the Senate never acted.

Academics mobilize against the bill. One important reason for the Senate's failure to act on the bill was a late lobbying effort by college and university presidents and faculty. Representatives of both groups pressed for a special provision in the bill that would exempt tenured faculty. The argument was that eliminating mandatory retirement for tenured faculty would threaten the tenure system and weaken the institution of higher education. This lobbying campaign was successful in muddying the waters and effectively stalling any legislative action on the bill during the regular session of the 97th Congress.

Business Objections to ADEA Enforcement Procedures

Some members of the business community have suggested that the right to a jury trial should be eliminated because older plaintiffs allegedly prevail more frequently in jury than judge trials in age discrimination cases. The argument is that because of the responsiveness of juries to emotional appeals, plaintiffs receive inflated damage awards from juries that are far higher than they would normally receive from a judge.

The right to a jury trial. The right to a jury trial was established by the Supreme Court in *Lorillard v. Pons,* 434 U.S. 575 (1978). The court was convinced that Congress had intended to include the right to a jury in the ADEA, since the ADEA was patterned after the Fair Labor Standards Act, which allowed jury trials. The 1978 Amendments to the ADEA reaffirmed congressional support for jury trials in ADEA actions.

No evidence that juries are biased toward older workers. Although no scientific data exist on jury trials and the ADEA, two surveys of personal injury cases (with are more emotional than ADEA cases) have produced conflicting results as to whether older plaintiffs prevail more frequently. In a 1974 study of personal injury cases based on 800 verdicts, the Jury Verdicts Research Company found the recovery rate was 59 percent for plaintiffs who are retired or are over 65, compared to a national average of 65 percent. A 1982 study of personal injury cases found the prevailing recovery rate for retired plaintiffs was 65 percent, which was *above* the national rate of 52 percent. The only conclusion that can be drawn from these studies is that there is no clear-cut evidence of bias in favor of older plaintiffs in jury trials. In general, no documented evidence has indicated that older plaintiffs prevail more frequently with juries than with judges under the ADEA.

Damage awards under the ADEA. In addition to the jury trial provisions, business lobbyists also want to eliminate the liquidated damage provisions of the ADEA. The claim is that liquidated damages are punitive and therefore have no place in antidiscrimination legislation. The remedies available under the ADEA, however, are the same as remedies available under the Fair Labor Standards Act of 1938 (FLSA). Section 7(b) of the ADEA incorporates the powers, remedies and procedures provided in sections of the FLSA. The FLSA provides that employers who violate its provisions shall be liable for unpaid minimum wages, unpaid overtime compensation, and an equal amount of liquidated damages for willful violations. However, in order to show a willful violation of the ADEA, the litigant must establish a "knowing and voluntary violation of the Act."

The narrow interests of some business lobbyists and of the academic institutions have effectively stalled efforts to improve legal protections for workers based on age. We may be in the midst of a political climate in which business leaders are concentrating their efforts on reducing the effectiveness of federal legislation rather than attempting to comply with intent of the legislation. The result, if this new climate continues, may be counterproductive to the broader social goal of equal employment opportunities for all age groups.

Conclusion

Public and employer opinions reveal a widespread belief that age discrimination is real. And, the recent upsurge in legal and administrative confrontations between older employees and their employers indicates that substantial numbers of older persons are acting on their beliefs.

The problem of age discrimination is not, however, confined to the oldest age groups (65 +). Certainly, age discrimination increases by age, but for a variety of reasons the oldest workers are not the ones seeking retribution. Rather, the typical age discrimination victim pursuing legal and administrative remedies is middle-aged, male and often from a managerial position. These individuals represent a new group of civil rights activists. They are not poor, minorities or women. They are predominantly white, middle-class individuals who have the resources to pursue an age charge and who believe they deserve better than they are getting after a lifetime of dedication to their employer.

The forms of age discrimination range from the more obvious mandatory retirement ages, to more subtle job harassment and early retirement incentives. Each of these forms represents not only a threat to the well-being of older individuals, but also undermines the economic stability of the nation. Age discrimination reduces the work efforts of older people, encourages premature labor force withdrawal, and increases the burden on an already burdened Social Security system and on private pension systems. Without adequate solutions to the problems of age discrimination and without incentives to encourage more older workers to remain employed longer, the nation could be facing a serious economic and social crisis.

Ironically, recent legislative attempts to bolster the Age Discrimination in Employment Act have been thwarted by special interest groups. In particular, business lobbyists have pushed to weaken the protections afforded by the ADEA, at a time when, if anything, the statute needs strengthening. Unfortunately, business is seeking ways of reducing costs during times of recession, an objective that is threatened in the view of some business leaders by civil rights legislation in general. Just as we should not tolerate weakening the Civil Rights Act, so we must also resist any attempt to undermine the ADEA. Rather, public policy efforts should strengthen protections for older workers, not only in the interests of individual rights but as a means of contributing to the nation's economic welfare.

Appendix I
Basic Protections of the Age Discrimination in Employment Act

The ADEA prohibits employers, employment agencies or labor organizations from discriminating on the basis of age in such matters as hiring, job retention, compensation and other terms, conditions and privileges of employment. The Act prohibits employment-related advertisements that show preference, limitation or discrimination based on age. And, labor organizations may not classify or refer persons based on their age.

In the 1978 Amendments, mandatory retirement was specifically oulawed for most federal workers at any age and for private sector and state and local employment before age 70. Furthermore, the 1978 Amendments to the ADEA specifically prevent employee benefit plans—such as retirement, pension or insurance plans—from including mandatory retirement provisions for protected workers.

Exemptions

The 1978 Amendments contained several important exemptions. First, executives and policymakers are protected only to age 65, if the individual has been employed in a "bona fide executive or a high policymaking position" for at least two years *and* is entitled to an annual retirement benefit provided by the employer of at least $27,000. Such high-level executives and policymakers can, therefore, be mandatorily retired upon their 65th birthday.

A second exemption applies to employee benefits. The legislative history of the 1978 Amendments left room for a subsequent Labor Department interpretive bulletin allowing employers to reduce certain employee benefits for workers age 65 and over. For example, pension contributions can be reduced or discontinued when an employee reaches age 65. Life insurance benefits may also be reduced if the employer can demonstrate that such benefits are more expensive for workers over age 65 than for those under 65. Employers were allowed to reduce health benefits until a 1982 Amendment required that workers between the ages of 65 and 69 be offered full coverage by the employer's health plan. Health benefits can be reduced and/or offset by Medicare after age 69.

Last, certain federal occupations were excluded from the Act—air traffic controllers, airline pilots, federal law enforcement officers, prison guards and firefighters, employees of the Alaska Railroad, Panama Canal Company, Canal Zone Government, Foreign Service and Central Intelligence Agency. These occupations are covered by provisions in separate statutes.

Procedural Issues

Several significant procedural changes were added to the ADEA in 1978, largely because of concern that the courts were dismissing lawsuits on procedural grounds, without consideration for the merits of the complaints.

Before going to court, an aggrieved individual must first file a "charge alleging unlawful discrimination" with the federal enforcement agency within 180 days of its occurrence (or 300 days if the alleged violation occurred in a state which has an agency empowered to grant or seek relief from age discrimination). After 60 days from the date of filing, or after conciliation efforts by the appropriate enforcement agency have failed, the charging party may file a private suit.

The statute of limitations—two years for nonwillful violations and three years for willful violations—may be tolled (extended) for up to one year, to allow the federal agency more flexibility to attempt conciliation. The tolling provision was added to the ADEA in 1978 to prevent those employers who may have violated the law from delaying conciliation with the idea of avoiding back pay liabilities because of the statute of limitations.

One of the most important procedural amendments of 1978 was that providing for a jury trial option. A jury trial is available to individuals in cases when alleged discrimination involves potential monetary liabilities, usually in the form of back pay.

Enforcement of the Act

Until 1979, the Department of Labor had jurisdiction over all aspects of the ADEA. With "Reorganization Plan No. 1 of 1978" the responsibility for ADEA enforcement shifted to the Equal Employment Opportunity Commission (EEOC). Enforcement responsibility by the EEOC for the federal sector became effective on January 1, 1979, and for private sector and state and local government employment it became effective on July 1, 1979.

NOTES

1. Louis Harris and Associates, "The Myth and Reality of Aging in America," conducted for the National Council on the Aging, Inc., 1974, available from the National Council on the Aging, Inc., 600 Maryland Ave., S.W., Washington, DC 20024; Louis Harris and Associates, "Aging in the Eighties: America in Transition," conducted for the National Council on the Aging, Inc., 1981.

2. Harris, "Aging in the Eighties."

3. In 1974, the Harris survey found that 66 percent of the American public "strongly opposed" age-based forced retirement. By 1981 this had increased by 12 percentage points to 78 percent strongly opposed.

4. William M. Mercer, "Employer Attitudes: Implications of an Aging Workforce," William M. Mercer, Inc., 1211 Avenue of the Americas, New York, NY 10036, November 1981.

5. William Graebner, *A History of Retirement* (New Haven: Yale University Press, 1980).

6. Ibid., p. 39.

7. Ibid., p. 38.

8. Section 715 of the Civil Rights Act of 1964 stated that, "The Secretary of Labor shall make a full and complete study of the factors which might tend to result in discrimination in employment because of age and of the consequences of such discrimination on the economy and individuals affected." Public Law 88-352, 2 July 1964.

9. U.S. Department of Labor, *The Older American Worker: Age Discrimination in Employment,* Report of the Secretary of Labor to the Congress under Section 715 of the Civil Rights Act of 1964, June 1965.

10. Ibid., p. 6.

11. The Age Discrimination in Employment Act of 1967, Public Law 90-202, 81 Stat. 602-08.

12. Differences in reporting procedures between the Labor Department and the EEOC make problematic any comparisons pre- and post-1979, the point at which enforcement duties were shifted between the two agencies.

13. Harris, "Aging in the Eighties."

14. U.S. Congress, House, Select Committee on Aging, *Age Discrimination: A Growing Problem in America,* Report by Chairman Claude Pepper, 97th Cong., 2d sess., 22 February 1982.

15. The EEOC filed only 89 lawsuits in FY 1981, and this constituted a record number for the agency. In FY 1982, however, the EEOC filed only 24 lawsuits.

16. Michael Schuster, "Analyzing Age Discrimination Act Cases: Development of a Methodology," *Law and Policy Quarterly* 4, no. 3 (July 1982), pp. 339-351.

17. It should be noted that all cases analyzed by Schuster were pre-1978. The ADEA was amended in 1978 and a jury trial option was added, an important procedural charge which some employers have recently argued gives a new advantage to the plaintiff.

18. U.S. Department of Labor, "Interim Report to Congress on Age Discrimination in Employment Act Studies," Report required by Section 5 of the Age Discrimination in Employment Act, submitted to Congress in 1981.

194

19. U.S. Congress, House, Select Committee on Aging, *Mandatory Retirement: The Social and Human Cost of Enforced Idleness,* 95th Cong., 1st sess., August 1977 (Out of print).

20. The arguments in favor of mandatory retirement include: (1) Older persons as a group are less well suited for some jobs than younger workers because they exhibit declining physical and mental capacity, an inability to learn, inflexibility and lower educational levels; (2) Individual assessments are not possible because of the absence of assessment technologies; (3) Mandatory retirement saves face for the individual; (4) Mandatory retirement provides a predictable situation allowing management and individuals to plan ahead; (5) Older workers are more expensive in terms of benefits and wages; and (6) Forced retirement opens opportunities for youth.

21. Benson Rosen and Thomas H. Jerdee, "Too Old or Not Too Old," *Harvard Business Review* 55 (1977), pp. 97-106; J. E. Haefner, "Race, Age, Sex and Competence as Factors in Employer Selection of the Disadvantaged," *Journal of Applied Psychology* 62, no. 2 (1977), pp. 199-202; J. O. Britton and K. R. Thomas, "Age and Sex as Employment Variables: Views of Employment Service Interviewers," *Journal of Employment Counseling* 10 (1973), pp. 180-186.

22. W. H. Bower, "An Appraisal of Worker Characteristics as Related to Age," *Journal of Applied Psychology* 36, no. 5 (1952), pp. 296-300.

23. H. Maher, "Age and Performance of Two Work Groups," *Journal of Gerontology* 10, no. 4 (1955), pp. 448-451.

24. N. W. Smith, "Older Worker Efficiency in Jobs of Various Types," *Personnel Journal* 32, no. 1 (1953), pp. 19-23.

25. J. A. Mark, "Measurement of Job Performance and Age," *Monthly Labor Review* 79, no. 12 (1956), pp. 1410-1414; H. M. Clay, "A Study of Performance in Relation to Age at Two Printing Works," *Journal of Gerontology* 11, no. 4 (1956), pp. 417-424.

26. W. H. Holley, Jr., H. S. Feild, and B. B. Holley, "Age and Reactions to Jobs: An Empirical Study of Paraprofessional Workers," *Aging and Work* 1 (1978), pp. 33-40; U.S. Department of Labor, Bureau of Labor Statistics, "Comparative Job Performance by Age: Office Workers," Bulletin No. 1273 (1960), p. 36.

27. James E. Birren, *The Psychology of Aging* (Englewood Cliffs: Prentice Hall, 1964); J. R. Sieman, "Programmed Material as a Training Tool for Older Persons," *Industrial Gerontology* 3, no. 3 (1976), pp. 183-190.

28. Sarah Paz, Testimony presented before the House Select Committee on Aging hearing on "The End of Mandatory Retirement," Washington, DC, 16 July 1982.

29. Rep. Claude Pepper, Opening statement before a hearing of the Select Committee on Aging on "The End of Mandatory Retirement," Washington, DC, 16 July 1982.

30. Michael Korda, *Power: How to Get It, How to Use It* (New York: Ballantine Books, 1975), pp. 201-204.

31. Cited in *Age Discrimination in Employment: A Growing Problem in America,* Report by Chairman Claude Pepper, Select Committee on Aging, U.S. Congress, House, 97th Cong., 2d sess., 22 February 1982, p. 7.

32. Korda, *Power,* p. 204.

33. V. Paul Donnelly, Testimony before the House Select Committee on Aging hearing on "Inside Views of Corporate Age Discrimination," Washington, DC, 24 February 1982.

34. Rose Darby, "More Firms Offer Early Retirement While Weighing Its Pros and Cons," *World of Work Report,* 7, no. 8 (August 1982).

35. Equal Employment Opportunity Commission v. Chrysler Corporation, U.S. District Court for Eastern District of Michigan, Docket No. 81-72347.

36. Equal Employment Opportunity Commission, "Final Interpretation: Age Discrimination in Employment Act," 29 CFR Part 1625.

37. Ibid.

38. U.S. Congress, House, Select Committee on Aging, *The Unemployment Crisis Facing Older Americans,* Report by Chairman Claude Pepper, 97th Cong., 2d sess., 8 October 1982.

39. Ibid.

40. Raymond Arnista, Testimony before the House Select Committee on Aging hearing on "The Unemployment Crisis Facing Older Americans," Washington, DC, 8 October 1982.

41. John Staley, Testimony before the House Select Committee on Aging hearing on "Inside Views of Corporate Age Discrimination," Washington, DC, 24 February 1982.

42. U.S. Department of Labor, "Employee Benefit Plans: Amendment to Interpretive Bulletin," 29 CFR Part 860.

43. U.S. Congress, House, Select Committee on Aging, *An Analysis of the Costs of Pension Accrual After Age 65,* 97th Cong., 2d sess., May 1982.

44. U.S. Department of Labor, "Interim Report on Age Discrimination in Employment Act," 1981.

45. Ibid. The Labor Department estimates that if pension accrual were required, 68,000 more older workers would remain in the labor force.

46. President Ronald Reagan, "Remarks of the President at the Signing Ceremony on Older Americans Month," 2 April 1982.

47. *Wall Street Journal,* Labor Letter Column, 13 April 1982.

48. Lawrence Meyer and Howie Kurtz, "Age Discrimination Opponents Suspect About-Face by Reagan," *Washington Post,* 3 June 1982.

Chapter 8
Financing Options
for Social Security

Alicia H. Munnell

Social security is the mainstay of the economic security of the elderly. In 1982 the aged, the disabled, their dependents and survivors will receive $156 billion in cash benefits from the Old-Age, Survivors, and Disability Insurance (OASDI) program and another $34 billion of medical care under the Hospital Insurance (HI) program. Approximately 90 percent of persons aged 65 and over are social security recipients, and for two-thirds of these recipients social security benefits account for more than half of total income.[1] With such enormous dependence on social security, any significant change in the program could affect the work and retirement patterns of older people.

In recent years, workers and beneficiaries alike have begun to question whether the system can continue to provide its current level of support. The widespread concern is a response to the repeated short-run financial crises and to the large deficits projected after the turn of the century as the baby boom retires. Confidence in the program can be restored only by bringing revenues and costs into balance so that the immediate shortfall is eliminated and the financial integrity of the system is insured for the long run. This paper explores possible solutions to both the current and projected deficits.

I. The Social Security Program Today

In 1982, the social security program covers 90 percent of the working population, including the self-employed. At present, the only significant categories of workers excluded from the program are civilian employees of the federal government under a retirement system of their own, 30 percent of state and local government workers, low-paid or very irregularly employed farm and domestic workers, and unpaid family workers. Railroad employees are also not covered directly, but their plan is thoroughly integrated with social security.

The social security system consists of three programs which are financed through separate trust funds. The Old-Age and Survivors Insurance (OASI) program, which pays benefits to retired workers, their dependents and survivors, is the largest program and will dispense $138 billion in benefits to almost 32 million beneficiaries in 1982 (see table 1). The Disability Insurance (DI) program, which pays benefits to disabled workers and their dependents, will pay $18 billion to roughly 4 million beneficiaries in 1982. The third program, Hospital Insurance (HI) or Medicare, pays benefits to workers covered by OASDI and the railroad retirement program. Benefit payments from this fund will be $34 billion in 1982.

Benefits Provisions

Old-age benefits are payable at age 65 to fully insured workers, that is, to workers who have one quarter of earnings in covered employment for each year since 1950 (or, if later, age 21) and the age of 62. Early retirement is possible as early as age 62 with reduced benefits. Disability benefits are payable to workers who have one quarter of coverage between 1950 (or age 21) and the onset of the disability.

Table 1
Benefits and Beneficiaries under Old-Age and Survivors Insurance (OASI), Disability Insurance (DI) and Hospital Insurance (HI), Selected Years 1950-1982

Year	Benefits ($ billions)				Beneficiaries (millions)			
	OASI	DI	HI	Total	OASI	DI	Total	HI
1950	1.0	—	—	1.0	2.9	—	2.9	—
1960	10.7	.6	—	11.3	13.7	.5	14.2	—
1970	28.8	3.1	5.1	37.0	22.6	2.6	25.2	20.4[a]
1980	105.1	15.4	25.1	145.6	30.4	4.7	35.1	27.6[a]
1982	138.5	17.7	35.1	191.3	31.5	4.4	35.9	28.5[a]

SOURCES: U.S. Department of Health and Human Services, Social Security Administration, *1982 Annual Report of the Board of Trustees of the Federal Old-Age and Survivors Insurance and Disability Insurance Trust Funds* (Washington, DC: GPO, 1982), Table 20, p. 51; Table 22, p. 54; Table 28, p. 65; Table A3, p. 84; Table A4, p. 86; U.S. Department of Health and Human Services, Social Security Administration, *1982 Annual Report of the Board of Trustees of the Federal Hospital Insurance Trust Fund* (Washington, DC: GPO, 1982), Table 6, p. 29; U.S. Department of Health and Human Services, Social Security Administration, Division of Medicare Cost Analysis, unpublished data.

a. This figure represents both aged and disabled beneficiaries. As of July 1, 1973 hospital insurance protection was extended to disabled persons entitled to monthly benefit payments under social security because of their disability.

The monthly benefits awarded to retired and disabled workers are computed in three stages. The first is the calculation of the worker's average indexed monthly earnings (AIME). To compute this figure, taxable wages in each year between 1950 (or age 21) and age 62 are revalued to reflect the increases in the average wage level and then the revalued earnings are averaged over the period, excluding five years of lowest earnings.

The second stage involves the calculation of the worker's primary insurance amount (PIA)—the benefit payable to a fully insured worker retiring at age 65. In 1982 this amount is determined by applying the following three bracket formula to the worker's AIME:

> 90 percent of the first $230 of AIME
> 32 percent of AIME between $230 and $1,388
> 15 percent of AIME over $1,388

Since the formula multiplies each successive increment of the worker's AIME by a declining percentage, low-wage workers receive a higher percentage of their pre-retirement earnings in benefits than high-wage workers. To maintain the progressivity and to insure that the average worker in each successive cohort receives the same replacement rate (benefit as a percent of pre-retirement earnings), the bend points in the benefit formula, that is, the amounts $230 and $1,388, are increased each year to reflect the average increase in wages in employment covered by social security.

The third stage in the benefit calculation is the determination of the actual benefit paid. This amount usually depends on the relation of the wage earner to the individual drawing the benefit and the age at which he claims it. A fully insured worker retiring at 65 receives a monthly benefit equal to 100 percent of his primary insurance amount; however, a worker can retire as early as 62, with an actuarial reduction in benefits of 5/9 of 1 percent for each month before the age of

65. A dependent spouse, a child, or dependent grandchild receives a benefit of up to 50 percent of the worker's primary insurance amount. If the worker dies, the widow or widower receives 100 percent of his primary insurance amount, while a surviving child or grandchild receives 75 percent. Dependents and survivors can also claim reduced benefits earlier than 65.[2]

Since social security payments are meant to replace earnings lost because of retirement or disability, the amount of earned income a person can receive while collecting social security benefits is limited until he reaches 72. This limit is known as the retirement, or earnings, test and is indexed to keep pace with the level of wages. For 1982, a beneficiary can earn up to $6,000 annually with no reduction in benefits. After that, a dollar of benefits is withheld for each $2 of earnings over $6,000.[3]

Social Security Taxes

The social security system is financed on a pay-as-you-go basis. Payroll tax contributions from the 115 million covered workers finance the benefits for the 36 million retired and disabled workers and their dependents and survivors. In 1982, the tax rate for retirement, survivors and disability insurance is 5.4 percent each for the employee and employer on the first $32,400 of wage income, with the ceiling scheduled to rise automatically with the wage level. Hospital insurance contributions raise the overall payroll tax rate to 6.7 percent each for the employee and employer.

Since social security benefits are funded essentially by the current flow of payroll taxes, the trust funds are designed only to provide a buffer against brief unanticipated economic fluctuations. The funds usually hold substantially less than one year's benefits, but a small trust fund should not be a source of concern in a social insurance program. A private pension plan must have sufficient assets to meet all prior and current commitments because it cannot be certain of receiving future premiums. In contrast, the social security program, which relies on the government's tax powers to meet its obligations, can continue to levy taxes on future generations of workers to pay social security taxes. However, pay-as-you-go financing can lead to short-run problems if economic fluctuations adversely affect receipts or outlays. Long-run financing problems can also arise if the size of the beneficiary population increases relative to the working population. The social security system now faces both of these difficulties.

II. Financing Social Security: An Overview

The trustees of the social security program each year prepare a report on the condition of and prospects for the OASI, DI and HI funds, both in the near and distant future.[4] Figure 1 compares the cost of the combined OASI and DI funds measured as a percentage of covered payrolls with the scheduled contribution rates for the employer and employee. The projections are based on the more pessimistic of the two central assumptions, II-B, in the trustees' 1982 report, and are shown through 2060, the end of the period for which official estimates are available.[5]

The easiest way to understand the OASDI financing situation is to divide the figure into three separate time periods—1982-1990, 1990-2014, and 2014-2060. In the first period, assuming a continuation of current law, OASDI has a considerable shortfall. Between now and 1985, expenditures substantially exceed income. Present law provides for borrowing from the hospital insurance fund during 1982, but without a continuation of the borrowing provision or additional income of some other source, the OASI fund would not be able to pay benefits after mid-1983. The scheduled

Figure 1
Estimated OASDI Costs as Percent of Payroll
and Scheduled Tax Rates
Intermediate Assumption II-Bᵃ, 1982-2060

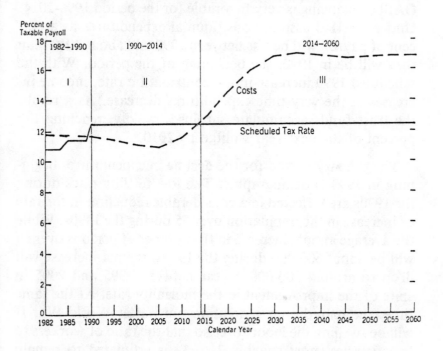

SOURCE: *1982 Annual Report of the Board of Trustees of the Federal Old Age and Survivors Insurance and Disability Insurance Trust Funds* (GPO, 1982), Table 27, p. 64.

a. Under Intermediate II-B assumptions, the ultimate percentage rates of increase for fertility, real wages and CPI are 2.1, 1.5 and 4.0 respectively.

1985 increase in the contribution rate brings the income and expenditure lines closer together, but the OASDI program continues to run a deficit.

In marked contrast to the first period, the outlook for OASDI financing is very favorable for the period 1990-2014. Under the II-B assumptions, annual expenditures as a percent of payroll will be less between 1990 and about 2010 than they will be in 1990, the beginning of the period. With the scheduled 1990 increase in the contribution rate, income increases at the very time expenditures decrease. As a result, the trust funds accumulate surpluses rapidly, reaching 177 percent of the next year's outgo by 2010.[6]

The primary reason for the decline in expenditures beginning in 1990 is demographic. The low fertility rates during the 1930s are reflected in a considerable reduction in the rate of increase in the population over 65 during the 1990s. While the average annual increase in the number of persons over 65 will be about 600,000 during the 1980s, the net increase will drop to around 300,000 a year between 1995 and 2005 in spite of the improvement in the mortality rate. At the same time, the baby boom generation born after World War II will be swelling the labor force so that the ratio of workers to beneficiaries, now roughly 3 to 1, is estimated to remain stable for the next 30 years. With a stable ratio of workers to beneficiaries, even modest productivity gains will reduce the cost of social security as a percent of payroll.

The third period is characterized by rapidly rising costs as the baby boom generation starts to retire. At the same time, the growth in the labor force slows markedly, reflecting the precipitous decline in the fertility rate which began in the mid-1960s. These two factors cause the ratio of workers to beneficiaries to decline from its current level of 3 to 1 to a ratio of 2 to 1. With a pay-as-you-go system, the decline in this crucial ratio produces a substantial increase in costs as a percentage of payrolls. Despite the increasing gap between costs and revenues, however, the large accumulated trust funds are sufficient under the II-B assumptions to carry the OASDI program through 2025.[7]

Figure 2 compares income and expenditures for the Hospital Insurance program from now until the year 2060. Because of the great uncertainty about the nature of the hospital system in the distant future, the Trustees traditionally have made cost estimates for HI for only 25 years as compared to 75 years for OASDI. However, projected costs for the entire 75-year period have been prepared by the Senate Finance Committee.[8] Under the HI program, expenditures consistently exceed contributions as a percentage of payroll. With unconstrained growth, which allows the hospital cost increases to match the increase in wages, the contribution rates scheduled under current law are clearly inadequate.

The following discussion of social security financing focuses primarily on the cash benefit program, OASDI, but it is necessary to consider the financial health of the HI program in evaluating alternative proposals for the short run, such as an extension of interfund borrowing, and for the long run, such as increase in payroll tax contribution rates.

Figure 2
Estimates HI Costs as Percent of Payroll
and Scheduled Tax Rates[a]
Intermediate Assumption II-B, 1982-2055

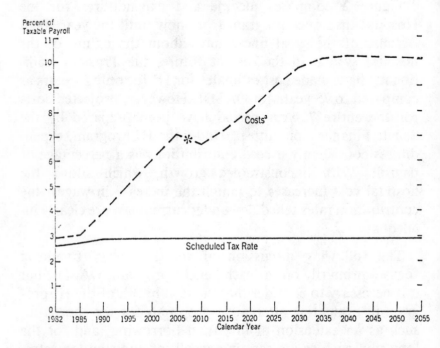

SOURCES: *1982 Annual Report of the Board of Trustees of the Federal Hospital Insurance Trust Fund* (GPO, 1982), Table 8, p. 37; Senate, Committee on Finance, *Staff Data and Materials Related to Social Security Financing,* Committee Print, 97 Cong. 1 Sess. (GPO, September 1981), Table 15, p. 31.

a. Costs for years after 2005 are prepared by Senate Finance Committee and are based on the assumption that medical care unit cost increases after the year 2005 will be equal to average wage increases in covered employment.

III. Short-Run Financing Problems and Options: 1982-1990

Under current law the OASI trust fund, the largest of the social security trust funds, will be unable to pay all benefits on time by July 1983. All three funds, OASI, DI and HI, together will be exhausted by the end of 1984. The immediacy of the projected shortfall has caused many to characterize the social security program's short-run problems as catastrophic and the press constantly refers to the impending "bankruptcy" of the system. In fact, the magnitude of the deficits forecasted for the next eight years is relatively small, less than 4 percent of annual outlays over the period, and numerous options are available for restoring solvency. This section explores the origins of the current deficits and some of the options available for reestablishing financial balance.

Origins of the Current Deficits

In 1977 Congress undertook an important restructuring of the social security program in order to insure its solvency. The congressional action was a response to dire predictions in the 1977 Trustees' report regarding both the short-run and long-run financing of social security. The report warned that the disability fund would be depleted by early 1979 and the OASI fund would be empty by the early 1980s. The short-run deficits were attributable to the high unemployment and inflation that accompanied the 1973-75 recession and to a continuing rapid increase in disability beneficiaries that would have depleted DI trust fund revenues even without the downturn in the economy. In addition, the 1977 report indicated that a significant long term deficit had emerged as a result of lower fertility rate assumptions and increasing replacement rates (the ratio of benefits to preretirement earnings) due to an overindexed benefit formula.

To restore solvency, the 1977 Amendments changed the way benefits were calculated in order to stabilize replacement rates, increased the payroll tax contribution rate, and raised the taxable earnings base. The legislation also reallocated the share of the payroll tax slated for DI trust fund. The principal changes in the financing provisions are shown in table 2. The largest increase in the tax rate occurred in January 1981, when the rate rose 0.52 percent for both employees and employers to a level 0.35 above what it would have been without the change in the law. The maximum wage base on which the tax is levied also increased substantially. For the years 1979 through 1981, the provision for automatic indexing of the base to changes in average wages was suspended and a series of large ad hoc increases was substituted. The consequence of the increases in the rate and base is that the maximum tax in 1982 was about 40 percent higher than the maximum tax under the old law. In view of the substantial increase in revenues and the reduction in benefit growth from correcting the overindexing, the Acting Commissioner of Social Security predicted that "with the signing of the Social Security Amendments of 1977 into law, the Congress and the President have assured the financial soundness of the social security program for the next 50 years."[9]

Less than three years later, however, the Trustees, in their 1980 report, again warned that as early as mid-1981 the OASI trust fund would not be able to pay retirement benefits as they came due. The obvious question is what changed in the intervening years to so dramatically revise the outlook for social security financing during the 1980s. The answer lies primarily in the poor performance of the economy.

Table 3 compares the assumptions underlying the 1977 Trustees' report to actual experience and to the assumptions underlying the 1980 Trustees' report. The 1977 projections were made on the traditional assumption that the rate of wage increase would equal the rate of increase in prices plus

Table 2
Social Security Financing Provisions Before and After the 1977 Amendments

Year	Tax rates[a] (percent)						Taxable base		Maximum tax	
	Old law			New law			Old law	New law	Old law	New law
	Total	OASDI	HI	Total	OASDI	HI				
1977	5.85	4.95	0.90	5.85	4.95	0.90	b	$16,500	$965	$965
1978	6.05	4.95	1.10	6.05	5.05	1.00	b	17,700	1,071	1,071
1979	6.05	4.95	1.10	6.13	5.08	1.05	18,900	22,900c	1,144	1,404
1980	6.05	4.95	1.10	6.13	5.08	1.05	20,400	25,900c	1,234	1,588
1981	6.30	4.95	1.35	6.65	5.35	1.30	22,200	29,700c	1,399	1,975
1982	6.30	4.95	1.35	6.70	5.40	1.30	24,300	32,400	1,531	2,171
1983	6.30	4.95	1.35	6.70	5.40	1.30	26,400	35,100d	1,663	2,352
1984	6.30	4.95	1.35	6.70	5.40	1.30	28,200	37,500d	1,777	2,512
1985	6.30	4.95	1.35	7.05	5.70	1.35	30,600	40,500d	1,928	2,855
1986	6.45	4.95	1.50	7.15	5.70	1.45	33,000	43,800d	2,079	3,132
1987-89	6.45	4.95	1.50	7.15	5.70	1.45	—	—	—	—
1990-2010	6.45	4.95	1.50	7.65	6.20	1.45	—	—	—	—
2011 and after	7.45	5.95	1.50	7.65	6.20	1.45	—	—	—	—

SOURCES: U.S. Department of Health and Human Services, Social Security Administration, *1982 Annual Report of the Board of Trustees of the Federal Old-Age and Survivors Insurance and Disability Insurance Trust Funds* (Washington, DC: GPO, 1982), Table E2, p. 105; John Snee and Mary Ross, "Social Security Amendments of 1977: Legislative History and Summary of Provisions," *Social Security Bulletin* 41, no. 3 (March 1978), Table 4, p. 18.

a. For employees and employers, each. Tax rates for the self-employed are approximately one and one-half times those for nonself-employed.

b. There is no provision in the "old-law" for the taxable base amount in 1977 or 1978.

c. Amount represents ad hoc increase specified by Social Security Amendments of 1977.

d. The taxable base amounts will be determined automatically on the basis of the annual increase in average earnings in covered employment.

Table 3
Comparison of Assumptions Underlying Trustees' 1977 Projections with Actual Experience and with Trustees' Assumptions[a]

| | Percentage increase in | | | | | | | | | Unemployment rate | | |
| | CPI | | | Wages in covered employment | | | Real wage differential[c] | | | | | |
Year	1977 Trustees	Actual	1980 Trustees	1977 Trustees	Actual	1980 Trustees	1977 Trustees	Actual	1980 Trustees	1977 Trustees	Actual	1980 Trustees
1977	6.0	6.5	--	8.4	8.0	--	2.4	1.5	--	7.1	7.0	--
1978	5.4	7.7	--	8.1	8.2	--	2.7	0.6	--	6.3	6.1	--
1979	5.3	11.3	--	7.8	8.8[b]	--	2.5	-2.6	--	5.7	5.9	--
1980	4.7	13.5	14.2	7.1	8.6[b]	9.6	2.4	-4.9	-4.6	5.2	7.2	7.2
1981	4.1	10.3	9.7	6.4	8.6[b]	9.5	2.3	-1.7	-0.2	5.0	7.6	7.9
1982	4.0	--	9.0	6.0	--	10.9	2.0	--	1.9	5.0	--	7.3
1983	4.0	--	8.6	5.75	--	9.9	1.75	--	1.3	5.0	--	6.6
1984	4.0	--	8.2	5.75	--	9.4	1.75	--	1.2	5.0	--	6.2
1985	4.0	--	7.8	5.75	--	9.1	1.75	--	1.3	5.0	--	5.9

SOURCES: U.S. Department of Health, Education and Welfare, Social Security Administration, *1977 Annual Report of the Board of Trustees of the Federal Old-Age and Survivors Insurance and Disability Insurance Trust Funds* (Washington, DC: GPO, 1977), Table 25, p. 45; U.S. Department of Health and Human Services, Social Security Administration, *1980 Annual Report of the Board of Trustees of the Federal Old-Age and Survivors Insurance and Disability Insurance Trust Funds*, Table 10, p. 41; U.S. Department of Health and Human Services, Social Security Administration *1982 Annual Report of the Board of Trustees of the Federal Old-Age and Survivors Insurance and Disability Insurance Trust Funds* (Washington, DC: GPO, 1982), Table 10, p. 32.

a. The 1980 assumptions are based on the intermediate alternative assumptions in the Trustees Report.

b. Estimates.

c. The difference between the percentage increase in average annual wages in covered employment and the percentage increase in the annual CPI.

1 or 2 percent for productivity growth. Since the 1977 projections, however, the traditional relationship between prices and wages has been reversed, with price increases exceeding wage growth. The projected balance in the trust funds is extremely sensitive to the assumed values of these economic variables. The rate of wage growth approximately determines the rate at which revenues grow, while the rate of increase in the CPI determines the rate at which benefit expenditures increase, since benefits are indexed to the CPI. Moreover, the higher unemployment predicted in the 1980 report further worsened the financial outlook since it implied that fewer people would contribute revenue into the trust funds and that more people, finding themselves unemployed, would be likely to take an early retirement or apply for disability benefits.

Despite the deteriorating economic conditions, however, the balance in the DI trust fund increased after 1977, due primarily to a tremendous reduction in the rate at which the eligible population was granted DI benefits. In 1975 the number of disability awards per 1,000 insured workers was 7.11, and in 1977, when the amendments were passed allocating a larger fraction of the combined OASDI tax rate to the DI program, the rate was still 6.54.[10] By 1978, however, it had fallen to 4.36 and, under the 1980 Trustees' intermediate assumptions, was forecasted to remain at about that level through 1982.

Since the Trustees sounded the initial alarm in their 1980 report, the economy has continued to weaken. Two legislative changes, however, have extended until July 1983 the date on which the OASI system will no longer be able to pay benefits on a timely basis. The Omnibus Reconciliation Act of 1981, which was signed into law on August 13, 1981, reduced benefits by about 2 percent through the elimination of students' benefits, capping family benefits for disabled workers and lowering Medicare costs.[11] Amendments to the

Omnibus Reconciliation Act, passed on December 29, 1981, authorized borrowing among the OASI, DI and HI trust funds until January 1983. However, a provision that permits borrowing for deficits up to six months in advance will insure sufficient revenues to carry the OASI fund through June 1983.

In addition to the legislation that extended the life of the OASI fund, the short-run financial health of the HI fund was improved by the Medicare provisions included in the Tax Equity and Fiscal Responsibility Act of 1982, which the President signed into law on August 20, 1982. To increase revenues for the HI program, the legislation extends the social security hospital insurance tax to federal employees. On the expenditure side, the new law substantially restricts Medicare reimbursement to hospitals. Over the three-year period, fiscal 1983-1985, the Tax Equity Act will increase revenues in the HI fund by about $10 billion.

The most recent projections for the short-run status of the OASI, DI and HI programs are presented in table 4. These projections are based on the 1982 Trustees' II-B assumptions, modified to take account of the 7.4 percent cost-of-living adjustment awarded in July 1982, the transfers under the interfund borrowing provisions, and the HI revenue increases and cost reductions from the Tax Equity Act. The obvious question, however, is whether these projections are reliable, particularly in view of the past experience with over-optimistic assumptions.

Table 5 presents forecasts of the change in the consumer price index, the average wage, the real wage differential and the unemployment rate from the 1982 Trustees' report and three independent forecasters, Chase Econometrics, Data Resources, Inc. (DRI) and the Wharton model. The table shows that the figures on which the Trustees based their projections are in the same range as the private forecasters for

Table 4
Estimated Operations of the OASI, DI, HI, and OASDHI Trust Funds Under Intermediate Assumptions, II-B, 1977-1990
(billions of dollars)

Fund performance	Actual				
	1977	1978	1979	1980	1981
Income	72.4	78.1	90.3	105.8	125.4
Disbursements	75.3	83.1	93.1	107.7	126.7
Fund at end of year	32.5	27.5	24.7	22.8	21.5
Fund as percentage of total expenditures during year[c]	47	39	30	23	18
Income	9.6	13.8	15.6	13.9	17.1
Disbursements	11.9	13.0	14.2	15.9	17.7
Fund at end of year	3.4	4.2	5.6	3.6	3.0
Fund as percentage of total expenditures during year[c]	48	26	30	35	21
Income	15.9	19.2	22.8	26.1	35.7
Disbursements	16.0	18.2	21.1	25.6	30.7
Fund at end of year	10.4	11.5	13.2	13.7	18.7
Fund as percentage of total expenditures during year[c]	66	57	54	52	45
Income	97.9	111.1	128.7	145.8	178.2
Disbursements	103.2	114.3	128.4	149.2	175.1
Fund at end of year	46.3	43.2	43.5	40.1	43.2
Fund as percentage of total expenditures during year[c]	50	41	29	29	23

(continued)

Fund performance	1982	1983	1984	1985	1986	1987	1988	1989	1990
					Projected[a]				
OASI[b]									
Income	137.7	136.5	149.2	167.3	180.9	194.5	209.1	223.9	257.0
Disbursements	141.9	156.5	173.0	190.9	208.5	226.3	244.5	263.2	282.2
Fund at end of year	17.3	-2.6	-26.4	-50.0	-77.6	-109.4	-144.9	-184.2	-209.3
Fund as percentage of total expenditures during year[c]	15	11	-2	-14	-24	-34	-45	-55	-65
DI[b]									
Income	16.6	26.1	29.6	37.5	42.0	46.5	51.3	56.5	69.6
Disbursements	18.1	19.0	19.9	21.3	22.7	24.2	25.8	27.6	29.4
Fund at end of year	1.6	8.7	18.4	34.6	53.8	76.1	101.6	130.4	170.6
Fund as percentage of total expenditures during year[c]	17	8	44	86	152	222	294	368	443
HI[b]									
Income	32.6	44.0	48.4	54.5	63.2	68.5	73.8	78.9	83.8
Disbursements	35.6	40.8	46.3	51.9	58.8	66.9	76.0	86.1	96.8
Fund at end of year	15.8	19.0	21.0	23.6	28.0	29.7	27.4	20.2	7.2
Fund as percentage of total expenditures during year[c]	53	39	41	41	40	42	39	32	21
OASDHI[b]									
Income	187.0	206.6	227.2	259.3	286.1	309.5	334.2	359.3	410.5
Disbursements	195.6	216.3	239.2	264.1	290.0	317.5	346.4	376.9	408.4
Fund at end of year	34.6	25.0	13.0	8.2	4.3	-3.7	-15.9	-33.6	-31.5
Fund as percentage of total expenditures during year[c]	22	16	10	5	3	1	-1	-4	-8

SOURCES: U.S. Department of Health and Human Services, Social Security Administration, Office of the Actuary, Health Care Financing Administration, Bureau of Data Management and Strategy, "Estimated Operations of the OASI, DI and HI Trust Funds Under the Laws Amended by the Tax Equity and Fiscal Responsibility Act of 1982," mimeographed (September 17, 1982), Table 3, p. 5; U.S. Department of

Health and Human Services, Social Security Administration, *1982 Annual Report of the Board of Trustees of the Federal Hospital Insurance Trust Fund* (Washington, DC: GPO, 1982), Table 10, p. 39; U.S. Department of Health and Human Services, Social Security Administration, *Summary of the 1982 Annual Reports of the Social Security Boards of Trustees* (Washington, DC: GPO, 1982), Table 4, p. 6; U.S. Department of Health and Human Services, Social Security Administration, *1982 Annual Report of the Board of Trustees of the Federal Old-Age and Survivors Insurance and Disability Insurance Trust Funds* (Washington, DC: GPO, 1982), Table 20, p. 51.

a. Based on Social Security Administration and Health Care Financing Administration estimates of impact of H.R. 4961, "Tax Equity and Fiscal Responsibility Act of 1982" on operations of the OASI, DI and HI Trust Funds under Intermediate Assumptions II-B of the 1982 *Trustees Report*, which were adjusted for OASI and DI to reflect the actual 7.4 percent benefit increase for 1982. The estimated operations for OASI, OASDI, and OASDHI and HI combined in 1983 and later are theoretical since, following the expiration of the present law interfund borrowing authority, the OASI Trust Fund would become depleted in July 1983 when assets would become insufficient to pay benefits when due. Authority for interfund borrowing among the OASI, DI and HI Trust Funds through December 31, 1982 was provided under H.R. 4331. The interfund borrowing provisions are contained in section 201(I) of the Social Security Act.

b. The income figures for 1982, and the end-of-year asset figures for 1982 and later, reflect the transfer of funds from the DI and HI Trust Funds to the OASI Trust Fund under the interfund borrowing authority provided by Public Law 97-123. Under Intermediate Assumptions II-B a total of $11.7 billion would be transferred to OASI in 1982, $6.2 billion from DI and $5.5 billion from HI.

c. Ratio of trust fund amount at beginning of year to total amount of outgo during year.

Table 5
Comparison of Projections for Change
in Selected Economic Variables, 1981-1984

Selected variables	1981	1982	1983	1984
Percentage increase in CPI				
Trustees	10.3	6.9	7.9	7.4
Chase	10.3	6.5	6.3	6.4
DRI	10.3	6.3	6.0	6.3
Wharton	10.3	6.1	6.1	5.7
Percentage increase in wages in covered employment				
Trustees	8.6	6.6	8.1	8.1
Chase	9.7	7.4	5.2	5.1
DRI	9.6	7.9	7.2	7.7
Wharton	9.6	7.6	6.4	6.2
Real wage differential[a]				
Trustees	-1.7	-.3	.2	.7
Chase	-.6	.9	-1.1	-1.3
DRI	-.7	1.6	1.2	1.4
Wharton	-.7	1.5	.3	.5
Unemployment rate				
Trustees	7.6	9.1	8.5	8.0
Chase	7.6	9.4	9.4	8.6
DRI	7.6	9.4	9.1	8.5
Wharton	7.6	9.3	9.0	8.5

SOURCES: U.S. Department of Health and Human Services, Social Security Administration, *1982 Annual Report of the Board of Trustees of the Federal Old-Age and Survivors Insurance and Disability Insurance Trust Funds* (Washington, DC: GPO, 1982), Table 10, p. 32; *Chase Econometrics, U.S. Macroeconomic Forecasts and Analysis,* Table 1.1, 1.2, 17.3, pp. D-1, D-2, D-33, D-34; Data Resources Inc., *Review of the U.S. Economy,* Table 10.4, p. 1.72: Wharton EFA, Inc., "The Wharton Quarterly Model," Table 1, p. 1.

a. The difference between the percentage increase in average annual wages in covered employment and the percentage increase in the annual CPI.

prices and wages, but are consistently more optimistic for the unemployment rate.[12] If, indeed, the unemployment rate averages one-half to 1 percent higher than the Trustees predicted, the financial picture will be bleaker than the estimates shown in table 4. Hence, any package of reforms designed to restore short-run financial solvency must provide enough of a cushion to enable the funds to pay benefits on a timely basis even if the economic conditions turn out to be worse than those anticipated in the 1982 Trustees' report.

Financing Options in the Short Run

The options for restoring financial balance to the social security program fall into three categories: benefit reductions, tax increases, or transfers from general revenues. Since even an extension of interfund borrowing can insure the timely benefit payments only through mid-1984, legislative action is needed immediately.

Benefit Reductions. While no one would advocate abrupt changes in the level of social security benefits, several proposals are being advanced to modify the way in which benefits are increased to maintain a recipient's standard of living. Some of the specific options for indexing changes are listed in table 6, and estimates prepared by the Congressional Budget Office indicate that the savings over the next three years would range from about $7 billion for a permanent shift in the cost-of-living adjustment from July to October to $21 billion for eliminating the cost-of-living increase scheduled for July 1983.

In addition to the obvious need for revenues, many argue that reductions in cost-of-living adjustments are justified as an offset to what they believe has been overindexing of social security benefits in the last few years. The overindexing is attributable to a soon-to-be corrected flaw in the CPI that gives excessive weight to mortgage interest rates and housing prices, components that have risen more rapidly than other prices in the recent past. If cost-of-living adjustments had been computed using an index that included a rental equivalence measure of housing costs, for example, benefits would now be 5 to 6 percent lower.[13]

Table 6
Social Security Outlay Savings
Under Different Cost-of-Living Adjustments (COLA)
Fiscal Years 1983-1985
(billions of dollars)

Proposal	1983	1984	1985	Total 1983-1985
Eliminate 1983 COLA	$2.2	$9.2	$9.5	$20.9
Delay COLAs from July to October	2.2	2.1	2.8	7.1
Cap COLAs at 4 percent	0.6	2.7	4.4	7.7
Set COLAs at growth in wages minus 1.5 percentage points[a]	0.2	0.9	0.9	2.0

SOURCE: U.S. Congressional Budget Office, "Statement by Alice M. Rivlin before the National Commission on Social Security Reform," mimeographed (August 20, 1982), Table 4, p. 11.

a. This option would result in small savings in outlays in the short run because of projected low productivity growth. Over the longer run, however, outlays could be either higher or lower than under current law, depending upon the relative behavior of wages and prices.

However, even if a rental equivalence measure of housing cost had been used, benefit increases would still have outstripped the growth in wages in the last five years. Hence, many argue that social security beneficiaries have received a degree of protection from the effects of inflation that has not been available to the wage earner. Thus, a reduction in future cost-of-living adjustments is viewed by some as a means of equalizing the treatment of workers and retirees.

The disadvantage, of course, is that reductions in current law cost-of-living adjustments lower the real value of social security benefits over time. Such a reduction would increase the incidence of poverty among the aged, particularly the very old, and among the disabled.

Tax Increases. A second option that would improve social security trust fund balances would be to increase taxes. Three separate approaches are available: (1) move forward the effective date of scheduled payroll tax increases; (2) extend coverage to federal workers and the 30 percent of state-local employees not currently covered by social security; or (3) tax a portion of social security benefits under the personal income tax.

Payroll tax rate increases are scheduled under current law for 1985, 1986 and 1990. According to the CBO, moving the 1985 and 1986 rate increases to January 1, 1984 would generate an additional $17 billion by the end of 1985. Moving all three scheduled increases to 1984 would generate $46 billion (see table 7).

Extending coverage to some or all of those workers not currently covered by social security is another way of increasing taxes. Full and immediate coverage of all non-covered government employees would produce about $46 billion by 1985. However, such a move may not be practical for political and constitutional reasons. Therefore, a more modest proposal such as extending coverage only to federal civil service employees may be more realistic.

The third approach would be to subject a portion of social security benefits—probably the half that is generally associated with the employer share of the payroll tax—to the personal income tax and to direct the $18 billion in new receipts over the next three years to the social security trust funds. Taxing benefits is equivalent, of course, to a benefit

Table 7
Additional Trust Fund Revenues Under Various Tax Changes
Fiscal Years 1983-1985
(billions of dollars)

Proposal[a]	1983	1984	1985	Total 1983-1985
Payroll tax rate increase				
a. Move 1985 and 1986 increases to January 1, 1984	--	$10.8	$6.2	$17.0
b. Move 1985, 1986, and 1990 increases to January 1, 1984	--	22.8	23.3	46.1
Extend Social Security coverage to federal, state and local government employees				
a. New employees only	$0.5	1.8	3.4	5.7
b. All employees	11.1	16.3	18.2	45.6
Tax 50 percent of OASI benefits[b]	4.5	6.5	7.0	18.0
Tax 50 percent of OASI benefits for recipients with income above $20,000 (individual)/$25,000 (couples)[b]	1.2	1.8	2.2	5.2

SOURCE: U.S. Congressional Budget Office, "Statement by Alice M. Rivlin before the National Commission on Social Security Reform," mimeographed (August 20, 1982), Table 5, p. 15.

a. Unless otherwise indicated, the effective date is January 1, 1983.

b. These estimates assume that the trust funds would receive the added revenues as income tax liabilities accrued, rather than when the income taxes were actually paid. Estimates are preliminary and subject to revision.

cut, but this approach would protect the poor elderly who do not pay taxes. Further protection could be gained for moderate income beneficiaries by imposing taxes only on those with incomes above a given level, such as $20,000 for an individual and $25,000 for a couple as in the taxation of unemployment benefits. While most experts acknowledge the desirability of taxing benefits, political opposition is so vehement that observers believe the proposal has little chance of success.

General Revenues. The third possible approach to increase social security revenues would be to transfer some funds from other parts of the budget. Such a transfer would, of course, require either an increase in other taxes, a reduction in other expenditures or a rise in the federal deficit.

The arguments for and against general revenue financing for social security rest in large part on one's view of the philosophical rationale of the social security program and its intended effect on the distribution of income. Some argue that social security is best construed as an annual tax-transfer program, which redistributes income from the relatively affluent wage earners to the relatively poor retired. The more common perspective sees social security in a lifetime framework, where payroll taxes are considered compulsory saving for retirement.

The annual view—that social security is part of the federal government's tax and transfer schemes—leads to an evaluation of the tax independent of the benefits, with the conclusion that the payroll tax clearly violates the ability-to-pay criterion for equitable taxation. The tax is levied without provision for the number of dependents, excludes income from capital, and exempts wages over the maximum. Advocates of the annual tax-transfer perspective would favor a more progressive source of revenue to finance social security. General revenues, most of which are derived from the personal income tax, would be preferable on distributional grounds, since the income tax includes unearned as well as earned income in the tax base, applies progressive rates, and makes allowance for dependents.

In contrast, many argue that the present program is best understood as a lifetime compulsory saving program in which people are forced to save during their working years in exchange for guaranteed income in retirement. In this perspective, where benefits and taxes are considered jointly, the payroll tax (with an earned credit for low-wage workers) can be seen as an appropriate method of financing a compulsory saving program.

Since the present social security system is a compromise between a strictly wage-related saving scheme and a program of income redistribution, it could be argued that a rationale exists for supplementing payroll tax receipts with general revenues. And indeed, several precedents exist for the use of general revenues within the social security system, such as the gratuitous wage credit granted to servicemen, transitional benefits for certain uninsured people, and general revenue financing of some hospital payments.

Two quite different groups have argued against the introduction of general revenues. One group, comprising people associated with social security during its formative years, argues that a switch to general revenue financing might mean a break in the perceived link between individual contributions and benefits, thereby creating a situation where social security might be transformed into a means-tested program. This argument may have lost some of its force, however, since the principles of social security may now be well enough established for the program to withstand an infusion of general revenues without undermining the earned-right aspect.

More recent opposition to the use of general revenues stems from those who fear there would be more of a tendency to expand social security without the countervailing constituency created by the payroll tax. This view reflects the judgment that increases in social security benefits should have a low priority because of the more pressing needs for general revenues. The argument that general revenues should be used to finance the non-wage-related components of the program is also not very compelling to those who feel that the program should be divested of its welfare function and that benefits should be based primarily on the earnings record of each participant.

A limited use of general revenues has been advocated repeatedly in the form of the proposal to transfer all or some of the financing of hospital insurance to general revenues and credit the scheduled increases in the HI tax rate to the OASDI funds.[14] Since hospital insurance benefits bear no direct relation to contributions or earnings in covered employment none of the program's underlying philosophies would be violated. However, opposition exists even to this limited proposal, because opponents fear that such a move might lessen the incentive to control the rapidly increasing costs of Medicare.

Summary

Establishing social security on a sound financial footing must be given a high priority in the next year. In view of the experience of underestimation of program costs during the last decade, the choice among solutions should be made at least partly according to the criterion that the program be sure of avoiding financial crises in the future. The pay-as-you-go nature of the program requires that workers whose taxes are supporting current retirees be certain of receiving benefits when they retire, a confidence that will be stronger if the program's ability to pay next year's benefits is not continually in doubt.

IV. Long-Run Financing Problems
and Options: 2014-2060

The large deficits projected for social security as the baby boom population retires in the first half of the 21st century confront policymakers with fundamental decisions about the future of the program. The options include raising taxes to maintain current benefit levels for a significantly larger aged population or reducing benefits in an effort to avoid major cost increases. Benefits can be lowered either through across-the-board reductions in the replacement rate or through extending the age at which workers are eligible for full benefits.

The Problem in Perspective

According to the 1982 Trustees' Report, under the most reasonable economic and mortality assumptions, the cost of the Old-Age, Survivors and Disability Insurance portion of the social security program is projected to rise from the current level of 11 percent of taxable payrolls to about 17 in the year 2030, remaining at that level through 2060 (see table 8, II-B). The sharp increase in costs reflects the changing demographic structure of the population. The ratio of the beneficiary population to covered workers is projected to rise dramatically as the sizeable post-World War II baby boom starts reaching retirement age after 2010. At that time, the working population will be composed of the relatively small group born during the period of low fertility that began in the late 1960s. Assuming that the fertility rate will rise gradually from the current level of 1.8 to a long-run rate of 2.1, the Social Security Administration projects that the number of beneficiaries per 100 covered workers will rise from 31 in 1982 to 50 by 2030, an increase of about 60 percent (see table 9). Since the social security program is financed on a pay-as-you-go basis, with tax contributions by today's workers paying for benefits to today's beneficiaries,

Table 8
Long-Run Projected Costs of the Old-Age, Survivors and Disability Insurance Trust Funds as a Percentage of Taxable Payroll, Under Alternative Assumptions[a]
Selected Years, 1982-2060

Year	Projected costs as percent of taxable payrolls under assumption				OASDI tax rates scheduled under current law
	Optimistic I	Intermediate II-A	Intermediate II-B	Pessimistic III	
1982	11.6	11.5	11.8	11.8	10.8
1990	9.8	10.5	11.6	12.9	12.4
2000	9.2	10.0	11.0	12.8	12.4
2010	9.5	10.7	11.5	13.9	12.4
2020	11.7	13.5	14.4	18.2	12.4
2030	13.0	15.8	16.8	22.6	12.4
2040	12.1	15.6	16.8	24.8	12.4
2050	11.4	15.5	16.7	26.9	12.4
2060	11.2	15.6	16.8	28.5	12.4
Average— 1982-2060	11.0	13.1	14.1	18.7	12.3

SOURCE: U.S. Department of Health and Human Services, Social Security Administration, *1982 Annual Report of the Board of Trustees of the Federal Old-Age and Survivors Insurance and Disability Insurance Trust Funds* (Washington, DC: GPO, 1982), Table 29, pp. 67-68.

a. The assumptions (in annual percentage rates of increase) are:

	Optimistic I	Intermediate II-A	Intermediate II-B	Pessimistic III
Fertility	2.4	2.1	2.1	1.7
Real wages	2.5	2.0	1.5	1.0
CPI	2.0	3.0	4.0	5.0

the projected increase in the aged population relative to the working population implies a similar increase in OASDI cost from 11 to 17 percent of taxable payroll.

Table 9
Projected Beneficiaries per Hundred Covered Workers Under Alternative Assumptions[a]
Selected Years, 1982-2060

Year	Projected beneficiaries per hundred covered workers under assumption			
	Optimistic	Intermediate		Pessimistic
	I	II-A	II-B	III
1982	31	31	31	31
1990	29	30	31	32
2000	30	31	32	34
2010	32	34	35	39
2020	38	43	43	51
2030	42	49	50	63
2040	40	50	50	70
2050	39	50	50	76
2060	38	50	50	80

SOURCE: U.S. Department of Health and Human Services, Social Security Administration, *1982 Annual Report of the Board of Trustees of the Federal Old-Age and Survivors Insurance and Disability Insurance Trust Funds* (GPO, 1982), Table 28, pp. 65-66.

a. The long-run ultimate levels of fertility under the alternative assumptions are;

	Optimistic	Intermediate		Pessimistic
	I	II-A	II-B	III
Fertility	2.4	2.1	2.1	1.7

Many view a combined employer-employee tax rate of roughly 17 percent as simply "too high," and considerable effort is currently directed toward devising alternative schemes to reduce long-run costs. The high rate, however, does not mean that the social security program will be any more generous in the future than it is today, but rather reflects the fact that after the turn of the century there will be a very large dependent aged population. These elderly and disabled people must receive support from some source—either social security, direct transfers from their children, private pension benefits or their own saving. Since the burden of a large dependent aged population is inescapable, a reduction in social security benefits may well lead to greater required expenditures for the elderly and disabled through other programs.

Moreover, those concerned about a combined employee and employer social security tax rate of 17 percent during the next century often ignore the fact that lower fertility results in fewer children per worker. If the economic burden on active workers is measured in terms of total dependents rather than just aged retirees, then the picture looks quite different. The total dependency ratio (the ratio of the number of people under age 20 and over age 65 per 100 people age 20-64) will be lower in the 21st century than it was in 1965 (see table 10). The rise in the aged will be more than offset by a decline in dependent children, thereby freeing resources which could be devoted to providing for the elderly.

Finally, while a projected tax rate of 17 percent represents a 60 percent increase over the current levy, it is considerably below the present payroll tax rates in many European countries. Austria, Italy, Sweden and the Netherlands all have rates for programs comparable to OASDI in excess of 20 percent of payroll. West Germany with 18 percent also already has a rate that exceeds the rate projected for the

United States as the baby boom retires after the turn of the century (see table 11).

Table 10
Actual Past and Projected Future Dependency Ratios
Selected Years, 1930-2060[a]

Year	Under 20	65 and over	Total
1930	69.6	9.7	79.3
1940	58.5	11.7	70.2
1950	59.2	14.1	73.3
1960	74.1	17.4	91.5
1970	71.1	18.4	90.0
1980	55.8	19.5	75.3
1990	49.4	21.5	70.9
2000	47.9	22.6	70.5
2010	44.7	23.6	68.3
2020	46.2	30.3	76.5
2030	48.1	37.8	85.9
2040	47.6	38.0	85.6
2050	47.9	37.4	85.3
2060	47.9	37.9	85.8

SOURCES: U.S. Congress, House, Select Committee on Aging, Hearings before the Subcommittee on Retirement Income and Employment, *Social Security,* "Statement of Robert M. Ball," 94th Cong., lst sess., 1975, p. 111. U.S. Department of Health and Human Services, Social Security Administration, *1982 Annual Report of the Board of Trustees of the Federal Old-Age and Survivors Insurance and Disability Insurance Trust Funds* (Washington, DC: GPO, 1982), Table A1, p. 79.

a. The dependency ratio is the total number of people under 20 and over 64 per 100 people aged 20 to 64.

Once the projected cost increases for social security are placed in perspective, maintaining current benefit levels and raising the payroll tax becomes a reasonable option. The alternative is to lower future costs by reducing benefits.

Table 11
Employee-Employer Tax Rates by Type of Program
Selected Countries, 1981

Country	All social security programs			Old age, invalids, and survivors insurance		
	Employer	Employee	Total	Employer	Employee	Total
Austria	27.80	15.90	43.70	11.35	9.75	21.10
Belgium	27.77	10.10	37.87	8.86	6.25	15.11[b]
Canada	4.49[a]	3.95	8.44	1.80	1.80	3.60
France	37.41	10.14	47.55	8.20	4.80	13.00[c]
West Germany	17.95	16.45	34.40	9.25	9.25	18.50
Italy	47.57	7.45	55.02	17.31	7.15	24.46
Japan	12.22	9.85	22.07	5.30	5.30	10.60
Netherlands	29.58	28.07	57.65	12.90	22.00	34.90[d]
Sweden	35.05	.15	35.20	21.15	—	21.15
Switzerland	8.24	9.48	17.72	4.70	4.70	9.40
United Kingdom	13.70	7.75	21.45	Not available on a comparable basis		
United States	11.35	6.65	18.00	5.35	5.35	10.70

SOURCE: U.S. Department of Health and Human Services, Social Security Administration, Office of International Policy, unpublished data.

a. Excludes work injury insurance.

b. Invalidity pensions financed through sickness insurance.

c. Invalidity and survivors benefits financed through sickness insurance.

d. Disability insurance also includes work-injury compensation.

Proposals to Reduce the Long-Run Deficit

Two major approaches have been proposed to reduce long-run social security costs—lowering replacement rates and extending the retirement age.

Lowering Replacement Rates. The specific suggestions for reducing replacement rates include the proposal by the 1976 Consultant Panel on Social Security[15] to index the benefit formula by prices rather than wages and the Reagan Administration's proposal to make a one-time ad hoc adjustment in the benefit formula.

The price indexing proposal involves reducing replacement rates by changing the method for adjusting the benefit formula. As noted earlier, the current formula consists of three brackets which apply declining percentages to increasing amounts of the worker's average indexed monthly earnings (AIME). The amounts separating the individual's AIME into intervals, that is, $230 and $1,388 in 1982, are called "bend points." Under current law, these bend points are increased automatically each year to reflect the growth in average wages. By adjusting the formula in this fashion, replacement rates remain constant over time. In other words, a worker with a history of average earnings retiring in the year 1990 will receive a benefit equal to the same percentage of his pre-retirement wages as a similarly situated worker retiring today. In contrast, if the bend points in the social security benefit formula were adjusted by prices rather than wages, the progressivity of the benefit structure would lead to lower replacement rates for future generations of workers as they moved up into higher real earnings brackets.

While the price indexing proposal would substantially cut costs, it would also create significant hardship for tomorrow's elderly. The problem arises because the rationale for price indexing is based on two fundamental assumptions, both of which are questionable.

The first assumption is that people's absolute level of real income rather than their position in the income distribution determines acceptable and desired standards of living. For example, under price indexing, a worker in 2060 with annual pre-retirement earnings of $15,000 in 1982 dollars would be assumed to have the same spending and saving habits and, therefore, retirement needs as a worker retiring today with earnings of $15,000; therefore, the worker retiring in 2060 would be given the same real pension amount as a worker retiring today. In fact, a worker retiring in 2060 will not have the same spending and saving habits as the worker earning the same real income today because he will be much poorer relative to the average.

The second assumption is that lower replacement rates in the future will be acceptable since individuals will be much better off, save more on their own and receive much greater private pension benefits. In fact, lower paid workers are simply not able to save for retirement since their incomes are barely adequate to cover current consumption. Even middle income workers are unlikely to undertake retirement saving because the widespread myopia with respect to retirement needs that provided the initial justification for the social security program will in all likelihood persist.

At first blush, a new emphasis on private pension plans may seem an appealing alternative to substantial increases in the payroll tax. Private pension benefits have increased dramatically as a source of retirement income, and private plans may meet a larger portion of the income needs for some groups of future retirees. The private pension system should not be viewed as a panacea, however, since it is plagued with problems of its own. The private system is incapable of offsetting the impact of inflation or of protecting workers who change jobs frequently. Moreover, less than half of the private nonfarm workforce is currently covered by private plans and pension benefits are concentrated among highly paid people; low-wage workers receive almost no private pension benefits.

Because industries with traditionally high pension coverage, such as manufacturing (see table 12), are expected to employ a declining share of workers, the percentage of the workforce covered by pension plans is not expected to increase significantly in the future. The people without pension coverage will continue to be primarily lower paid employees, precisely those people who are incapable of saving on their own. For these individuals, social security will remain the sole source of support in retirement. Lowering social security replacement rates for these workers through price indexing, on the assumption that such a reduction will be acceptable because they will have higher real incomes, will simply force a substantial portion of future retirees to suffer a dramatic decline in economic well-being upon retirement.

Most of the problems associated with reducing replacement rates by price indexing are equally applicable to lowering benefit levels through a one-time adjustment of the bend points in the benefit formula.[16] The only factor in favor of an ad hoc adjustment is predictability so that corporations and the pension industry will know the level of protection to be provided by social security in order to establish meaningful private pension benefits and realistic integration provisions. Under the price indexing proposal future replacement rates are not predictable but rather depend on the rate of growth of real wages. For example, in the absence of productivity growth, replacement rates would remain constant for the average worker; with positive real wage growth they would decline; and with price increases in excess of wage growth, as has been the case in the last few years, replacement rates would actually rise.

The advantage of price indexing over an ad hoc adjustment is that it allows for a more gradual reduction in replacement rates. Avoiding abrupt changes in the level of benefits is essential in order to provide people with enough time to revise their saving plans in response to the lower levels of replacement under social security. Lowering replacement rates, however, either through price indexing or by adjusting the benefit formula may be an inferior option to extending the age at which individuals are eligible for full benefits.

Table 12
The Percentage of All Workers Covered by a Pension Plan
By Age Group and Industry, 1979

Industry	Age group	
	25-64 (percent)	16 and over (percent)
Mining	74	70
Construction	46	37
Manufacturing	73	66
Transportation	70	66
Trade	41	29
Finance	58	50
Services	36	30
All private, nonfarm	55	46

SOURCE: President's Commission on Pension Policy, *Coming of Age: Toward a National Retirement Income Policy* (Washington, DC: Government Printing Office, 1981), Table 11, p. 27.

Extending the Retirement Age. While 65 was the most acceptable age for retirement when social security was established in 1935, dramatic changes in the characteristics of the elderly population and the economy argue for postponing retirement past age 65 in the 21st century. Tomorrow's elderly will have improved life expectancy, better health, and more education than those retiring today. Older workers will also be in greater demand as the growth in the labor force slows and as an increasing proportion of employment is generated by the service industries where the work is less physically stressful.

Although most of the startling gains in life expectancy during this century are attributable to a substantial reduction in neonatal mortality and elimination of childhood diseases, the life expectancy of older workers has also increased significantly (see table 13). As a result, workers will have at least as many years left after age 68 during the first half of the next century as they did after age 65 in the early years of social security. Actuaries at the Social Security Administration recently calculated the retirement age that would be equivalent to retiring at age 65 in 1940. Under any of four measures, the 1980 equivalent to age 65 retirement was 69 years and the 2000 equivalent was more than 71 years.[17]

The projected health of tomorrow's elderly is equally as important as longevity in assessing their ability to work past age 65. Current studies reveal that a large majority of the elderly who are under 70 appear free of physically disabling limitations.[18] This may be attributable partly to the significant progress that has been made in treating arthritis and cardiovascular diseases, two of the most serious barriers to good health at older ages. Most of the evidence indicates that increased life expectancy will be accompanied by a corresponding increase in the physical well-being of the aged.[19]

Older workers after the turn of the century will also be better educated than their counterparts today. The baby boom generation has already achieved a higher level of formal schooling than any previous generation. In 1979, about 85 percent of those aged 22 to 29 had graduated from high school, compared to only 50 percent of the same age group in 1950 and 60 percent in 1960. Over half of those aged 25 to 29 in 1979 had some college education, compared with less than 20 percent of the same age group in 1950. Improved education and training will enable them to adapt to the changing technological demands of the workplace.[20]

Table 13
Life Expectancy at the Age of 65, by Sex
Selected Years, 1930-2060[a]

Year	Male	Female	Both sexes
1930[b]	11.8	12.8	12.3
1940	12.0	13.7	12.9
1950	12.9	15.4	14.2
1960	13.0	16.1	14.6
1970	13.2	17.2	15.2
1980	14.3	18.7	16.5
1990	15.3	20.3	17.8
2000	15.8	21.1	18.5
2010	16.1	21.6	18.9
2020	16.4	22.0	19.2
2030	16.7	22.4	19.4
2040	17.0	22.8	19.9
2050	17.3	23.2	20.3
2060	17.6	23.6	20.6

SOURCES: U.S. Department of Health and Human Services, Social Security Administration, Office of the Actuary, *Social Security Area Population Projections, 1981,* Actuarial Study no. 85 (July 1981), Table 18, p. 42; U.S. Department of Health and Human Services, Social Security Administration, Office of the Actuary, unpublished data.

a. Intermediate alternative life expectancy rates.

b. Data based on the average of deaths over a three-year period, 1929-31, as a percentage of the population in the census year.

The changing conditions in the labor market will most likely lead also to an increased demand for older workers. The growth in the labor force will taper off at the turn of the century, since the low birth rates of today will result in considerably fewer new workers. Unlike the past when the rapid growth in the supply of workers strained the nation's capacity to provide enough new jobs, the new environment should create a tight labor market where the experience and skill of older workers will be in increasing demand. Their employment will be further facilitated by the long term shift in the industrial structure from mining and manufacturing where health hazards are relatively high, to trade and services, where older workers can perform with less strain and threat to their health.

In recommending an increase in the retirement age, however, it is essential to remember that some older workers will not be able to engage in gainful employment past age 62 and must have access to some form of income support. If they are prevented from working by physical disability, the appropriate way to provide for them is an expanded disability insurance program. While current law makes some allowance for age in determining disability by applying a more liberal test to those aged 50 or older, more explicit recognition of the interaction of age and physical impairment may be required.

In addition, some older workers may not be able to find jobs because they have been displaced by automation. These aged will not have access to disability insurance and may face a severe loss of income as a result of extending the social security retirement age. The changing characteristics of the workplace, however, indicate that the number of healthy unemployed aged may be quite small. While retraining older workers is generally considered impractical today, restructuring jobs for older employees may become economical in the tight labor markets forecasted after the turn of the century. However, it may be necessary to establish an expanded unemployment insurance program for older workers.

The issues raised by the older disabled worker and the worker displaced by technology highlight the potential dangers in raising the age at which full social security benefits are available. Unless some provision is made for these workers, the costs of later retirement will be borne by the most disadvantaged aged. Expanding the disability program, however, necessarily reduces the cost savings of extending the retirement age. After adjusting for increased disability outlays, proposals which involve a gradual increase of the retirement age from 65 to 68 yield a long term reduction in costs of about 1 percent of taxable payroll.[21] The major reductions would come after the turn of the century when the new retirement pattern would lead to a cost saving of about 1.6 percent of taxable payroll. With the retirement age at 68 rather than 65, costs in the year 2030 would be 15.4 rather than 17 percent of taxable payroll.

Summary

A large dependent elderly population creates an inescapable burden which is reflected in the required increase in the social security tax to about 17 percent of payroll after the turn of the century. The first question is whether to schedule future tax increases to cover these costs or to reduce benefits as the baby boom generation retires. If benefits are to be lowered, a second question is whether to reduce replacement rates or extend the retirement age. Several arguments can be marshalled for maintaining current benefit levels and raising taxes. (1) Higher social security taxes in the next century will be offset by a decline in the resources required for the clothing, feeding and education of children. (2) The scheduled tax rates, while high by current U.S. standards, are actually lower than the current payroll tax levy in many European countries. (3) Finally, if the large elderly dependent population is not supported through social security, the working population will probably end up providing equivalent support through some other program, in light of the historical inability of people to save for retirement and the inadequacies of the private pension system.

We may be unwilling, however, to commit the working population in the 21st century to transferring 17 percent of their payroll to the retired and disabled. In that case the relative merits of alternative approaches to reducing long-run costs become important. The improved life expectancy and health of the elderly and the likelihood of increased pressure for older workers to remain in the labor force argue for raising the retirement age, provided that expanded disability benefits are available for those too incapacitated to work. The alternative of lowering replacement rates in a society where only half the workers have private pension coverage will cause a significant portion of workers, primarily those with low earnings, to suffer a disastrous decline in income after retirement.

NOTES

1. U.S. Department of Health and Human Services, Social Security Administration, Office of Research and Statistics, *Income of the Population 55 and Over, 1978,* prepared by Susan Grad, Staff Paper no. 41 (Washington, DC: GPO, 1981), Table 32, p. 54.

2. Wives, divorced wives and husbands are eligible for permanently reduced benefits at age 62. Widows, divorced widows and widowers can receive permanently reduced benefits as early as age 60.

3. Workers retiring before age 65 can only earn $4,440 without a reduction in benefits.

4. The following discussion is based on an analysis of social security's financing problems presented in Robert M. Ball, "The Financial Condition of the Social Security Program," mimeographed (Washington, DC, April 1982).

5. U.S. Department of Health and Human Services, Social Security Administration, *1982 Annual Report of the Board of Trustees of the Federal Old-Age and Survivors Insurance and Disability Insurance Trust Funds* (Washington, DC: GPO, 1982) (hereafter cited as *1982 Trustees Report*).

6. *1982 Trustees Report,* p. 71.

7. Ibid.

8. U.S. Congress, Senate, Committee on Finance, *Social Security Financing*, Committee Print no. 97-8, 97th Cong., 1st sess. (Washington, DC: GPO, 1982).

9. John Snee and Mary Ross, "Social Security Amendments of 1977: Legislative History and Summary of Provisions," *Social Security Bulletin* 41, no. 3 (March 1978): 3-20.

10. Mordechai E. Lando, Alice V. Farley and Mary A. Brown, "Recent Trends in the Social Security Disability Insurance Program," *Social Security Bulletin* 45, no. 8 (August 1982), Table 3, p. 7.

11. See U.S. Congressional Budget Office, "Statement by Alice M. Rivlin before the National Commission on Social Security Reform," mimeographed (August 20, 1982), p. 6 (hereafter cited as "Statement by Alice M. Rivlin").

12. In part, the discrepancy may be due to the fact that the Trustees' set of assumptions was developed slightly earlier than the other forecasters.

13. "Statement by Alice M. Rivlin," p. 12.

14. This proposal was advanced by the 1979 Advisory Council of Social Security. Moreover, previous Advisory Councils, beginning in 1965, have recommended using general revenues to finance some portion of HI.

15. *Report of the Consultant Panel on Social Security to the Congressional Research Service*, 94th Cong., 2d. sess. (Washington, DC: GPO, 1976).

16. In May 1981, President Reagan proposed a plan under which the bend points would be adjusted to reflect only 50 percent of the increase in average wages over a five-year period. This proposal, however, was never submitted to Congress.

17. U.S. Department of Health and Human Services, Social Security Administration, "Equivalent Retirement Ages: 1940-2050," prepared by Francisco R. Bayo and Joseph F. Faber, Actuarial Note no. 105 (Washington, DC: GPO, 1981).

18. University of Massachusetts and Joint Center for Urban Studies of M.I.T. and Harvard University, *Understanding the Health and Social Service Needs of People Over Age 65*, prepared by L.G. Branch and submitted in partial fulfillment of grants 90-A-641/01 and 90-A-641/02 from the U.S. Department of Health, Education and Welfare, Administration on Aging (1977).

19. See discussion in National Commission of Social Security Reform, *Social Security in America's Future—Final Report of the National Commission on Social Security* (Washington, DC: GPO, 1981), pp. 124-126 (hereafter cited as *Final Report of National Commission on Social Security).*

20. U.S. Bureau of the Census, Population Division, *Education,* Special Report P-E, no. 5B, Table 5 (Washington, DC: GPO, 1950); U.S. Bureau of the Census, Population Division, *Educational Attainment,* Report PC (2), no. 5B (Washington, DC: GPO, 1960), Table 1; U.S. Bureau of the Census, Population Division, *Educational Attainment in the United States: March 1979 and 1978,* Current Population Report P-20, no. 314 (Washington, DC: GPO, 1980), Table 2, pp. 20-28.

21. For example, see *Final Report of the National Commission on Social Security,* Table 5-2, p. 125.

Chapter 9

Private Pensions, Inflation, and Employment

James H. Schulz

Some Prefatory Comments on Social Security

Attention continues to be riveted on issues and problems associated with OASDHI, almost as if the other parts of our system to provide financial security during old age were free of troubles. The list of fears and criticisms is now well known: Social Security is going bankrupt; we "can't afford" the cost of future benefits; Social Security depresses savings and hence economic growth; various provisions of the insurance programs are inequitable and discourage work; and at a time when we are trying to balance the budget and reduce the size of the federal government, Social Security continues to grow at an uncontrolled pace.

All these criticisms are debatable, of course. In fact, the arguments continue hot and heavy—both in the policymaking arena and in academia. As a strong supporter of Social Security, I only point out here that while public anxiety—fueled by political rhetoric—has reached unprecedented levels, public support for Social Security remains high; people want Social Security made secure—not dismembered—*even if that requires higher taxes.*[1] Moreover, every bipartisan government commission appointed to review the system has emphasized the viability of the OASDHI programs and has recommended only marginal improvements.

241

Of course, most critics of Social Security today also profess to support the system. They argue, however, that major long-term changes are needed. Their proposed changes are almost all pointed in one direction—drastic cutbacks in benefits to reduce program costs. The logical question that follows from proposed action of that kind is: what else changes in reaction to cutbacks in Social Security (i.e., what takes the place of Social Security)?

In examining the ability of alternatives to pick up the slack from a pared down Social Security program, we should not ignore economic history. Despite what Martha Derthick says about bureaucratic elites engineering the expansion of Social Security, the development of OASDHI was to a very large extent a reaction to the failure of the alternatives—namely employment of the old and providing for old age through personal savings.[2] The vicissitudes of our economic system over the years have made both these alternatives largely untenable:

a) Past periods of unemployment and inflation have made financial planning and preparation for retirement extremely difficult for individuals, if not impossible.[3]

b) An inability to achieve sustained full employment—except in periods when the nation was preparing, fighting, or recovering from war,[4] has caused the government to actively discourage employment by older workers and to develop pension mechanisms that encourage retirement.

c) Finally, both Social Security and private pensions also have a long history as tools of business management to deal with cyclical and long-term shifts in demand.[5]

What then are the alternatives proposed today? Not surprisingly, we find that they are the same as in the past; private saving, private insurance and employment of the old. The focus of this conference is on employment, and my assignment is to relate private pensions to it. I shall restrict myself, therefore, to the relationship between pensions and employment opportunities.

But one must begin by recognizing that there is some large measure of unreality in talking about employment as an alternative to Social Security—especially at a time when unemployment is at double-digit levels. Many economists insist that policy development should focus on the labor force disincentives created by various aging programs, especially Social Security, implicitly assuming that a full-employment economy was, is, and will be the reality. Worse yet, some analysts confuse the issues in a major way by failing to distinguish between theory and assumption on the one hand and the realities of the American market-oriented economy on the other. For example, a recent analysis by the Congressional Budget Office states:

> Increasing numbers of nonworking older persons could reduce the amount of goods and services produced in the economy as well as personal incomes. This decreased production could also put upward pressure on prices and increase inflation. The smaller labor force of older workers probably would reduce overall unemployment, however, because many jobs not taken by older persons would go to younger ones.[6]

Of course, other things being equal, withdrawal of any substantial number of persons from the labor force will reduce potential national output. But as has been emphasized above, we have all too frequently failed to achieve our potential. Perhaps we should develop better policies to achieve sustained economic growth before agonizing about the problems the elderly may create if we are successful in meeting that goal.

We know with great certainty that demographic trends will lead to a decrease in the ratio between the population of traditional working age and the older population (but not necessarily to dependent population of young and old combined). What we do not know is whether we will be able to do any better in the future than we have in the past in employing the potential labor force. Yet full employment is seen by many as the simple and obvious solution to most of Social Security's current and future problems.

Even if it is assumed that we will be able to generate sufficient jobs for all age groups in the future, including more jobs for the aged—we need to confront two other major issues: the fact that the elderly strongly prefer retirement to full-time work and the fact that increased longevity does not necessarily mean more surviving older persons will be able to work. With regard to the former, voluminous data[7] now indicate quite clearly that workers have a high degree of preference for retirement over continued employment—even when pension benefits are relatively low.[8] The data are much less clear with regard to the implications of increased longevity, but certainly available statistics do not indicate any marked turn-around in ability to work in the later years. Rather than the expected decrease in the proportion of men age 50-69 unable to work because of illness, data from the National Health Interview Survey show that the proportion actually increased between 1970 and 1980.[9]

There are still many health factors at work that reduce mortality but also reduce the employability of older persons. Examples include: improved survival for myocardial infarction among the disabled; the persistence of the incidence of arthritis or any of a number of other disabling conditions that do not generally cause death; the successful treatment of individuals with problems such as diabetes that previously caused early deaths but that are still disabling, and alcohol or drug abuse.

Robert N. Butler, former director of the National Institute on Aging, recently summarized the issue as follows:

It is not clear that morbidity rates in the older population are improving. While mortality from heart disease and stroke has gone down, the data do not clarify whether this means disease has been prevented and people are not at risk, or whether more people are surviving with impairments, thanks to medical and other support. A number of leading demographers and epidemiologists share the view that morbidity in later life probably is rising. One recent paper (by L. A. Colvez[10]) indicates that morbidity and attending disability increased rapidly from 1966 to 1976. The increases were sharpest for those aged 45 to 64.[11]

Benefit Levels in Private Pensions

Putting aside the issue of the extent to which we can and should rely on public versus private mechanisms for income in old age, what is the impact of private pensions on employment in the later years? It is now commonplace for analysts to cite the dramatic drop in labor force participation rates among older persons and to point a suspicious finger at public and private pensions, especially the liberalization of coverage and benefit levels that has occurred over recent decades. Gordus for example, writes:

In 1870, about 20 percent of the males 65 years of age and over were retired. In 1970, nearly 75 percent of the male population over 65 had withdrawn from the labor force. This trend toward retirement reflects a demographic shift, a rising average age at death. The incomes of retired Americans are now maintained through benefits from private pension plans and from social security benefits. For over a century, demographic change and the gradual development of pension benefits have combined to produce a relatively new phenomenon, retirement. More recently, the extension of pension benefits to those younger than 65, in combination with other factors, has produced an even newer phenomenon, early retirement.[12]

While pension developments have undoubtedly had an important impact on labor force behavior and decisions to retire, any precise quantification of the impact or a completely satisfactory explanation of "the retirement decision" has yet to be achieved. The four excellent reviews of our knowledge in this area by Mitchell/Fields, Foner/Schwab, Morgan, and Clark/Barker indicate the complexities of the issues and the limitations of research done thus far.[13]

With regard to private pensions, the literature discusses a variety of factors that may encourage employees to retire earlier. Mandatory retirement provisions are still very common in companies with private pensions. Private disability benefits are usually a part of private plans, complementing disability coverage from other programs. Benefits are usually paid only if an employee stops work and separates from the company. Pension benefit accruals, especially given the tax treatment of pension reserves, typically represent a sizeable accumulation of personal wealth—wealth available for consumption needs, however, only in the latter part of the life cycle. Finally, private plan formulas and payment provisions are often structured in ways that discourage continued employment.

Based on the most recent studies, there seem to be relatively strong indications that higher private pension benefit levels do in fact encourage retirement. This raises the question of what the level of private benefits is and the extent to which they have been changing over time.

We have just completed a study of these two questions at the Brandeis Policy Center on Aging.[14] The major purpose of this study was to analyze the 1979 benefit levels—both retirement and survivor benefits—in a representative sample of private pension plans. Pension benefits were calculated for hypothetical workers retiring in 1979, using U.S. Bureau of Labor Statistics (BLS) data on 1,010 pension plans covering workers in establishments meeting certain minimum employment size criteria (50 to 250 workers, depending on industry).

Median pension replacement rates were estimated separately for male and female workers in various industries, by years of service. Distributions of replacement rates were also presented by sex and years of service. Total replacement rates were calculated by combining Social Security and private pension benefits. Using replacement rate targets necessary to maintain living standards in retirement for men whose earnings had been equal to the median wage, estimates were made of the proportion of such workers where pension benefits (together with Social Security) would achieve those targets.

Results of the 1979 survey analysis were compared with a prior BLS survey of 1,467 defined benefit plans in 1974. Because the 1979 survey did not include many of the large multiemployer plans, the comparison was restricted to single employer plans in 1974.

The median private pension replacement rate in the 1979 plans, for workers with 30 years of service and average earnings, was 27 percent for males and 34 percent for females. Median replacement rates varied from a low of 23 percent in the service industry to a high of 35 percent for females in manufacturing. Comparison of the 1979 and 1974 data suggests that a small improvement in plan benefit levels had occurred over the five-year period between surveys.

The *total* replacement rate (Social Security plus private pension) for a hypothetical male worker with 30 years service was compared for each plan with the "target replacement rate" necessary to maintain living standards in retirement without other income supplementation. Very few workers, 6 percent, were in plans that achieved that target in 1979. But if the spouse benefit under Social Security was included (e.g., the case of a married male worker with a nonworking wife), the proportion in plans achieving the target replacement rate rose dramatically to 59 percent.

Probably the most important limitation of the study is the fact that benefit level estimates were made assuming long and uninterrupted work histories of 20 and 30 years. In reality, many workers shift jobs frequently. And even if they acquire vested benefits before leaving a job, two or three vested pensions will rarely produce a combined benefit as large as one based on 20 or 30 years of continuous employment. Thus, the hypothetical calculations in the study should not be used to predict the adequacy of pensions for actual workers. Instead, they can be used to indicate the *potential* contribution of private plans to retirement income and to show the wide variation in benefit levels that occurs among plans.

If we keep in mind the long tenure assumption, the replacement rates calculated in the Brandeis study do give a good indication of the potential magnitude of private pensions as part of total pension income. Table 1 shows the median of the replacement rates provided by the 1979 plans in various industries and also estimated Social Security replacement rates. Earnings levels used in calculating the replacement rate for hypothetical workers were based on tabulations of data from the Social Security Administration's "Current Work History Sample of Covered Workers" (CWHS).[15]

Table 1
1979 Median Replacement Rates for Hypothetical "Average" Workers, by Sex and Industry

Industry[a]	Private pensions[b]	Social Security[c]	Total
Males:			
Manufacturing	27	28	55
Transp/Comm/Util	34	25	59
Trade	24	30	54
Fin/Insur/Real Est	30	28	58
Service	23	32	55
All industries	27	28	55
Females:			
Manufacturing	35	41	76
Transp/Comm/Util	34	36	70
Trade	26	46	72
Fin/Insur/Real Est	26	40	66
Service	23	44	67
All industries	34	38	72

SOURCE: Based on data in James H. Schulz et al., *Private Pension Benefits in the 1970s—A Study of Retirement and Survivor Benefit Levels in 1974 and 1979* (Bryn Mawr, PA: McCahan Foundation, 1982).

a. The mining and construction industries are omitted because of small sample size.

b. Based on BLS, Level of Benefits Survey, a representative sample of U.S. establishments (excluding Alaska and Hawaii) with a minimum size of 50 to 200, depending on industry. Because this survey samples establishments rather than plans, inference is appropriate only to those establishments meeting the BLS size criteria and to the pension plans found in such establishments. Thus, the survey cannot be used as a guide to benefit levels (a) in very small establishments or (b) in those large plans (particularly multiemployer plans) covering many small establishments.

c. Calculated using the legislated benefit formula and rules appropriate for 1979. Benefits were calculated assuming that the worker was employed in Social Security covered employment during the years without private pension coverage, if any. Spouse benefits are not included.

In three of the five industries studied, the private pension replacement rate of a long-term, "average" male worker equaled or exceeded the Social Security replacement—indicating the major role that private pensions can play in the total pension income of some workers. For women, the role is smaller; Social Security replacement rates for women always exceeded the private ones. This is a result of the lower earnings levels of women and the weighted Social Security formula favoring low earners.

To the extent that the size of pensions is related to the retirement decision, the data indicate that private plans probably play a major role. However, the factor of inflation complicates any assessment of impact. Unlike Social Security, which is fully indexed, hardly any private plans automatically adjust benefits in payment status for inflation. Such adjustment that does take place is typically done on an *ad hoc* basis and rarely comes close to keeping up with the CPI. We would like to know the extent to which the failure of private pensions to adjust for inflation affects the employment decisions of older workers.

Inflation and the Elderly

Older persons living on fixed incomes used to be one of the most inflation-vulnerable groups in our society. Times have changed, however. Today, elderly persons have important protections against inflation:

- Social Security, federal supplemental security income (SSI) benefits, federal pensions, and food stamps are all indexed fully against inflation.
- Medicare and Medicaid benefits help to keep pace with medical costs that rise in part due to inflation.
- Most of the assets of the elderly are held in the form of real estate—the value of which has risen in most cases faster than inflation.

- The rising Social Security benefits of the elderly are not subject to federal income tax and hence not subject to erosion as a result of progressive tax brackets defined in money rather than real terms.[16]

There are two major sources of elderly income, however, that are still highly vulnerable to inflation: financial assets and private pensions. Most financial assets—bonds, checking accounts, savings accounts, and insurance policies—do not adjust when the general level of prices changes. Common stocks and mutual funds may promise better protection over the long run, but no guarantee of complete security from inflation over any particular short run period. As indicated above, almost all private pension plan commitments during retirement are specified in money terms, with no guarantee of any adjustment for inflation.

The possibility of continuing high levels of inflation in the years to come requires that we think seriously of providing appropriate safeguards for the most economically vulnerable age group of our population. The most serious problem of this kind at the present is the vulnerability of the "near-poor" aged. An overwhelming majority of elderly live on incomes *above* the official poverty level, but below $10,000 a year. Many of these elderly families depend on their financial savings and their private pensions to provide the margin of support necessary for a modest but more comfortable life style.

Rising government expenditures caused by automatically indexed Social Security benefits have resulted in increased scrutiny of the adjustment mechanism and of the appropriateness of the Consumer Price Index (CPI) for making such adjustments. During inflationary periods, the prices of various goods change by different amounts. Since the expenditure patterns of individuals and families differ, the impact of any particular pattern of price increases will vary, depending on the expenditure patterns of various individuals.[17] For example, if food and housing prices go up faster than the prices of other goods and services and if the aged spend a large share of their income on food and housing, the result is a larger increase in prices paid by the aged than the non-aged.

Thus there is a concern that the CPI, which is the measure used to adjust Social Security benefits, does not correctly reflect the buying patterns of the aged. Some organizations that speak for the aged argue that the CPI underestimates the impact of inflation on the elderly and advocate a special index for the elderly. More recently, others have argued that Social Security increases based on the CPI are too generous.

How well the CPI measures changes in living costs of the elderly depends on: *what* prices are rising or falling; how *rapidly* particular prices are changing; and the *reactions* (i.e., changing expenditure patterns) of particular groups of the elderly. All the studies of these issues suggest that using special price indexes for subgroups of the population like the aged will not necessarily be more equitable than using the regular CPI.[18] Thus, the present indexed Social Security system seems to do a relatively good job of reducing the uncertainty and anxiety facing older persons in periods of rapid inflation.

Instead of a new index for the aged, we need to improve the existing CPI. The recent BLS change in handling housing costs is a step in the right direction, but a more general problem exists. There is a systematic, upward bias in the CPI, primarily due to the lag in accounting for new products and for quality improvement in products and services. With regard to quality change, the CPI does not measure the impact of changes in product performance. For example, the prices of motor oil, tires, light bulbs, appliances, etc. have increased. But because the service life of many such products has also increased, not all the price increases are truly inflationary.

Economists have written about these problems for many years. Over 20 years ago a prestigious committee headed by economist George Stigler recommended major changes in the CPI. Unfortunately little has been done since then. With the amount of indexing that now takes place, it is imperative that we reassess the situation. I would like to see a major review of ways to moderate the existing bias in the CPI. By doing this, the costs of pension indexing could be reduced without hurting the living standards of pensioners.

As has been mentioned, while the impact of inflation on the elderly has been reduced, the two major remaining problems are the erosion of savings and the fact that private pensions do not fully adjust for price rises *during* retirement. The latter problem has received increasing attention in recent years, and consideration is being given to the ways that plans can be redesigned to reduce it.[19] However, a related problem has been largely ignored.[20] Most vested benefits are frozen when a worker changes jobs. The worker does not benefit from subsequent improvements in the plan formula or even the inflation protection of many plans that base benefits on average earnings just prior to retirement. For example, given the inflation rates of the post-war period, a vested pension for someone changing jobs at age 45 (with, say 20 years of coverage) will give a worker almost nothing at retirement.

Why is so little attention given to this vesting problem? In part, it is because private pensions are so new. Many people affected by the problem (i.e., vested workers) are still many years from retirement. Yet, given the serious implications of the vesting-inflation issue for the future, the problem needs to be addressed. Perhaps an even more important reason that the issue has been ignored is cost. Employers with defined benefit plans currently keep their pension costs down by giving little or no benefits to workers who leave the firms' employ in their early years. To deal with this problem effectively would require a major increase in pension expenditures by employers.

The Impact of Inflation
on Retirement Decisions

Given the recent high rates of inflation and the fact that private pensions do not keep up with inflation, many observers have supposed that current workers will be reluctant to retire as early as recent cohorts of retirees. For example, Sheppard recently speculated that "there might be a new retirement consciousness developing in this country, which is making older workers reexamine the costs of retiring prematurely."[21]

While longitudinal data bearing on this question are relatively sparse, most of the available evidence indicates that retirements have slowed somewhat in recent years, but not in any appreciable way. An analysis by Parnes of the National Longitudinal Survey (NLS) data found that "the trend toward earlier retirement that had been discernible in the longitudinal data between 1966 and 1976 continued without interruption between 1976 and 1978."[22] Parnes also found among *retired* men only slightly more interest in post-retirement jobs in 1978 than in 1976. (Parnes is currently analyzing data from a more recent NLS survey and will soon have additional information on this question.)

The Panel Study of Income Dynamics also provides longitudinal data bearing on the impact of inflation on retirement decisions. In 1979, the panel was asked whether inflation had caused them to change their attitudes toward retirement. According to Morgan, "the startling finding from the responses was the small effect of inflation."[23] The actions or plans of those already retired had changed hardly at all. With regard to those age 45 or older who were not yet retired, however, there was a small but significant change in plans or expectations regarding retirement. About a fifth of the interviewees in that group indicated they would not be retiring as early as previously planned.

One of the most useful indicators of retirement trends is Social Security data on new benefit awards. Table 2 shows the number of Social Security benefits newly awarded and the proportion of these beneficiaries receiving reduced benefits for retirement before age 65. From 1973 to 1978 the trend was clearly in the direction of more early retirement. Since then the data indicate a relatively sharp drop in the proportion of men awarded benefits before age 65, but a very small decline for women.

What available evidence we have, therefore, indicates that the inflation of recent years may have moderated the rush to early retirement that developed in the 1960s and 1970s. The proportion of people retiring early, however, still remains very high, and we should not be surprised if the trend resumes its upward climb once inflation moderates.

Pension Retirement Incentives

While inflation's impact on benefit levels may be reducing the number of workers currently retiring at early ages, it is important to be aware of a number of factors in the design of private pension plans (in addition to benefit levels) that encourage retirement. It is clear that it is relatively easy to encourage workers in a broad spectrum of occupations and industries to retire at early ages through various pension incentive mechanisms. Probably the most important way to encourage early retirement is by simply making pensions available at early ages. Data on defined benefit plans covering about 23 million workers in 1974 show that 70 percent of these workers were eligible for early retirement benefits at least by age 60 (provided service requirements, if any, were met).[24] Over half could retire as early as age 55, and 15 percent were in plans with even earlier eligibility ages (or no age requirement at all).

Table 2
New Social Security Worker Beneficiaries and the Proportion Receiving Reduced Early Retirement Benefits, 1968-1980

Year	Men		Women	
	Number (000s)	Early retirement[a] (percent)	Number (000s)	Early retirement[a] (percent)
1968	677	54	435	71
1969	691	53	449	71
1970	749	53	496	70
1971	752	57	507	73
1972	b	b	b	b
1973	897	54	650	66
1974	766	63	606	69
1975	873	61	539	80
1976	808	66	569	77
1977	855	68	616	78
1978	754	70	578	77
1979	811	67	612	77
1980	850	65	621	76

SOURCE: Table Q-6, published quarterly in the *Social Security Bulletin* (Washington, DC: U.S. Government Printing Office).

a. Reduced benefits awards currently payable as a percent of all awards moving to payment status (currently payable regular awards plus those originally awarded as not currently payable that moved to payment status).

b. Data are not available.

A Bureau of Labor Statistics analysis of a sample of private plans in 1978 indicates that retirement age policies have been significantly liberalized since 1974. "In 1978, approximately three out of four plans allowed retirement at age 55 or earlier, as compared with two out of three in 1974."[25] Moreover, many plans have lowered their normal retirement age (i.e., the age at which unreduced benefits are paid) below age 65, and other have eliminated age requirements entirely.

These numbers do not tell the whole story, however. When a worker retires before the "normal" retirement age, his or her benefit is usually reduced. But a large number of employers encourage their employees to retire early by absorbing some of the costs of paying pensions over a longer period of time. While some plans reduce benefits by the full actuarial discount, many plans, in effect, give actuarial bonuses to workers who retire early. Our study of defined benefit plans in 1974 indicates that powerful economic incentives are provided in many plans. For example, in 1974 there were about seven million workers covered by defined benefit plans that permitted retirement at age 60 with less than a full actuarial reduction in benefits. More recently The Urban Institute has tabulated early retirement reductions using the 1979 Bureau of Labor Statistics Level of Benefits Survey. They found that 78 percent of participants in plans with early retirement provisions were subject to less than full actuarial reductions in benefits.[26]

In addition to encouraging retirement through regular retirement plans, many corporations have developed special and more limited benefit "offers" to encourage their employees to retire. A recent report on special incentive programs by Towers, Perrin, Foster and Crosby (TPFC) looks at the evolution of these mechanisms.[27] As pension consultants to major corporations, TPFC state at the beginning of their report: "Early retirement benefits are not always enough to make retirement affordable and attractive, especially during periods of high inflation and economic uncertainty. Yet these are precisely the times when companies may need to encourage early retirement on a selective basis.''

As part of its report, TPFC discusses the special programs that have been instituted in ten major corporations. The average acceptance rate among those employees offered the special plans was 48 percent. In six out of the ten companies, moreover, over half the eligible employees took advantage of the inducements to retire early, with the acceptance rate going as high as 73 percent in one company and 67 percent in another.

Employment Policies and Older Workers

Even while employers struggle to allocate jobs equitably and efficiently in an economic environment of shrinking and shifting demand, we have been shocked by people proposing what was once thought to be unthinkable. It is now frequently recommended that the normal retirement age for Social Security be raised and/or that early retirement under Social Security be heavily penalized. Such proposals are stimulated in large part by rising pension costs and declining labor force participation among older workers.

Currently there is high unemployment and no general shortage of labor. But as the age structure of the population shifts, employers may be faced with an entirely different situation. Unlike the past—when both employers and unions encouraged workers to retire at increasingly early ages—employers of the future may want older workers to stay longer. But will employee attitudes also change? Most older workers want to retire as soon as possible; once retired, they adjust well to their new status in society and enjoy their increased leisure.

Any proposal to mandate a longer period of work life in the later years is likely to meet strong resistance from American workers, especially older workers. Pension plans were developed to provide compensation based on years of service on the job rather than on need per se. Thus, as observed by Friedman and Orbach in their excellent survey of retirement research, pensions have emerged "as an 'earned right' and (have) become instrumental in defining retirement status as appropriate for the older workers."[28] It will be difficult to turn back the clock and convince future generations of workers that they are required to postpone their enjoyment of the retirement period currently enjoyed by so many older Americans.

There are two basic approaches to getting workers to remain in the labor force—the carrot and the stick. Which is better? Which should be emphasized? Should we achieve higher labor force participation on the part of older workers by severe penalties or by mandating work (compulsion), or should we emphasize incentives that will increase voluntary participation?

I think we should emphasize the carrot approach. Along these lines, there are many things we can do. For example, we must get management and workers to speed up the development of more flexible work opportunities and encourage a more positive attitude toward older workers. That is hard to do in an environment of high unemployment. I would recommend—

- that there be more research and demonstrations to help employers understand the feasibility and profitability of flexibility in work environments;
- that mandatory retirement be completely abolished (more for attitudinal and symbolic reasons than for its labor force impact, which would be negligible);
- that the Social Security retirement test be significantly liberalized.

The last of these recommendations deserves elaboration. The retirement test is currently $6,000 for persons age 65 to 71 and $4,400 for those age 62 to 64. For many years I have urged major liberalization of the test, rather than abolition. In an opening address to "Committee One"[29] of the 1981 White House Conference on Aging, I recommended that the test be set at the level of "average wages covered under Social Security." In 1981 that would have been about $13,000. At this level, benefits would go mostly to those in need and those with modest incomes, i.e., the cost would be much, much less than if the earnings test were completely abolished. For example, if the test were set at $10,000 in 1983, only about $900 million would have to be paid out in additional benefits.[30] In contrast, complete abolition of the test at all ages would cost about eight billion dollars and, furthermore, would distribute the benefits in a very inequitable way. A simulation study on abolishing the retirement test that I carried out revealed that half of the new benefits from abolition of the test would have gone to the top one-third of aged income recipients, with incomes over $10,000.[31] Twenty percent would have gone to those with incomes over $20,000!

The White House Conference Committee, after considering both a liberalized retirement test and abolishment of the test, formally adopted my proposal as a recommendation. Unfortunately, the present Administration took the recommendations of all the Committees and selected only a few that were generally consistent with their ideological predilections. These selected recommendations wre the only ones put into the primary conference report ("A National Policy on Aging"), and included a recommendation from another committee that supported abolition of the earnings test. Thus, the recommendation for a liberalized retirement test was eliminated in this manipulative process. But the fact remains that the majority of a cross-section of Americans who were delegates to the conference chose liberalization of the retirement test over its complete abolition when presented with a choice between the two.

Conclusion

We are entering into a new era of pension policy. The early years entered around, first, gaining acceptance of the idea of collective retirement income and, second, the actual implementation of both public and private pension plans. Now that these pension programs have been in operation for many years, attention has shifted to assessing how well they operate and projecting what they will cost. Issues of pension adequacy, pension equity, and pension burdens have moved to center stage.

During the past two decades we have witnessed a tremendous push toward early retirement. Social Security early retirement benefits now go to the majority of new retirees. Federal employees can retire on full benefits at age 55 with 30 years of service; in fact, the President's Commission on Pension Policy recently reported that 59 percent of retiring male civil servants (fiscal 1978) were age 60 or younger. Most state and local government employee plans also have very liberal retirement provisions. Early retirement is usually possible after 20 to 30 years of service—often as early as age 50 or 55.

While Social Security and public employee pensions are important, what I have tried to do in this paper is to emphasize the equally important role played by private pensions—not just in providing benefits for retirement, but in influencing employment/retirement decisions. Today private pensions play a key role and, as a consequence, they deserve the increased scrutiny and understanding of both academics and policymakers.

NOTES

1. See, for example, the public opinion survey for the National Commission on Social Security: Peter D. Hart Research Associates, Inc., *A Nationwide Survey of Attitudes Toward Social Security,* a report prepared for the National Commission on Social Security, mimeographed (Washington, DC, no date).

2. Martha Derthick, *Policymaking for Social Security* (Washington: The Brookings Institution, 1979). See, for example, Roy Lubove, *The Struggle for Social Security, 1900-1935* (Cambridge, MA: Harvard University Press, 1968); Gaston Rimlinger, *Welfare Policy and Industrialization in Europe, America, and Russia* (New York: Wiley, 1971); William Graebner, *A History of Retirement* (New Haven, CN: Yale University Press, 1980); W. Andrew Achenbaum, "Did Social Security Attempt to Regulate the Poor? Historical Reflections on Piven and Cloward's Social Welfare Model," *Research in Aging* Vol. 2 (December 1980).

3. See "Providing Retirement Income," Chapter 4 in James H. Schulz, *The Economics of Aging* 2nd ed. (Belmont, CA: Wadsworth, 1980), pp. 73-82.

4. Robert J. Gordon, "Postwar Macroeconomics: The Evolution of Events and Ideas," in *The American Economy in Transition,* ed. Martin Feldstein (Chicago: University of Chicago Press, 1980), pp. 101-182.

5. William Graebner, op. cit.

6. U.S. Congressional Budget Office, *Work and Retirement: Options for Continued Employment of Older Workers* (Washington: U.S. Government Printing Office, 1982).

7. See the summaries in James H. Schulz, Testimony. In U.S. House Committee on Ways and Means, Subcommittee on Oversight, *Strategies to Encourage Older Workers to Voluntarily Extend Their Worklives,* Hearings (Washington: U.S. Government Printing Office, 1980) and James H. Schulz, *The Economics of Aging* 2nd ed. (Belmont, CA: Wadsworth, 1980), Chapter 3.

8. Some would say this results from disincentives built into pension programs. While these disincentives play some role, I think the data indicate that declining health status, a declining "work ethic," rising leisure opportunities, and quick adaptation to the supposed "role loss" of retirement play a much larger role. See Ethel Shanas et al., *Old People in Three Industrial Societies* (New York: Atherton, 1968); Gordon F. Streib and Clement J. Schneider, *Retirement in American Society* (Ithaca, NY: Cornell University Press, 1971); and Robert C. Atchley, *The Sociology of Retirement* (New York: Wiley/Schenkman, 1976).

9. Jacob J. Feldman, "Work Ability of the Aged Under Conditions of Improving Mortality," Statement Before the National Commission on

Social Security Reform, mimeographed (Washington, DC, 21 June 1982).

Disability in the statistics reported by Feldman refers to persons who are not able to work at all because of one or more chronic conditions. Total recovery or rehabilitation for these disabled tends to be relatively rare.

10. L. A. Colvez and M. Blanchet, "Disability Trends in the United States Population, 1966-76: Analysis of Reported Causes," *American Journal of Public Health* 71 (1981), pp. 464-471.

11. Robert N. Butler, Testimony Before the National Commission on Social Security Reform, mimeographed (Washington, DC, 1982).

12. Jeanne Prial Gordus, *Leaving Early—Perspectives and Problems in Current Retirement Practice and Policy* (Kalamazoo, MI: W. E. Upjohn Institute, 1980), p. 16.

13. Olivia S. Mitchell and Gary S. Fields, "The Effects of Pensions and Earnings on Retirement: A Review Essay," NBER Working Paper No. 772, mimeographed (Cambridge, MA, 1981); Anne Foner and Karen Schwab, *Aging and Retirement* (Monterey, CA: Brooks/Cole, 1981); James N. Morgan, "Antecedents and Consequences of Retirement," in *Five Thousand American Families—Patterns of Economic Progress,* ed., M. S. Hill, D. H. Hill and James N. Morgan, Vol. IX (Ann Arbor, MI: Institute for Social Research, 1981), pp. 207-243; Robert L. Clark and David T. Barker, *Reversing the Trend Toward Early Retirement* (Washington, DC: American Enterprise Institute, 1981).

14. James H. Schulz, T. D. Leavitt, L. Kelly, and J. Strate, *Private Pension Benefits in the 1970s—A Study of Retirement and Survivor Benefit Levels in 1974 and 1979* (Bryn Mawr, PA: McCahan Foundation for Research in Economic Security, 1982).

15. The median earnings used were based on earnings for four-quarters workers age 50 to 59 in 1974—differentiated by sex and industry. Earnings were assumed to have risen at a five percent average rate up to 1974 but at actual average rates as measured by the percentage increase in average Social Security covered earnings for the years 1974 through 1978.

16. Indexing of federal income tax brackets is scheduled to go into effect and will provide this protection for all age groups.

17. I refer here both to what might be called customary patterns and also to *new* patterns resulting when people adjust their spending because of price changes.

18. A summary of the earlier studies appears in James H. Schulz, *The Economics of Aging* 2nd ed. (Belmont, CA: Wadsworth), pp. 45-46. More recent studies include Data Resources, Inc., *Inflation and the Elderly,* mimeographed (Lexington, MA, 1980); Michael J. Boskin and

M. D. Hurd, "Are Inflation Rates Different for the Elderly?" NBER Working Paper No. 943 (Cambridge, MA: National Bureau of Economic Research, 1982); and Paul L. Grimaldi, "Measured Inflation and the Elderly, 1973 to 1981," *The Gerontologist* 22, No. 4 (1982), pp. 347-353.

19. Keith H. Cooper, "Pensions, Inflation, and Benefit Indexing." In Aspen Institute for Humanistic Studies, *The Quiet Crisis of Public Pensions,* Report on a Workshop (New York: The Institute, 1980), pp. 43-46.

20. Munnell's discussion of the problem is an exception. See Alicia H. Munnell, *The Economics of Private Pensions* (Washington: The Brookings Institution, 1982), pp. 170-177.

21. The National Council on the Aging, "Is Inflation Slowing Retirement," Press Release, mimeographed (Washington, DC, 17 August 1981).

22. Herbert S. Parnes, "Inflation and Early Retirement: Recent Longitudinal Findings," *Monthly Labor Review* 104, No. 7 (July 1981), pp. 27-30.

23. Morgan, op. cit.

24. Tabulation of a BLS survey of plans covering 100 or more employees.

25. Robert Frumkin and Donald Schmitt, "Pension Improvements Since 1974 Reflect Inflation, New U.S. Law," *Monthly Labor Review* 102 (April 1979), pp. 32-37.

26. The Urban Institute, *Financial Incentives in Private Pension Plans,* Report submitted to Pension and Welfare Benefit Programs, U.S. Department of Labor (Washington: The Institute, 1982).

27. Towers, Perrin, Foster, and Crosby, *Limited Period Early Retirement Incentive Programs* (New York: no date).

28. Eugene A. Friedman and H. L. Orbach, "Adjustment to Retirement." In Silvano Arieti, ed., *The Foundations of Psychiatry,* Vol. 1, *American Handbook of Psychiatry,* 2nd ed. (New York: Basic Books), pp. 609-645.

29. Committee One was entitled "Implications for the Economy of an Aging Population." See Recommendation Number 2 as printed in *Final Report, the 1981 White House Conference on Aging* Vol. 3, Recommendations (Washington: undated).

30. Congressional Budget Office, op. cit.

31. James H. Schulz, "Liberalizing the Social Security Retirement Test—Who Would Receive the Increased Pension Benefits?" *Journal of Gerontology* 33 (March 1978), pp. 262-268.

Chapters 8 & 9
Discussion
Bert Seidman

When I discuss papers at meetings I usually find myself in the position of disagreeing fundamentally with the authors, but that is not true on this occasion. I have seldom had the opportunity to comment on two papers that offer so much sense and sensitivity, especially when so much nonsense and insensitivity are abroad about the issues that these papers treat.

A formulation that James Schulz used in his paper seems particularly appropriate. These papers do, indeed, distinguish between theory and assumption on the one hand and the realities of the American market-oriented economy on the other. I think it is very important that we do not get bogged down in theories and that we look at the realities.

Let me begin with Alicia Munnell's paper. I am in basic agreement with her overview of the Social Security system. In particular, I agree with the separation of the fiscal outlook of Social Security into three separate periods—the period up until 1990, the period from 1990 to about 2015, or perhaps more appropriately until 2025, and then the period after that. I will not repeat her analysis, but I believe that it correctly portrays the nature and extent of the fiscal problems that Social Security faces during each of the three periods as well as for the entire period until about 2060. I do not want to emphasize that, contrary to the allegations of some who are for drastic cuts in Social Security protection, those of us who oppose such cuts are not refusing to face up to the fiscal problems that Social Security faces. We who op-

265

pose Social Security cutbacks fully recognize that there is an immediate short term problem which must not be ignored. Indeed, it must be dealt with no later than the early months of next year, because if we do nothing at all it may not be possible to pay full benefits on time as early as 1984. But as Munnell has made crystal clear, there are readily available ways of meeting this short term problem that do not curtail benefits. Some of them are probably more politically feasible than others; but let me indicate what some of them are.

In the first place, it is possible to move up to 1984 the increases in the tax rate that are scheduled to take effect between now and 1990. Are people willing to pay increased taxes for Social Security? The answer is already "yes"; poll after poll has shown that although people's confidence in Social Security has been shaken by scare headlines, they are nevertheless quite willing, if necessary, to pay more in order to assure the solvency of the system and to guarantee that the protection they rightly expect will be available to them. If the scheduled increases in payroll taxes were moved up to 1984, it would be possible to credit part of the Social Security tax for income tax purposes. To make sure that poor people who pay little or no income tax are not adversely affected, there could be a refundable feature similar to the earned income tax credit in current law. This proposal has actually been made by a conservative organization, the Committee for Economic Development, which is made up exclusively of business organizations.

Another possibility would be to eliminate the deductibility for income tax purposes of the employer's share of the payroll tax and earmark the funds for Social Security. My own feeling is that this is probably less feasible politically, and probably less desirable. However, if either of those proposals were to be adopted, we could be reasonably sure that the Social Security trust funds would be adequate until 1990.

But to provide absolute assurance, there should be authority for the Social Security trust funds to borrow, if necessary, from the general fund. This would make it possible to get along with trust funds at lower levels than if we had to depend entirely on them for benefit payments even under the most adverse circumstances conceivable. Afer 1990, the fiscal outlook for Social Security improves greatly. A surplus begins to develop rapidly, and it would then be possible to repay to the general fund whatever loans may have been made to the Social Security trust funds.

With respect to the long term outlook, there are many imponderables. All we know is that we will have more elderly and fewer young people than we do now. But what we do not know is how many people will be employed or unemployed, the levels of wages and prices, the level of immigration and a host of other factors that could influence the fiscal outlook for Social Security after the first quarter of the next century.

Some of these factors have rarely been taken into consideration in discussions of Social Security's long term outlook. For example, the fact that wages are taxed for Social Security purposes but fringe benefits are not means that how much the system collects in payroll taxes depends markedly upon the proportions of total compensation represented by wages and by fringe benefits, respectively. The assumptions one makes about this issue can have a very considerable impact on the long term fiscal outlook of Social Security. The actuaries in the Social Security Administration have been assuming that fringe benefits as a proportion of total compensation will continue to rise indefinitely in the future at the same rate as they have in the past. I think that is highly unlikely; the dependence of workers on their money wages for daily living requirements will put a limit on how much of their compensation they will be willing to take in the form of fringe benefits.

Munnell makes a point in her paper that deserves additional emphasis. It is true that in the future we will have more older people in relation to those still in the labor force. However, if you consider what is called the total "dependent" population—a term that I do not particularly like—including both persons 65 years of age or over and children under the age of 18, the ratio to active workers 40 or 50 years from now will be lower than it has been in recent years. I see no reason why we will not at that time be able to transfer to the elderly resources which had previously gone to meet the needs of (larger numbers of) young people. Indeed, the strong political force that will be created by the large number of older persons at that time will almost guarantee that the necessary reallocation of resources will be accomplished.

Now I wish to say a word about James Schulz's paper. He and others in this conference have rightly emphasized that changes in policies and programs should not be made on the assumption that there will be ample and suitable employment opportunities for the elderly; in other words, that we should not put the cart before the horse. We should not legislate cutbacks in Social Security protection now, either for the near term or the long term, because of unknown factors that may or may not occur in the distant future.

This admonition is especially relevant to the proposals for raising the retirement age for Social Security eligibility. This is an issue on which Munnell and Schulz seem to disagree. It is my understanding that Munnell sees some merit in a decision now to gradually raise the retirement age to 68 as a way of reducing the long term program costs. In his paper, Schulz points to all the problems and hardships that this would cause, and advocates use of the carrot rather than the stick in order to avoid these difficulties. That is, he would emphasize incentive mechanisms that would increase voluntary participation in the labor force but not penalize those who either because of bad health or lack of suitable employment opportunities or both—and it is the combination of the two that afflicts many older people—would be unable to work. We are not sure of employment opportunities for the aged or of decreasing morbidity rates. (Robert Butler, until recently Director of the National Institute on Aging, has pointed out that morbidity rates may not be improving even though people are living longer.[1]) We certainly should not. therefore, commit ourselves now to raising the retirement age in the future.

It is ironic that nobody is proposing to prohibit paying full private pensions to early retirees. As a matter of fact, we in the labor movement would oppose such a prohibition. However, if the retirement age under Social Security is raised, we would be faced with the paradox that the more fully protected workers who have both pensions and Social Security would have to wait even longer than they now do to get their Social Security benefits.

Neither paper takes account of the special needs of the "old-old"—people over the age of, say, 75. With increasing longevity, especially for women, and with no assurance that improved health will accompany longer life we will have a much larger and growing group of the very old with greater needs for income and services. This could require increasing expenditures if the old-old are to be adequately provided for, and could mean that we would have to allocate to our Social Security program as high a proportion of our total income as many of the European countries have done for a long time. But with a higher level of real national income that will prevail when the problem becomes acute, there is no reason to assume that this could not be done while still permitting active workers and their families to enjoy a level of living considerably higher than that enjoyed by today's employed.

---

1. Statement before the National Commission on Social Security Reform, June 21, 1982.

Chapters 8 & 9
Discussion
James R. Swenson

Alicia Munnell and James Schulz are to be congratulated for their excellent, comprehensive papers. I wish to expand on several points made in those papers and discuss several of the authors' assertions.

The Munnell paper credibly describes the short and long term financing problems confronting the wage replacement portion of the Social Security program, namely the OASDI benefits. The short term problems, which have been caused by adverse economic conditions, were described by Senator Heinz as "critical but manageable." That is a reasonable characterization and is supported by information provided in the paper.

The long term problems are much more significant, particularly when the Medicare program is considered. The Munnell paper only makes a brief reference to the Medicare program. Since the Medicare program is of critical importance to both the financial and physical well-being of most Social Security beneficiaries, it should be considered within the context of the resources to be transferred from current workers to those beneficiaries.

In addition to the short and long term financing problems, the Social Security program is faced with a severe lack of public confidence. Headline stories about imminent bankruptcy have helped to create this reaction. Young workers are concerned that there will be no program when they reach retirement age. A survey conducted in 1979 found that three of every four persons between the ages of 25 and

44 had little or no confidence that funds will be available to pay their retirement benefits.[1] Faced with uncertainty, many of the elderly are terrified. They are afraid their benefits will be drastically cut. No responsible study group has ever recommended the kinds of cutbacks that many of the elderly fear. Furthermore, our legislators would not enact such Draconian measures.

It is essential that confidence be restored. The elderly must be reassured and their anxiety eliminated. Young people have to be convinced that the program will survive so that they will continue to be willing to pay the taxes needed to support benefit payments. I strongly agree with Munnell that the best way to restore confidence is to enact changes that bring revenues and expenditures into balance for both the short and long term. I further submit that confidence will best be restored by honestly achieving financial balance without resorting to the sham of general revenue financing; it is painfully apparent there are no general revenues available considering the projected budgetary deficit of $150 billion or more.

However, there are reasonable solutions available that do not require general revenues and that do not require that any current benefits be cut. The consequences of such solutions will not be severe if timely action is not taken.

As indicated earlier, the short term problems are the result of unfavorable economic conditions. High rates of unemployment have contributed to a reduction in expected revenues. However, of even greater importance is the fact that prices, as measured by the faulty CPI, have increased much more rapidly than average wages. During the three years 1979 through 1981, CPI indexed benefits rose by 40 percent, whereas average wages rose by only 30 percent.[2] If benefits had risen by 30 percent, current benefit outlays would be approximately $11 billion less this year and for many years in the future, and short term financing problems would have been avoided. Moreover, intergenerational equity between workers and beneficiaries would have been preserved.

Presently, revenue growth depends on wage growth, while benefit growth depends on the CPI. Economist Henry Aaron of the Brookings Institution, in his testimony before the National Commission on Social Security Reform, said that this results in an "unstable" situation that should be corrected. This "unstable" condition must be addressed if future financing problems are to be avoided.

In an August 10, 1982 article appearing in the Wall Street Journal, Charles Schultze, Chairman of the Council of Economic Advisers to President Carter, argues persuasively for replacement of CPI adjustment in all federal entitlement programs with a wage index reduced by 2 or 2.5 percent. This deduction exceeds the assumed future increase in real wage growth. Therefore, he concludes that Congress could periodically decide if ad hoc adjustments are warranted.

The long term financing problems are much more serious, particularly if the Medicare program is considered, as it should be. The long term problems are largely the result of demographics. The tidal wave of the "baby boom" generation will have to be supported by the relatively smaller "baby bust" generation, and the problem will be compounded by every increasing longevity.

There are currently 3.2 workers supporting each beneficiary. Even after assuming an increase in birth rates, this is expected to decrease to a 2 to 1 ratio once the baby boom generation is retired.[3] This projection is of minor concern to some who point out that the total dependency ratio, considering both those under 20 and those over 64, will not change dramatically and that resources can therefore be shifted from support of dependent children to support of the elderly. While this is true in part, it must be recognized that the elderly receive a level of support three times as large as that received by children because the elderly maintain independent households.[4] This fact gains significance when one realizes that the percentage of U.S. population over age 65 will exceed the proportion of the current population residing in Florida once the baby boom generation retires.

I am both a representative of the baby boom generation and a father. My children are part of the baby bust generation. Unless changes are made in the benefits that have been promised to my generation, my children and their employers will be required to pay taxes equivalent to 34 percent of payroll to support the wage related benefits discussed by Munnell and the Medicare benefits.[5] I believe it is neither fair no reasonable to leave that legacy to my children.

Incidentally, this 34 percent cost estimated is based upon the II-B "best estimate" assumptions, which project an increase in birth rates, a slowdown in the rate of mortality improvement, and a return to the very favorable economic conditions of the 1950s and 1960s. Costs would be even higher if these assumptions prove to be optimistic, as has been the case during the last decade.

Since the long term problem is a demographic problem, it warrants a demographic solution. The proposal to gradually increase the retirement age, as Munnell suggests, is a reasonable solution. Most study groups have recommended such an increase, and a New York Times survey conducted last year found public support for such a change by a 5 to 4 margin.

James Schulz correctly points out the fact that people do favor early retirement. Therefore, the approach being developed by House Ways and Means Social Security Subcommittee Chairman Pickle that would still permit actuarially reduced benefits to begin as early as 62 is preferable to approaches that advance the early retirement ages as the normal age increases.

Like Schulz, I too favor the "carrot to the stick." However, demographic developments force our country to make some difficult choices. Since Social Security is an intergenerational transfer program, the difficult choices must be framed within the context of the following question: At what point in time can parents realistically expect that their children will be able to support them?

Several years ago, President Carter appointed the President's Commission on Pension Policy to examine all aspects of retirement income. This Democratic controlled Commission concluded that "the nation has become too dependent on pay-as-you-go programs like social security to provide retirement income for elder citizens." They recommended a long term shifting of dependency to a balanced program of employer sponsored pension plans, social security and individual saving.[6]

The Schulz paper points out the fact that private pension plans can provide a very significant level of retirement income for those who are covered. Munnell points out that only one-half of the workforce is covered by such plans. However, that statistic is misleading, since many of those who are not covered do not yet meet the ERISA participation standards of age 25, one year of service and 1000 hours of employment. Among that portion of the workforce who must meet these standards, more than two-thirds are covered.[7] Furthermore, more than 90 percent of married couples can expect to receive employer pension benefits when they retire.[8]

Besides helping to assure an adequate level of retirement income, private pension plans offer an important advantage in that they offer flexibility to meet different needs and circumstances. For example, some industries, such as steel, have jobs that are more physically strenuous. Therefore the United Steel Workers of America have typically negotiated pension plans offering generous early retirement benefits. This type of flexibility is virtually impossible to achieve with a monolithic plan covering all Americans. It is just one of the reasons why the government should actively seek to encourage the expansion and adoption of such plans.

Both authors have noted that private pension plan benefits to retirees have not kept pace with inflation despite periodic ad hoc adjustments. I regard this as a significant problem that employers must address. In Canada, there is increasing awareness of this issue, and the employer community is beginning to respond by supporting an approach referred to as the "excess interest method." Under this method, excess investment return, resulting in large part from inflation, is used to provide additional benefits. This approach has been used by the Rockefeller Foundation in the U.S.

However, the best way to solve these inflation-related problems is by adoption of appropriate fiscal and monetary policy designed to control inflation. While the Federal Reserve has been following such a course, neither Republican nor Democratic politicians have had the courage to do so.

Finally, individual savings can provide a very significant source of retirement income or can reduce the need for other sources of income. I agree with Munnell that individuals at the lowest income levels are not able to save. However, I strongly disagree that middle income workers will not be able to save if proper tax incentives are provided along with convenient means to facilitate the saving. As evidence, it should be noted that 72 percent of persons over age 65 live in their own homes, and 84 percent of those homes are mortgage free.[9] Our tax policies have encouraged home ownership and the public has responded.

As another example, my employer, The Prudential Insurance Company of America, provides a thrift plan to all employees after one year of service. The company fully matches the first 3 percent of salary set aside by the employees. Beyond that, the employee can save up to an additional 10 percent of salary. Since the company contribution vests very quickly, it is not surprising that 90 percent of the eligible employees participate in the program. Moreover, contrary to Munnell's contention, two-thirds of the participants are able to set aside additional savings, and the levels of savings are very significant at every income level. For example, the total savings rate for all participants, including the company's 3 percent share, is 10.5 percent of salary. The only salary group with a savings rate less than 10 percent are those earning less than $10,000 per year, whose rate was 9.7 percent.

In addition, last year's Congressional legislation permitting all wage earners to establish tax-deferred IRAs was a major step to encourage people to save for their retirement. The public has responded very favorably, and our company alone will have established approximately one-half million IRAs in this first year of eligibility. This figure is especially impressive considering that only one-tenth of all IRAs have been set up through insurance companies, and that Prudential accounts for only 10 percent of the total insurance industry.

Evidence of these kinds leads me to believe that the majority of the population is capable of setting aside significant savings for retirement. What has been needed are the proper incentives and the means to set aside such savings. National policy should continue and expand efforts to develop such arrangements.

In conclusion, Social Security is the essential base for providing retirement income, and steps should be taken to restore public confidence in the program. Those steps should honestly restore financial balance for both the short and long term so that it will continue to serve its vital role not only for this generation but for future generations as well. Private pension plans and individual savings can and should play a major role in providing retirement income. Those plans offer flexibility needed to meet different needs and circumstances. In addition, those plans avoid the potential for inter-generational conflicts inherent in pay-as-you-go financed programs. Thus, there is need for legislation and regulation designed to encourage rather than discourage these sources of income. Retirement income can best be provided by a balanced program of Social Security, private pension plans and individual savings. Such a balanced program will assure adequate and secure sources of retirement income for all Americans.

NOTES

1. Survey conducted by Peter D. Hart, Research Associates, *Social Security in America's Future, Final Report of National Commission on Social Security* (Washington, DC: GPO, March 1981), p. 378.

2. U.S. Congress, Senate, Committee on Finance, *Social Security Financing,* Committee Print, No. 97-8. 97th Cong., 1st Sess. (Washington, DC: GPO, September 1981), p. 50.

3. U.S. Department of Health and Human Services, Social Security Information, *1982 Annual Report of the Board of Trustees of the Federal Old-Age and Survivors Insurance and Disability Insurance Trust Funds* (Washington, DC: GPO, 1982) (hereafter cited as *1982 Trustees Report),* pp. 65 and 66.

4. *Social Security Financing and Benefits, Reports of the 1979 Advisory Council on Social Security* (Washington, DC: GPO, December 1979), pp. 309-313.

5. *1982 Trustees Report,* p. 64 and unpublished results of studies conducted by Actuarial Division, Health Care Financing Administration, U.S. Department of Health and Human Services.

279

6. *Coming of Age: Toward a National Retirement Income Policy, President's Commission on Pension Policy* (Washington, DC: GPO, February 1981), pp. 7 and 9.

7. Sylvester J. Schieber and Patricia M. George, *Retirement Income Opportunities in an Aging America: Coverage and Benefit Entitlement* (Washington, DC: Employee Benefit Research Institute, June 1981), p. vii.

8. Employee Benefit Research Institute, *Retirement Income Opportunities in an Aging America: Income Levels and Adequacy* (Washington, DC: Employee Benefit Research Institute, 1982), p. vii.

9. Dallas Salisbury, Employee Benefit Research Institute.

Michael K. Taussig

Alicia Munnell and James Schulz have produced two stimulating papers on various aspects of social pension policy. Munnell's paper gives an excellent, clear presentation of the main issues in social security financing. Schulz's paper is harder to describe; its title is somewhat misleading because he has as much to say about social security as about private pensions. His discussion of both these subjects includes a number of important, provocative points about pension policy issues. On the whole, the two papers complement each other well.

Munnell and Schulz do clash sharply on one crucial factual matter. Schulz argues that the available evidence shows that improvements in longevity have not been matched by similar improvements in the health of the aged. Munnell comes to the opposite conclusion. Pension policy decisions depend critically on who is right. We expect that continued improvements in medical care and technology will—in the absence of nuclear war or some other catastrophe of comparable magnitude—cause a large increase in the number of persons who survive until, and well past, the traditional retirement ages in this country. We do not yet know, however, whether the expected increase in longevity will cause a corresponding increase in the number of *dependent* aged persons. If the aged worker of tomorrow is healthier than her or his counterpart today, and if there are sufficient attractive job opportunities, then increased longevity will not necessarily mean increased dependency. Unfortunately, I am not an expert on this complex subject and I cannot resolve the disagreement between the authors of the two papers. The fact that two such eminent authorities on social pension policy disagree about the weight of the available evidence suggests to me that this is a high priority area for more research.

Instead of dwelling further on the details of the papers, I will now briefly sketch my own perspectives on some of the issues in social pension policy. The basic features of social security financing in the United States today are remarkably simple. The system is financed almost entirely by a payroll tax levied on the wages and salaries of current workers. If payroll tax revenues into OASDI are not sufficient to pay the benefits payable under existing formulas to retired and disabled workers and to their dependents and survivors, then either more revenues have to be found or benefits have to be cut, or some combination of both. None of the options today for solving the short-run financing problems of the system is painless. However, the magnitude of the problem is too often exaggerated. As Munnell shows, the current short-falls in OASDI revenue are small relative to the size of existing benefit commitments and are not expected to persist for more than the next half dozen years or so.

In my view, solving the short-run financing problems of social security by cutting benefits is wrong because it means breaking government commitments to dependent retired and disabled persons who are, for the most part, helpless in coping with large, unexpected cuts in their incomes. Any payroll tax increase would be preferable because it would spread the pain of reductions in living standards much more widely and fairly. My own preferred solution to the short-run financing problem of the OASDI system is to extend coverage immediately to all federal government employees. This step is long overdue on the basis of fairness to virtually all other workers. It is my experience that people become instant cynics about the federal government and about social security in particular when they learn that the Congress chooses to exclude itself and social security bureaucrats from the "protection" of the social security programs they legislate and administer for almost all the rest of the population. The extension of coverage to federal government employees would end this scandal and would most conveniently solve completely all financing problems for social security until well into the next century.

As Munnell explains, the long-run financing problems of social security around the year 2014 and for some time thereafter are largely due to the aging of the baby boom cohorts and the expected continuation of the very low fertility of the 1960s and 1970s. I find it impossible to share the prevalent concern about this distant crisis because I believe there is little we can do now to affect the situation some 30 or 40 years in the future. We could, of course, sharply increase payroll tax rates in order to build up substantial OASDI trust funds. Economists throw cold water on this idea by observing that such a measure would help only if it caused a substantial increase in real capital formation and a higher rate of national economic growth. Even if it were guaranteed to work, I doubt that it would be acceptable to current workers. They would in effect have to pay for their own retirement benefits as well as for the benefits of current retirees. Alternatively, we could be more conservative about the level of benefits promised to current workers. As Munnell explains, one way this could be done is to switch from the current system of wage indexing of covered earnings to price indexing. Such a step would reduce the replacement rate under OASDI if real wages increase in the future. It should be obvious that this change would also be most unattractive to current workers looking ahead to retirement in the next century. If such measures are rejected, then the social security financing problems of 2020 will have to be solved in 2020.

These thoughts lead me to question what Munnell calls the "individual lifetime perspective" as the rationale for a social security disability and retirement system. Both it and the annual tax and transfer perspective are valid in specific circumstances, but I lean more to the tax-transfer view. Every generation has to make a decision about the size and distribution of the net transfer from its current workers to its dependent nonworkers. We can try now to influence this transfer in the year 2020 by promising our young workers the present replacement rates in OASDI, but any such promise has to be fulfilled by the workers then alive. If we make promises now that the workers of 2020 refuse to honor, they will have ample means to cut drastically the size of the transfer. Thus, all the lifetime insurance aspects of social security could be swept away if any generation refuses to repay the compulsory savings of its retired and disabled workers.

Even if we could do something now to avert the expected long-run deficits of OASDI, it is not obvious to me that we should do anything. First, babies may come back into fashion in the 1980s and 1990s and grow up just in time to work and pay taxes to alleviate the expected social security financial problems. Second, as both Munnell and Schulz say, the opportunities for work are likely to be more attractive for older workers in 2020 than today. If continued work becomes attractive enough, both financially and otherwise, then the burden of dependency to be borne by social security could turn out to be far less than we project today. Third, if tight labor markets do exist in 2020 and if older workers are not interested in taking the available jobs, then allowing more immigration of young workers might be an attractive policy on many grounds. For one thing, the young immigrants could help pay for the social security benefits promised to the retired and disabled. Such optimistic scenarios are not to be confused with scientific predictions, of course, but in my opinion, they are on the same footing as the projections of the OASDI actuaries. I derive great amusement from the spectacle of intelligent and well-informed people who take the official social security actuarial projections so seriously despite the fact that these projections have turned out to be dead wrong time after time. It would be an interesting exercise to trace the history of the social security actuarial projections for fertility, mortality, wages, prices and labor force participation against what actually occurred. Finally, as Munnell shows, even if we accept the pessimistic official projections for 2020 and beyond, the tax rates required of the relatively rich workers with few dependent children at that time are not out of line with the social security tax rates paid now by workers in other industrialized, democratic countries.

I will conclude my discussion of the two papers with a mention of important aspects of social pension policy that neither author addressed. The elderly have important sources of income other than earnings or OASDI and private pensions. Supplementary security income is an important source of income support for the poor and near-poor elderly. Also, many elderly persons still depend on support from their children, sometimes as members of extended families living in the same household. On the other end of the income spectrum, a small number of elderly persons finance their retirement largely out of accumulated personal saving. If the new rules affecting individual retirement accounts are effective, private savings will become a more important and widespread source of retirement income by 2020. I believe it is important to examine the possible growth of these alternative income sources for the elderly in assessing the sufficiency of pensions in the next century.

A related point is that both papers concentrate too much on the replacement rates provided by public and private pensions as a criterion for the sufficiency of such benefits. The focus of some recent research has been on direct measurement of the total incomes of the elderly relative to the nonelderly. In some recent work of this kind, Sheldon Danziger, Jacques van der Gaag, Eugene Smolensky, and I have found that the elderly fare surprisingly well relative to the nonelderly when all relevant factors, such as the number of persons sharing the household income, are taken into account as much as current data allow. One of our findings of particular interest for this conference is that the elderly fare particularly well relative to the nonelderly at the same level of pretransfer income. Compared to the elderly, some other groups, such as children in one-parent families, are much worse off and are much less protected by our system of transfers.

DATE DUE

OCT 01 '90			